*THINKING
FASCISM*

# THINKING FASCISM

## Sapphic Modernism and Fascist Modernity

ERIN G. CARLSTON

*Stanford University Press   Stanford, California*

Stanford University Press
Stanford, California
© 1998 by the Board of Trustees of the
Leland Stanford Junior University

Printed in the United States of America

CIP data appear at the end of the book

*In memory of my sister*
*Catherine Alice Carlston Brisbois (Kim Eun Sook)*

# *Acknowledgments*

To paraphrase a Zen prayer: innumerable labors brought me this book. I would like to take this opportunity to thank some of those who contributed to its writing. Research for and writing of some sections were facilitated by generous grants from the Stanford Humanities Center, the Lurcy Foundation, and the Whiting Foundation, and by the resources made available to me by the École Normale Supérieure in Paris. I am also indebted to the curators of the Djuna Barnes Papers at McKeldin Library at the University of Maryland for permission to use materials from the collection; to the curators of Natalie Barney's papers at the Bibliothèque Jacques Doucet in Paris for permission to view the correspondence between Barney and Marguerite Yourcenar; and to Yvon Bernier for spending a most enjoyable and informative afternoon with me in Northeast Harbor, Maine, discussing Yourcenar. Helen Tartar and Nathan MacBrien of Stanford University Press provided helpful and thoughtful editorial advice.

More personally, I wish to thank some of the many colleagues, friends, readers, and teachers who have generously proffered ideas, criticism, help with translations, and numerous other kindnesses: Russell Berman, Joe Boone, Terry Castle, Heesok Chang, Pamela Cheek, Hélène Cixous, Vilashini Cooppan, Arnold Davidson, Regenia Gagnier, Linda Garber, Krystyna von Henneberg, Miranda Joseph, Marcia Klotz, Julia Kristeva, Stephanie Lysyk, Marcelle Marini, Lee Medovoi, Diane Middlebrook, Kirsten Nussbaumer, Ben Robinson, Jeff Schnapp, Helen Solanum, Michael Tratner, and Priscilla Wald. I am particularly grateful to Trip McCrossin for locating a rare copy of the 1934 edition of *Denier du rêve* for me. Andrea Webber and John McDonald provided patient, dedicated, and sometimes heroic assistance with research. Marjorie Rauen did all that, and so much more that no words could measure my gratitude.

In closing, I would like to thank my family for their support; and finally, and most fondly, the Niblings, for helping me keep my priorities straight.

# Contents

1. Women Writers / Thinking / Fascism  1
2. Political Bodies  18
3. "The Learned Corruption of Language": *Nightwood*'s Failed Flirtation with Fascism  42
4. Neither Right nor Left: Marguerite Yourcenar and the Crisis of Liberalism  86
5. Another Country: Virginia Woolf's Disloyalty to Civilization  136

Coda: Back to the Future  187

*Bibliography*  195

*Index*  209

*THINKING FASCISM*

CHAPTER I

# *Women Writers / Thinking / Fascism*

> The history of fascism must be interlocked with the whole history of modern Europe—not treated on one side as an ulcerous growth or a temporary nightmare. Fascism is as much an organic part of modern Europe as liberalism or communism.
>
> H. R. Kedward,
> *Fascism in Western Europe 1900–45*

This book is an analysis of the work of three women writers—Djuna Barnes, Marguerite Yourcenar, and Virginia Woolf—who wrote texts in the 1930s that engage, directly or indirectly, with fascist politics and ideology. It has been said that fascism constitutes the "potent 'political unconscious' " of Barnes's 1936 novel *Nightwood* (Marcus, "Laughing," 222). Yourcenar's *Denier du rêve* (1934) was, at least by its author's account, the first novel in French to address the problem of fascism; and *Three Guineas* (1938) is, of course, Woolf's most sustained piece of political argument, a feminist analysis of fascism and militarism. In my readings of these texts, I attempt to refine the discussion about the relationship between women intellectuals and the various aesthetic and ideological practices collected under the names of modernism and fascism. My work is indebted to and situates itself between two important revisionist projects that have developed since the 1970s and that are still very much under way: feminist rereadings of modernism on the one hand, and studies of fascist culture on the other. Hence the double valence of the title *Thinking Fascism*, which evokes both the ways in which women modernists *thought* or conceptualized fascism and the idea of a *thinking* or intellectual fascism.

1

In the early 1980s, feminist literary critics began to call into question the characterization of the modernist canon, promulgated by critics like Hugh Kenner and Edmund Wilson, as that body of experimental writing produced by a group of expatriate men between about the turn of the century and World War II. Feminists argued that this androcentric vision of literary modernism distorted a history in which women had in fact been central, as authors, critics, editors, and publishers; they rediscovered the work of long-neglected women writers and asserted that in addition to the established mandarins of masculine modernism—T. S. Eliot, James Joyce, Ezra Pound—women like Djuna Barnes, H.D., and Mina Loy were writers who deserve inclusion in any canon of modernism. Furthermore, feminists claimed, the politics and thematics of gender and sexuality also played a formative role in the developments of a modernist poetics: modernism not only treated, but was also determined by, gender issues (Rado, "Lost," 5).\*

Critics like Shari Benstock even went so far as to suggest that women writers of the period—many of whom could be considered lesbian or bisexual, in contemporary terms if not always their own—were excluded from a "male modernism" that was inherently reactionary and misogynist, and constituted an entirely different literary movement: Sapphic Modernism. Reviewing the work of Benstock, Sandra Gilbert and Susan Gubar, and other prominent feminist analysts of modernism, one critic noted that by 1994 we could "document the production of a formidable and hard-won piece of turf, now occupied by 'female modernism' " (Jacobs, 273).

---

\* Some of the most important feminist work on women and modernism from this period includes Shari Benstock's *Women of the Left Bank*; Benstock, "Paris Lesbianism and the Politics of Reaction, 1900–1940"; Mary Lynn Broe, ed., *Silence and Power: Djuna Barnes, a Reevaluation*; Mary Lynn Broe and Angela Ingram, eds., *Women's Writing in Exile*; Sandra M. Gilbert and Susan Gubar, *The War of the Words*, vol. 1 of *No Man's Land*; Susan Stanford Friedman's work on H.D. and Jane Marcus's on Virginia Woolf; and the writings of Bonnie Kime Scott. The essays in Lisa Rado's 1994 collection *Rereading Modernism* offer excellent accounts of this earlier work and point to exciting new possibilities for contemporary modernist studies.

These battles are far from over, as an examination of current syllabi for university courses on modernism will reveal: many reading lists are still largely or entirely devoted to men writers. Nonetheless, in the 1990s some feminist writers—including a few of those who helped to shape the concept of a "female modernism"—began to argue that although focusing on women writers unquestionably offers an invaluable corrective to gender-blind accounts of modernism, it may overcompensate by exaggerating the differences between men and women modernists and by minimizing their personal and professional interdependencies. These critics, among whom I number myself, have tried to articulate descriptions of gender and gender relations in modernism that steer between the relentless sexism of masculinist versions of modernism on the one hand and an overemphasis on separate spheres on the other.* Reexamining the intricate network of relationships in modernist communities, they have rewritten misogynist accounts of male masters and their less-talented female acolytes as a story of reciprocal influence between colleagues, thus opening up new possibilities for interpretation of writing by both men and women. This approach permits us, for example, to reconsider the possibility that there *are* convergences between H.D.'s poetics and Pound's, or between *Mrs. Dalloway* and *Ulysses*, without having to assume that such comparisons must work to the detriment of one writer or the other.

Debates about the role of gender in modernism and in modernist studies are an aspect of even larger questions about the nature of modernism itself. Contemporary criticism has challenged the very notion of modernist canonicity, claiming that modernism was not one movement or even two or three, but many, a literary/social/historical constellation informed by (at the least) the nationality, gender, sexuality, race, and class status of the writers who participated in it. New work is proliferating on lesbian, African-American, nonexperimental, and pop-cultural texts from the modernist period. Thus, according to many of those in contemporary

*See especially Bonnie Kime Scott, *Refiguring Modernism* (1995), the essays collected in her *Gender of Modernism* (1990), and Rado's *Rereading Modernism*.

modernist studies, in referring to the literary production of the first half of this century we cannot speak of Modernism, but only of modernisms. And, taking this trend toward expansion of the canon one step further, Marianne DeKoven and others argue in favor of looking beyond written texts and broadening the discipline of modernist studies to include cultural studies. DeKoven writes that "at the current juncture in feminist scholarship, we ought to expand our sense of the connections between feminism and modernism: to move beyond analyses of women modernists, their separate tradition and their complex relations to canonical male modernism in order to include a much broader historical provenance and a much wider range of cultural work" (DeKoven, 344).

Although the present volume is a work of literary criticism, I have undertaken my examination of women modernists and fascist thought in this spirit, in the name of expanding our sense of the "historical provenance" of modernisms, of their political context and of the role gender plays in modernist political history. Although masculinist critics have generated considerable discussion about the relation between men modernists and fascist politics, much of this critical work has tended to overlook both women writers and questions of gender and sexuality in the political movements of the modernist period. At the same time, readers who *have* addressed these questions have frequently assumed that women writers were necessarily antagonistic to fascist ideologies. Reed Way Dasenbrock, for instance, asserts flatly that "profascist sympathies are found exclusively among male Modernists" (Dasenbrock, 82). Sapphic Modernism in particular is often aligned with a politically progressive "modernism of the margins"; feminist critics cite the correspondences many women writers draw among members of marginalized groups (women, homosexuals, Jews, blacks), and some interpret this gesture as a revulsive reaction against the rise of fascism.* And as recently as 1995 Bonnie Scott claimed that "unlike many of their celebrated male modernist colleagues," women writ-

*See, for example, Susan Stanford Friedman, "Modernism of the 'Scattered Remnant'" and "Exile in the American Grain: H.D.'s Diaspora"; and Jane Marcus, "Laughing at Leviticus."

ers like Woolf, Dorothy West, and Barnes rejected fascism out of hand (Scott, *Refiguring*, 2: xviii).

But a third trend has emerged in critical writings on women and fascism, especially in analyses of the cultural productions of German and Italian women who lived under fascist regimes. This work suggests that any systematic division of political tendency along gender lines is inadequate as a description of the complex effects of what Dasenbrock terms the "fascist imagination" in writing by both men and women.* Proponents of this view argue, instead, that intellectuals of both genders and all political persuasions were preoccupied during the interwar period by the commodification of culture and sexuality, the erasure of liberal bourgeois concepts of the individual and the work of art in mass society, and the failure of social institutions to provide transcendence and immediacy in this materialist and alienated age.

Rereading modernist texts from this perspective reveals that women writers like the Sapphic Modernists, and conservative or fascist men modernists, often articulate surprisingly similar conceptions of and reactions to these *maux de siècle*, which suggests that fascism cannot be posed as the absolute Other of politico-cultural thought in the interwar period. Even the correspondences among marginalized groups established by the "modernism of the margins" are themselves derived from a chain of equivalences established by the constellation of late-nineteenth-century discourses about the body that also gave rise to the rhetoric of fascist modernity. My goal in this work is not only to demonstrate that fascist discourses share a vernacular with non- and antifascist discourses of the same period, but also to argue that fascism itself could supply the vocabulary and the methodology of even the most rigorously antifascist critiques, such as Woolf's in *Three Guineas*. While the personal political views of the three authors treated in this study ranged, during the interwar years, from Woolf's outspoken antifascism to Yourcenar's moderate conservatism to Barnes's apparent

---

* See, for example, Marie-Luise Gättens, *Women Writers and Fascism*, and the essays collected in Elaine Martin's *Gender, Patriarchy, and Fascism in the Third Reich* and Robin Pickering-Iazzi's *Mothers of Invention*.

apoliticism, none of their texts holds a position entirely outside the terms of fascist discourses. The following readings examine the different ends to which each of these works, as it attempts to "think fascism," deploys discourses that also inform fascist cultural productions.

Before that discussion begins, however, a number of brief explanations and definitions may be required: what is *meant* here by "Sapphic Modernism"? By "intellectual fascism"? These are highly contested terms, and my definitions are, intentionally, provisional, adapted for the purposes of the current work. Although I adopt the term Sapphic Modernism, for example, I wish to call into question some of the assumptions about sexuality and gender that may seem implicit in its usage. The word "Sapphic" in conjunction with "Modernism" tends both to imply a transparent relation between biography and literary production and to apply an anachronistic conception of lesbian identity to the sexual cultures of the early twentieth century. During that period there certainly existed a lesbian community in Paris that self-consciously modeled itself on Sappho's circle, but the three writers under discussion here, like many other women-loving women artists of the time, were only tangentially related to it; and their lives and works do not otherwise lend themselves to any easy definition of lesbianism or bisexuality, or of lesbian writing. Yet all three experienced (homo)sexuality as an aesthetic problematic and political *enjeu*, as well as a private problem or pleasure. "Sapphic modernism," writes Benstock, "constitutes itself through moments of rupture in the social and cultural fabric" (Benstock, "Expatriate," 198n3). In my readings, it is in the writer's attentiveness to these "moments of rupture" that her Sapphism manifests itself; "Sapphism" will, then, be taken to express itself not as an organized identity or as a *mise-en-texte* of biography, but as a hypersensitivity to sexuality in, and as, the aesthetic and the political.

To some extent I have taken a similarly nonontological approach to gender. It should go without saying that there are salient differences in political perspective as well as style among works written by women. Certainly *Nightwood*, *Denier du rêve*, and *Three*

*Guineas* differ considerably from each other in their treatment of fascism, which indicates the difficulty of defining a simple correspondence between gender and ideology. Barnes retreats from the fascist implications of *Nightwood*'s decadence into a deeply pessimistic if resigned Catholicism, while Yourcenar proposes an alternative to fascist culture in a renewed focus on the individual and Western cultural values, and Woolf calls for a socialist/feminist revolution. But all three texts also differ in important ways from much contemporary work by men, notably in their rejection of patriarchal/fascist ideologies of maternity and militarism.

As we will see in the readings below, for example, one of the few commonalities among Barnes, Yourcenar, and Woolf is an emphasis on the sinister complementarity of patriotism and what I term "matriotism," an ideology of motherhood that buttresses patriarchy and militarism. Matriotism conceals gender inequity behind an idealization of maternity, harnesses women's (reproductive) labor in the service of the State, and suppresses women's sexuality in favor of their maternal role. Using images of childbirth and maternity in quite different ways to ridicule or undermine fascist ideologies, Barnes, Yourcenar, and Woolf nonetheless coincide in drawing a distinction between women's actually existing experiences of pregnancy, childbirth, and motherhood and fascism's manipulations of those experiences in the service of the *patria*. This convergence in their approaches to gender and fascism, otherwise so distinct, seems especially significant given that, in general, even their male contemporaries on the Left were not particularly concerned with disentangling reproductive labor from its ideological valences. The importance of gender in my analysis of these works does not lie in the "fact" of the writers' sex, then, but is instead derived from the uses they make of gender difference in their texts.

Finally, I have identified "Modernism" not in terms of period or a group of canonized authors, but in terms of a set of textual tropes. In this work I have characterized the defining feature of modernisms of all stripes as a close engagement with questions emerging from nineteenth-century discourses about individual and social bodies: questions not only about sexuality but also about the definition of the nation, the significance of racial difference, and the meaning of individuality and subjectivity in an age of mass culture.

In doing so I join the often heated discussions about the political valences of the various modernist and avant-garde movements. The question of the relation between the Left, the Right, and the modern is deeply perplexed. Georg Lukács and others have maintained that Continental modernism was elitist and reactionary, relying for its reception on a highly educated community sharing the same haut-bourgeois or aristocratic sources and values. In the Anglo-American tradition, some claim that the associative verse or "open poem" created by writers like Yeats, Eliot, and Pound "demanded for its completion not the free mind of democratic man, but the rich mind of the privileged within a hierarchical society" (Craig, 71). And feminists have pointed out that the dense, multilingual allusiveness of work like Joyce's or Pound's particularly excluded women readers who generally had not benefited from a classical education.

In contrast, critics and writers of the Left, from Theodor Adorno to Stephen Spender, have argued that avant-garde aesthetics were a kind of realist response to contemporary mass culture: "Modern art is as abstract as the real relations among men" (Adorno, *Aesthetic Theory*, 45). At worst, then, in this view, modernist art simply reflects the alienated conditions of its own production. But at best, as a representation of interior or psychological reality, modernist literature could be deeply and objectively true in a way that socialist realism, which treated only surfaces, was not. And some critics, including some women modernists, have even asserted that modernist art was more democratic than the realist work. Modernism aestheticized the banal, the humble; it rescued people from what Mina Loy called "stabilized culture" and reinfused them with a joyful sense of the aesthetic possibilities of daily life. "Modernism," wrote Loy,

> has democratized the subject matter and *la belle matière* of art; through cubism the newspaper has assumed an aesthetic quality, through Cézanne a plate has become more than something to put an apple upon, Brancusi has given an evangelistic import to eggs, and Gertrude Stein has given us the Word, in and for itself.

Would not life be lovelier if you were constantly overjoyed by the sublimely pure concavity of your wash bowls? The tubular dynamics of your cigarette? (Loy, 298)

The thread joining these competing versions of modernism is their relation to the bourgeois aesthetics of the previous century. Whether modernist artists envisioned art as the exclusive province of an educated elite, defended modernism as an objective response to alienated culture, or welcomed the populist and even revolutionary potential of avant-garde aesthetics, they all rejected liberal bourgeois aesthetic and ethical values. For conservative and fascist modernists, bourgeois liberalism represented mediocrity, the lowering of aesthetic standards to the lowest common denominator and the subordination of art to capital. For left-wing modernists, it represented elitism, the hegemony over culture of the ruling classes—and the subordination of art to capital. Loy's love affair with futurism (and with the Italian futurist F. T. Marinetti) epitomizes the numerous conjunctions between right and left modernisms: in both cases, the declared goal is to wrest art from the tired conventions of an outdated bourgeoisie. Loy's assertion that modernism democratizes art by bringing aesthetic consciousness to bear on the banal overlaps with the claim of radical Italian fascists to be bringing art to the people by aestheticizing every aspect of daily life.

A definition of fascism is, of course, at least as hard to establish as a definition of modernism; and a good deal more would seem to be at stake, politically and ethically. One dominant approach ever since the war, both in scholarship and in the popular media, has been to subsume all fascist phenomena under the history of the Nazi regime. This is an understandable strategy from an emotional or moral perspective; it seems wrong to speak of fascism without keeping its victims in the foreground. And if an insistence on the unique catastrophe of the Holocaust tends to close what the liberal philosopher Benedetto Croce called the "parenthesis in history," to try to contain fascism by defining it as an unreproducible aberration, perhaps this is in one sense simply the manifestation of a natural hope that it could never happen again. But such a "narrow" definition of fascism reads history backwards; it is inevitably informed, and perhaps distorted, by our retrospective knowledge of the horrors of World War II.

Theoretical work on fascism has therefore increasingly tended toward a "broad" definition of fascism, taking into account the numerous manifestations of fascist influence on European political, cultural, and intellectual life between the wars. To make the "f" lowercase, reserving the term "Fascist" for the political parties that applied the word to themselves, has been only the first step toward acknowledging the plurality of fascist thought and movements. Much of the most important critical work on fascism, dispensing with the idea that National Socialism can or should be the final reference point of any treatment of fascism, has been devoted instead to a careful delineation of the historical and political specificity of other national fascisms.*

Proponents of this method may object that my own definition of fascism in this work is broader still, and indeed that I have conflated distinct national phenomena and emphasized different and sometimes contrary aspects of fascist thought to suit my own purposes. This book, however, does not purport to treat a particular national fascism, but rather the response of writers of various nationalities *to* fascisms, whose nature and significance often seemed as unstable and vague in the 1920s and 1930s as they do today. When Barnes, Yourcenar, and Woolf "thought fascism," fascism could mean to them, variously or simultaneously, National Socialism or Italian Fascism, Oswald Mosley's British Union of Fascists or Jacques Doriot's *Parti Populaire Français*—or something else, some still-evolving and amorphous set of concepts, images, and

---

*The field of "fascist cultural studies" is even wider than that of feminist modernist studies, including as it does significant scholarship in and on half a dozen different countries, and it is more difficult to provide a comprehensive list of major sources. A few of the texts that have been most pertinent to my own research include, in addition to the feminist works already cited, Alexander De Grand, *Italian Fascism*; Victoria De Grazia, *How Fascism Ruled Women*; Alastair Hamilton, *The Appeal of Fascism*; all of Andrew Hewitt's work; Alice Kaplan, *Reproductions of Banality*; Zeev Sternhell, *Neither Right Nor Left*; and the essays collected in Richard J. Golsan's *Fascism, Aesthetics, and Culture* and Walter Laqueur's *Fascism: A Reader's Guide*.

political practices, which these writers themselves were trying to identify and define. Even though Yourcenar might set *Denier du rêve* in the specific context of Mussolini's Italy, for instance, that novel and her other contemporary works are often informed as well by her concern with Prussian history and French reactionary movements. If at one moment I choose Ernst Jünger as an exemplar of a particular tendency in fascist thought, and at another Pound or Louis-Ferdinand Céline, it is not because I take them all to typify a hypostatized fascism, but precisely because I wish to examine the multiple meanings "thinking fascism" took on for intellectuals in the interwar period, whether they identified themselves with fascism or opposed it.

While my subject thus requires that I rely on a broad and flexible characterization of fascism, this approach, which insists that fascist modernity was *not* a parenthesis—in history, in culture, in "civilization"—does present some real hazards, as theorists of fascism and culture have generally been quick to acknowledge. First, arguing that fascism constituted one configuration of cultural discourses shared by non- and even antifascist ideologies may seem to accord it an intellectual seriousness and respectability that at best trivialize it, and at worst legitimate it. As one critic has written, "We have tended to refuse" to engage with fascism as an intellectual problem "in order to preserve in ourselves the emotional recoil upon which our disgust for it is based"; to do otherwise might encourage tolerance for tendencies that World War II ought to have rendered definitively intolerable (Craig, 262).

Yet we must also realize that the refusal to acknowledge that fascism had deep intellectual, aesthetic, and ideological roots in European culture falsifies its history, and ours. It forces us to deny the alliance between culture and politics upon which fascism itself insisted and from which it drew so much force: "Stunned by the horrors of the established Nazi state, we forget that fascism took hold in Europe partly as 'radical chic,' that it was gaily disseminated by poets and critics" (Kaplan, 170). In addition, refusing to treat intellectual fascism seriously frequently leads to a demonization or pathologization of fascist intellectuals that borders on bad faith: as Russell Berman notes, an intellectual antifascism that is satisfied with "denouncing barbarism as merely barbaric. . . . denies itself the possibility of investigating intellectual lineages, perhaps even its own. Has it constructed a self-serving alibi?" (Berman, "Wandering Z," xiv; see also Craig, 262)

A second danger attendant on the cultural analysis of fascism is that, if we admit that fascism and culture might have something to do with each other, we are faced with the troubling problem of figuring out whether and to what degree artists or cultural artifacts can be held "responsible" for fascism—a problem that has produced a great deal of impassioned, confused, and sometimes hypocritical debate ever since fascist intellectuals found themselves on trial for treason after the war. The fear that literary texts might, in this case, stand in a direct causal relation to political events, and particularly to the Holocaust, tends to provoke a mad rush by critics to try to rescue their favorite authors from charges of collaboration, by showing some profound divergence from the fascist program in their texts, or pointing to the writers' actual persecution by fascist regimes.

The first defense, however, would be valid only if fascism had some consistent and clearly articulated program, which it did not. It has often been argued, indeed boasted by fascists themselves, that it is this extreme flexibility, the refusal to abide by any static ideological scheme, that is the very hallmark of fascism: the fascist philosopher Giovanni Gentile, for instance, asserted fervently in 1925 that fascism was a "mystical state of the soul" and that therefore the Fascist Party had "no need to define its doctrine and set its agenda" (Gentile, 95–96). Fascist ideologies are perhaps better characterized as hybrid and highly opportunistic conglomerations of beliefs, themes, and images, none of which is necessarily present in any given articulation of fascist thought. As soon as we attempt to define some element fundamental to fascism—say, the adoration of a heroic leader—we can find an apparently fascist writer in whose texts this element does not appear—Céline, for example—and have therefore to conclude either that Céline was not a fascist in any meaningful sense, or, more probably, that the adoration of the hero may not be essential to all fascist thought. This is not to say that fascist discourses have no typical or common features; they have many.* But they are rarely found all together, and the absence of any particular "ideologeme"—one of the rhetorical figures, tropes, and themes that constitute ideological discourse—does not necessarily mark a text as nonfascist; to claim otherwise is disingenuous at best.†

As for the assertion that censorship or persecution by a fascist regime proves an individual's essential antifascism, it is obvious that such an argument would, at its nonsensical limit, mark the German expressionist painter Emil Nolde or the Italian writer Curzio Malaparte as antifascists. In fact, the silencing and persecution of numerous fascist intellectuals by fascist regimes demonstrates little more than fascism's insatiable appetite for eating its elders as well as its young. The fact is that for at least part of their careers Nolde, Malaparte, Céline, Pound, Gabriele D'Annunzio, Jünger, Martin Heidegger, Marinetti, and many other intellectuals

*Many critics of fascism have listed the "ideologemes" they feel to be most characteristic of fascist thought. I would like to cite from one of these lists at some length, because it includes numerous features typical of many different national ideologies at various stages, and thus gains in scope what it may lose in precision. Dieter Saalmann lists, as features common to both many fascisms and the avant-garde,

the irrational tendencies of the *fin-de-siècle*; Nietzsche's plea for *Lebenspathos*, or a vitalistic disposition; moral relativism; the cult of the instinct; an emphasis on action; aristocratic inclinations toward the state as the only purveyor of values; an anti-capitalist mentality nurtured by utopian and romantic notions; an overt racism and virulent anti-semitism; an elitist aestheticism coupled with an occasional extreme form of *Weltfremdheit*; a deep-seated aversion to the parliamentary form of government; a profound anti-modernist conviction exacerbated by capturing, in a very genuine way, a pronounced sense of the loss of national self-esteem and a distinct feeling of distrust vis-à-vis the Western world and the modern age in general; a frame of mind dedicated to the principle of *épater le bourgeois*; an emphasis on the power of the free will reinforced by an anarchist drive to determine the pattern of life . . .; a ruthless readiness to cast aside the human element in favor of ideology; a resolute denial of mediocrity and the conforming habits of the herd instinct under the impact of Nietzsche's demand on the individual to conquer himself and to rid himself of his false sense of inferiority; and, finally, the dichotomy between aesthetic and economic considerations, between the spiritual values of the "new myth" and its plutocratic aspects, a point that figures prominently in Brecht's and Benjamin's discussion of fascist aesthetics. (Saalmann, 223)

†This kind of defensive maneuver, while increasingly discredited, could still be met with as recently as the late 1980s. During the ardent debates of

openly identified themselves with fascism, up to and sometimes even after the moment when they provoked the displeasure of a fascist leader or regime. And incurring the wrath of the regimes did not necessarily require an act of outspoken resistance; the political tendencies of many fascist intellectuals were simply too idealistic and anarchic to conform entirely to the demands of established power, and fascist politicians generally mistrusted even their "pet" intellectuals.

In judging the culpability of individuals, then, it seems at least provisionally useful to call anyone a fascist who called him- or herself one, regardless of his or her relationship to fascist institutions; and to hold individual artists and intellectuals accountable, not for causing the Holocaust, but for whatever they actually said, did, and wrote. It hardly constitutes an apology for fascism, after all, to acknowledge that many fascists neither foresaw nor willed the end results of Hitler's military and racial policies; that fact does not render them blameless.

But this said, it is more important to acknowledge that limiting our discussion of fascist texts to the question of the "guilt" or "innocence" of their authors prevents us from recognizing the hegemonic influences of the fascist discourses circulating in those texts. One critic writes:

> It could indeed be argued that the postwar politico-juridical machinery sought principally to reduce and confine the meanings of texts by writers . . . in order to contain the broader significations that might have emerged following the war as French and much of European society confronted the genocidal consequences of the racist and ethnocentric discourses that had proliferated in the period immediately preceding and during World War II. (Scullion, 195)

Again it seems that the effect, if not actually the goal, of the effort to "other" fascist thinkers and fascist thought—to define them as aberrant, pathological, or, in the case of the judicial analysis of fas-

---

those years about Pound's relationship to fascism, Leon Surette maintained that although Pound did eventually fall victim to fascist propaganda, he could not have been in general agreement with fascist doctrines because he was skeptical of conspiracy theories—as if a belief in conspiracy theories were the determinant feature of all fascist ideology (see Surette, 343–48).

cism, criminal—is principally to relieve the investigators of the need to pursue a line of inquiry that could prove embarrassing, to say the least. And while it is understandable that the postwar "juridical machinery" was required to make a sharp, and sometimes fatal, distinction between collaborators and the "innocent," the machinery of literary criticism can surely afford a less trenchant and more self-critical approach, an undertaking endangered by an overemphasis on individual biographies.

If biographically based criticism is one way of containing the far-reaching effects of fascist discourse, formalist criticism is another and equally effective method. A third, and very serious, possible consequence of an analysis that attempts to explore the intellectual origins of fascism is that by refusing to begin with the ending we might end by dismissing it from our theory altogether. It is easy enough to explode the idea that writers and intellectuals like Gottfried Benn or Jünger—and how much less Marinetti or Pound—were responsible for the death camps. But a formalist reading of their texts can lead us so far from the thought of the death camps that we end up in some very compromising positions indeed. The study of fascist aesthetics, for example, has tended to privilege Mediterranean fascisms and protofascisms, uncannily recapitulating certain racial stereotypes in the process: if Nazism was ruthlessly efficient, bureaucratic, and humorless, then Italian Fascism was spirited, sexy, and *fun*, not to mention well dressed. (Even Hannah Arendt, not generally given to aesthetic tergiversation, tends toward this conclusion in *Eichmann in Jerusalem*, as we will see in Chapter 4.) It is not too far a slide down this particular slope before we arrive at the conclusion that there was nothing wrong with fascism except its racism, and that there was, therefore, nothing wrong with Italian Fascism at all; this argument was used, with some success, by Alessandra Mussolini in her campaign for Italy's reconstituted neofascist party. The ethical challenge posed by "thinking fascism," then, is always to keep the vision of "where it all ended" in the 1940s on the horizon of our speculations, without letting that knowledge paralyze our investigation of the paths it took to get there.

Fourth and finally, treating fascism as an intellectual and cultural phenomenon always entails the risk that, as we widen our definition of fascism to include all of its diverse origins and manifestations, we may arrive at a uselessly broad concept of fascism as virtually everything that happened in Europe in the first half of the twentieth century, and "protofascism" as everything that happened before that (Spackman, *Genealogies*, 211–12). Fascism would thus become identical with modernity, and, consequently, equally impervious to both analysis of its specificity, and condemnation.

It is true that as we delve into the cultural history of fascism we may begin to feel like the proverbial hysteric who is always seeing Germans under the bed. Like the hysteric, however, we must ask what part our own illegitimate desire plays in our fear, and consider the possibility that the real anxiety underlying the criticism of a broad definition of fascism is that such an approach might reveal the fascist elements of texts that we have always read with "innocent" pleasure, and even force us to acknowledge the seductiveness of more clearly fascist texts we would love to hate. The goal of an investigation of the "intellectual lineages" of fascism must be neither to tar all of modernity with a fascist brush nor to exonerate particular fascist works or authors, but rather to understand, in order to counteract, the deep and widespread fascination and appeal of the cultural discourses that led, for many, to a fascist politics. If such an investigation has occasionally had uncomfortable consequences for some intellectuals—the potential stigmatization of deconstruction, for example, in the wake of disclosures about Paul de Man's collaborationist activities during the war—then it is all the more necessary that our analysis should be thorough, careful, and precise.

Heesok Chang has proposed a model for thinking fascism in this way, posing a question about Martin Heidegger that can be asked of many modernist texts: "If we are neither attempting to show a troubling complicity of his thinking with Nazism, nor trying to salvage a buried thought which is antifascist in its essence, for what else then are we reading?" (Chang, 32). Following Derrida's work on Heidegger, Chang suggests that we are instead reading fascist texts, or reading texts in relation to fascism, in order to articulate a difficult but surely necessary critique of fascism "from the inside." Such a critique accepts that its own methodology has already been determined by fascism's successful "recentering of critical focus on the terrain of the politico-cultural," and that it is not, therefore, possible—and was not in the interwar period—to produce texts that treat fascism while remaining wholly Other to it, outside the terms of fascist thought.

Before approaching the three works that are the principal focus of this book, I would like to explore the topography of that politico-cultural terrain in greater detail. In the next chapter, I identify the salient ideologemes circulating in European cultures at the end of the nineteenth century and the beginning of the twentieth, and so describe the cultural context from which both fascist modernity and the various modernisms arose.

CHAPTER 2

## *Political Bodies*

> [They seek] out . . . cases of inversion in history, taking pleasure in recalling that Socrates was one of themselves, as the Israelites say of Jesus that he was a Jew, without reflecting that there were no abnormal people when homosexuality was the norm, no anti-Christians before Christ, that the opprobrium alone creates the crime. . . .
>
> Marcel Proust, *Sodome et Gomorrhe*

Michel Foucault coined the phrase "the technology of sex" to describe the system under which, during the nineteenth century, class-based notions of genealogy were transformed into a preoccupation with heredity, sexual behaviors became associated with distinct biological types, and ontogeny and phylogeny were linked in the conceptual "series composed of perversion-heredity-degenerescence," each term referring to the others in such a way that, in this system, an unhealthy heredity could produce a sexual pervert, and sexual perversion could exhaust the pervert's line of descent (Foucault, 118).

In the ideological net thus woven around the concepts of race, disease, sexuality, gender, and class, Jewishness and homosexuality were perhaps the densest knots of signification, both capable of recalling all the meanings invested in each term. One critic has written that in the nineteenth century "the representations of both syphilis and the Jew are informed by particular constructions of gender and sexuality" (Geller, 23), and the reverse is also true: representations of the newly created class of "homosexuals" were, as we will see below, modeled on familiar figures of Jews and Jewishness, as well as on prototypes of disease.

For conservative and nationalist discourses, these marginalized Others were frequently objects of fascination and revulsion. Yet the horror provoked by Jews, homosexuals, and, in some areas, Gypsies cannot be explained simply by reference to the marginal; it was the way those at the margins of society made the borderlines of gender and nationality blur and shift that threatened to tear apart the very fabric of the patriarchal nation-state as it had been constituted. This threat was perhaps especially acute in Germany, whose identity as a unified nation was so tenuous.

But it is important to recall that the technology of sex furnished the vocabulary of explanation for the epoch, and not merely for conservatives. The conceptual connection between Jews and homosexuals, and more generally between nationality, class, and sexuality, also constituted the discursive terrain where numerous banners besides that of nationalist racism were unfurled. When we find Jews and homosexuals adapting this rhetoric, it may not always be meaningful to refer to "Jewish self-hatred" as Sander Gilman has, or to what we would now called "internalized homophobia"; I will claim that progressive and emancipatory discourses of sexuality, for example, could also draw on this shared vocabulary.

In order to understand the varied ways in which the technology of sex was implemented, we must first investigate the context in which it arose in the nineteenth century. Historian George Mosse writes that the technological changes spawned by the industrial revolution "introduced a new velocity of time that menaced the unhurried pace of life in an earlier age." The struggle to resist this velocity produced a sense of disorientation, the feeling that human beings were incapable of adapting themselves to a pace of life ordained by machines (Mosse, "Beauty," 25). In 1895, adapting the theories of B.-A. Morel and the Comte de Gobineau, Max Nordau diagnosed the root of this malaise as "degeneration." According to Nordau, modern Europeans, especially the upper classes, were suffering from a degeneration caused by the combined effects of urbanization. Neurasthenic symptoms of "nervous exhaustion" were provoked, according to Nordau, by contemporary opera and theater, tobacco, alcohol, narcotics, the "fatigue" induced by novel sensations like electricity, and overwork; the result of these stresses, particularly on constitutions already debilitated by generations of consanguineous marriages and the dissipated habits of the upper classes, was that people were now aging faster, giving birth to enfeebled children, and dying sooner (Nordau, 9–11, 39–40). Nordau and many others claimed that European society as a whole was, like imperial Rome and other great civilizations before it, sliding into decline.

In addition to causing physical and psychological stress, the rise of industrial capitalism also thoroughly disrupted Western culture's organizing hierarchies and boundaries of class, race and place, and gender. Especially in Europe, the decline of established codes of social differentiation and the effort to consolidate the diverse European nations provoked a growing concern with the human body as the site and marker of difference—difference of gender, race, class, nationality, and the newly created category of sexuality. The customs, accents, gestures, education, state of health, kind of work, and even (with the arrival of mass-produced ready-to-wear) the clothing that had formerly permitted groups to differentiate themselves from each other were becoming more and more mixed, democratized, and homogenized. But concepts drawn from the biological sciences (the survival of the fittest, the biological basis of all human characteristics, the transmissibility of traits) suggested more essential differences among human beings, differences that were inscribed on their bodies.

> It was the basic claim for all of the various offshoots and parallels of scientific discourse during the latter half of the century: that human nature and the psyche are but reflexes of biology and that it is this that determines humanity's place in the world. . . . Whether Darwinian or Lamarckian, whether Herbert Spencer's social darwinism or Ernst Haeckel's biological recapitulation, all the variations on the biological model used their paradigms to explain the nature of human difference. (Gilman, 213)

It was, perhaps, in part in reaction to a way of life that was increasingly mechanized that many embraced "organicist" ideologies like Social Darwinism so eagerly; being a mere animal was still better than being a machine. While such ideologies were not uncontested, the scientific discourses that proclaimed that human nature could be reduced to the biological traits of the organism, and that the characteristics of both groups and individuals could be explained by reference to biological "laws," eventually penetrated every domain of nineteenth-century life, including institutional politics.

Although biologistic thinking influenced radical as well as conservative ideologies, it lent itself especially well to the effort to contain revolutionary movements. Nordau attributed anarchism and socialism to the revolutionaries' incapacity to adapt "to existing circumstances" (Nordau, 22, 43). In particular, biologism provided an apparently empirical and rational foundation for racist discourses. In Foucault's words, "An entire social practice, which took the exasperated but coherent form of a state-directed racism, furnished this technology of sex with a formidable power and far-reaching consequences" (Foucault, 119).

Within an organicist model, for example, the idea of the nation-state as a unified, organic body politic eventually became quite literalized. Thus, in the discourse of degeneration, the principal culprits in the perceived decline of the polis were often thought to be those who confused boundaries of race and place, particularly Jews and Gypsies, who came to be described, in influential texts like Nordau's, as symbols and symptoms of the nervous decline of races and nations. In the words of Walter Rathenau in 1897, Jews were "not a living part of the people (*Volk*) but a strange organism in its body" (Rathenau, 454).

In an age of rapid urbanization, furthermore, Jews were identified with the "inorganic" landscape of the city. The eternal land—in its multiple senses of soil, nature, and nation—was contrasted with the speed, noise, anonymity, and dirt of the modern industrial city. Jews and other "outsiders" concentrated in urban populations, like homosexuals, were then linked in a chain of equivalent elements perceived to threaten propriety and property, with their associated notions of cleanliness, rectitude, ownership, belonging, and place. Big cities and their inhabitants became for many the symbol of the mechanical, abstract, and unnatural (Mosse, *Nationalism*, 137). Jews, it was held, "thrived in 'mechanical' rather than 'organic' situations. They thus flocked to Berlin—the very embodiment of 'Judaized' society—for there, as Heinrich Laube put it, even spiritual exercise was the product of mechanical forces" (Aschheim, 227). "From the nineteenth century on," claims Mosse,

> the guardians of nationalism and respectability felt menaced by the big city, the apparent center of an artificial and restless age. Such cities were thought to destroy man's rootedness. They led to alienation—and unbridled sexual passion. . . . Sexual deviance was once again linked to conspiracy, darkness, and stealth. The village or small town close to nature possessed no dark bowels within which vice could flourish. It symbolized those eternal values that stood outside the rush of time. Here the nation and manliness were at home; here one could still recall the healthy, happy past. The city was home to outsiders—Jews, criminals, the insane, homosexuals—while the countryside was the home of the native on his soil. Such notions, common by the middle of the nineteenth century, were to be repeated almost word for word by Heinrich Himmler during the Third Reich. (Mosse, *Nationalism*, 32)

Such a conservative, nationalist ideology was in fact widely promulgated in the first decades of the twentieth century, not only by Nazi officials but also by reactionary intellectuals like Oswald Spengler, and Maurice Barrès and Charles Maurras in France. They underlined the conflict between a rural scene invested with the eternal values of tradition, blood, and community, and the metropolis—impersonal, anonymous, and devoted to the pursuit of material pleasures. In *The Decline of the West*, Spengler contrasts the peasant's farmhouse, "the great symbol of settledness," with the "giant cities" that house the "intellectual nomad." These urban intellectual nomads become too alienated from "the primitive values of the land" ever to return to their roots: "Even disgust at this pretentiousness, weariness of the thousand-hued glitter, the *tædium vitæ* that in the end overcomes many, does not set them free. They take the City with them into the mountains or on the sea. They have lost the country within themselves and will never regain it outside" (Spengler, 2: 90, 97, 102).

Furthermore, the city, like the Jew, "means not only intellect, but also money" (Spengler, 2: 97). For reasons related to but going beyond their historical ties to moneylending, Jews were firmly associated with what Spengler calls *"Gelddenken"* or "money thinking," the logic of abstraction, mediation, and exchange value: the logic of liberal capitalism. Judaism was indeed inseparable from Enlightenment thought itself; liberalism was essentially Jewish.

> Worldliness, conservatives argued, threatened to destroy the organic basis of society, to trample on traditional values of honest labor and authentic community. For such circles the process of "Judaization" was the consequence of the decline of religion. The triumph of the Enlightenment, of the French Revolution and liberalism, had destroyed the Christian state and the old social order and prepared the way for the rule of Judaism. (Aschheim, 232)

In 1903 the conservative and notoriously anti-Semitic Jew Otto Weininger remarked with distaste that indeed, "Judaism is the spirit of modern life" (Weininger, 329).

After World War I, similar anti-Semitic and racist themes gained in intensity. In its "milder" form, fascist racism expressed itself as simple xenophobia; the Other might very well be in his place, or as Céline expressed it, "Over there they were great guys, here they bug me." But with the increasing stress on the organic cohesion of the national community, elements perceived as alien were bound to be viewed as intolerable threats, whether they were seen as evil in themselves or only out of place: to be out of place was, indeed, to be intrinsically evil. The Jew, especially though not exclusively in Germany, thus became the focus of wide-ranging anxieties about the integrity of culture and the stability of the nation.

Conservative and fascist ideologies adapted the notion that Jews were alien to the national community to a cultural critique that attributed the inauthenticity of contemporary mass culture to Jewish influence. Jews, not having a fixed location, could not share in cultures rooted in the community of blood or soil and were therefore reduced to the imitation of other cultures, to artifice. This accusation was, of course, no newer than other anti-Semitic ideas; the idea that Jews lacked originality was prevalent in the nineteenth century, and indeed harked back at least as far as the sixteenth (Gilman,

62–63). But fascism updated the concept with its insistence that the *Verjudung*, or Judaization, of society was responsible for the atomization and commercialization of mass culture:

> If there were no significant additions to the idea of *Verjudung* during the Weimar period, there was a kind of updating, fitting it into the *Zeitgeist* of an unprecedented permissiveness and placing it within the new era of technology and consumerism. This, at least, was the emphasis of racist ideologues and self-proclaimed "culture critics" like Alfred Rosenberg and others. "Judaization" now became the metaphor for the critique of mass society. . . . It was the Jews who relentlessly tried to remove individual personality and "replace it with the chaos of those cosmetic leveling phrases of Humanity, Fraternity, and Equality." The modern city was the creation of, and dominated by, the "Jewish spirit"; its result was mass, atomized man. . . . The major instrument of "Judaization" was mass culture. (Aschheim 238; quotations are from Rosenberg, "Der Jude")

Mass culture was also, of course, one of *fascism*'s major instruments of control. Fascism constituted itself on the terrain of the cultural; throughout Europe, fascist movements and, later, fascist regimes were preoccupied with controlling cultural forms and made use of cultural media to an unprecedented degree. Antifascist critique, as I argue at greater length in Chapter 5, was obliged to follow; it was "the political success of fascist culture" that forced the reorientation of Marxist criticism toward "a focus upon the 'political' at the very moment of its production" in the superstructure (Chang, 19).

Benjamin's famous pronouncement that fascism is the aestheticization of politics is in some regards more provocative than descriptive, but it has the virtue of acknowledging the way in which fascism invaded the cultural domain and the new cultural media created by technological advances. In Italy, Marinetti's "radical chic" and D'Annunzio's elegant militarism contributed to the creation of a politics of style that infiltrated or assaulted public consciousness by means of radios, loudspeakers, and the mass distribution of futurist-style pamphlets. In Germany, especially once the Nazi regime was installed, "what becomes apparent is the microscopic attention the Nazi hierarchy accorded the observation and regulation of all aspects of cultural life in the Reich" (Barron, 10). Radios were jokingly referred to as *Goebbelschnauzen*, such was the ubiquity of the *Reichsminister für Volksaufklärung und Propaganda*. Under the Nazi administration, thousands of new pieces of music were composed to glorify National Socialism, and the film industry produced over a thousand feature films, of which only one-sixth, according to one estimate, were explicit propaganda; the rest enacted fascist principles or aesthetics in more subtle ways (Meyer, 173–74). Mass media became the means of indoctrinating the masses.

In every aspect of culture, fascism strove to recuperate a notion of authenticity that contrasted with commodified, inauthentic, or "Jewish" culture. The idea and importance of the authentic was so widely recognized that the Belgian Rexist movement could call its publication simply *Pays réel*, automatically invoking an image of the "real" or "true," fascist, Belgium. Cultural authenticity was located in different domains by different aspects of fascist thought: for Jünger, for example, the "authentic" might be represented by the transcendent emotion of battlefield experience. Céline strove to re-establish what he called an "authentic" French literature, and the fascist implications of his concern with authenticity are particularly manifest in works like *Bagatelles pour un massacre*, in which Bolshevist/capitalist/Jewish elements introduce sexual debauchery and miscegenation into "authentic" rural French communities. For conservative German nationalists, similarly, the "authentic" continued to be represented by a pastoral image of the *Volk*, and the "inauthentic" by the urban Jewish or "Jewified" intellectual: for them, "[Weimar] Berlin was a loveless metropolis of left-wing intellectuals, pornography, and mass consumption" (Herf, 35).

As the participation of Jews in cultural institutions threatens, in the discourse of authenticity, to contaminate the purity of national cultures, the presence of Jews within national boundaries threatens to destabilize the nation, whether defined in terms of a shared culture, soil, language, or blood. It could be argued that the need to contain the influence of the Jew on the cultural domain is both provoked by, and an expression of, the anxiety occasioned more generally by the attempt to define the nation.

While the notion of the nation-state as the highest form of social organization prevailed throughout Europe after World War I, the question of where and how to draw the boundaries of particular nations—literally and figuratively—was deeply perplexed. For example, the tropes of nationality and exile recur insistently in both fascist rhetoric and modernist literature. Fascist nationalism has sometimes been contrasted with the supposedly intrinsic internationalism of modernism; but in truth we find both tendencies crossing and conflicting in modernist/fascist texts.

Many of the writers who made their literary debut in the interwar period were expatriated for part or all of their lives; and yet they frequently remained preoccupied with defining (their own relation to) the "national character" of the *patria* they had left behind. For some, the experience of exile was emblematic of modernity itself and was essential to a conception of modern(ist) marginality that many writers concretized in the figure of the Jew—as, too, did fascism. As we will see in Chapter 3, Barnes embodies her concerns with alienation, mediation, and the significance of bodily difference in Jewish and half-Jewish characters, Guido and Felix. Joyce chose to represent his own experience of exile and alienation in the person of the Irish Jew Bloom. Pound, the chief exponent of an "internationalist" modernist poetics, espoused the nationalist and anti-Semitic rhetoric of fascism, finding in Mussolini's Italy the closest parallel to what he viewed as an authentically American tradition. Christopher Isherwood and W. H. Auden went into exile, as one critic has said, "as the only way . . . finally to effectively insult England"—or in Auden's words, "to break away from it all"—but we will see in Chapter 5 that the obsessive recurrence of literal and symbolic frontiers in their work suggests that the break with their own nation did not free them from their preoccupation with the concept of "the nation" (Martin Green, 372; Maugham, 203).

Barnes, Yourcenar, and Woolf also dealt, in both their lives and their writing, with the meanings of nationality and exile. Barnes and Yourcenar were expatriated from their native countries for much of their lives; and Woolf, who stayed her whole life in or near London, was particularly preoccupied by the question of the relation between women and the nation, a question articulated most explicitly in *A Room of One's Own, Three Guineas, The Years*, and *Between the Acts*. For both Barnes and Yourcenar, exile became not only a theme of their writing but, apparently, a precondition for its production: as if it was necessary for them, in order to write in the ornate, almost Shakespearean English of the one, or the pure classical French of the other, to distance themselves from the reality of the spoken mother tongue.* For her part, Woolf, in her corner of Bloomsbury, wanted to create a "woman's sentence," a language that would express women's distinctive relationship to the national tongue—and to the nation.

Fascist ideologies, though explicitly nationalist, were also troubled by the instability of their own (conceptual) borders. National Socialism itself, the most nationalist of doctrines, "deliberately cut across all national boundaries," as Arendt points out, noting that, "Historically speaking, racists have a worse record of patriotism than the representatives of all other international ideologies together" (Arendt, *Origins*, 161). It is in part for this reason that Mussolini, as a good patriot, originally rejected racialist thinking—which did not hinder him in the least from pursuing his vision of an imperial Italy across the national frontiers of Ethiopia. In every European country except Germany, radical nationalists were confronted during the war with a conflict between their allegiance to fascism and their nationalism: was the French fascist, for example, supposed to embrace the German invaders in the name of international fascism and a vision of a united fascist Europe, or to cling determinedly to a nationalist ideology for which Germany was the traditional archenemy?

As Alice Kaplan notes, "a confusion about identity and nationality in general can be collapsed into the word *Jew*" (Kaplan, 152–53), underlining the crucial role ideologies of Semitism, whether anti- or philo-Semitic, play in these conflicting discourses. A similar confusion and ideological *density*, as it were, is indicated by the word "homosexual," a term that, as my earlier remarks suggest, is

*Josyane Savigneau offers a similar hypothesis in her biography of Yourcenar; see Savigneau, 331.

thoroughly involved in European culture with concepts of the Jew and Jewishness. Furthermore, the connection between homosexuals and Jews, like the significance of Jewishness itself, must be understood within the context of the conceptual associations among abstraction, exchange value, liberal capitalism, the inorganic, and the unnatural.

Thus in the late nineteenth and early twentieth centuries, both homosexuals and Jews were accused of being sterile or of causing sterility, homosexuals for obvious reasons, and Jews because their lustfulness, it was charged, provoked them to corrupt gentile women, "thus preventing the birth of healthy children." Jews in particular were said to frequent gentile prostitutes; here, a kind of bourgeois sexual moralism merged with the popular prejudice that portrayed Jews as arch-capitalists, as they were attacked for treating gentile women as commodities (Mosse, *Nationalism*, 134–44). Jews, homosexuals, and women were all thought to lack control over their carnal desires ("The Jew is always more absorbed by sexual matters than the Aryan," wrote Weininger [311]). The nineteenth century's economic model of sexuality described sexual force, embodied in sperm, as a limited resource that had to be carefully conserved; those who indulged their lusts, especially nonprocreatively, were said to be squandering their life energies. Consequently, Jews and homosexuals were typically portrayed, on stage and in other media, "as fragile, close to death, the victims of premature old age." And, although it was known that Jewish culture was in fact strongly patriarchal and family-oriented, Jews were not portrayed with children, because doing so would have de-emphasized their supposed exclusion, along with homosexuals, from bourgeois family life (Mosse, *Nationalism*, 134–35).

For Weininger, homosexuality, like Judaism, was a symptom of a material and effeminate culture in which the transcendent values of virility were in decline: he observed darkly, "Our age is not only the most Jewish but the most feminine," and promptly surmised that "the enormous recent increase in a kind of dandified homosexuality may be due to the increasing effeminacy of the age" (Weininger, 329, 73). The peculiar logic of this "chain of equivalences" culminated in the notion that Jews actually invented homosexuality. For Arthur Trebitsch, another conservative, anti-Semitic Jew: "The 'secondary spirit' of the Jews is manifested in their sexuality, since their perversions are a reflection of their inability to relate at all to primary experiences, such as love. The Jews are the inventors of masturbation and homosexuality, both of which reveal their true nature, as they are only mechanical sexual acts, acts without any true relationship between the sexual partners" (Gilman, 250).

The menace these marginalized elements represented was accentuated by the fact that neither Jews nor homosexuals were necessarily recognizable as such. It is worth noting that, as intense as racism toward Africans was throughout the history of colonialism, in Germany and France at least it seems never to have attained the degree of hysteria provoked by the idea of a freemasonry of Jews and homosexuals. The recognizable Other might have his (subordinate) place, but hidden he could insinuate himself anywhere. The paranoia this idea induced manifested itself in conspiracy theories that stretched, sometimes, to include nearly everyone except the individual conspiracy theorist. The forgery of the *Protocols of the Elders of Zion* is only the most notorious example of the lengths to which some were willing to go to demonstrate that Jews, homosexuals, and masons all over Europe were infiltrating positions of power in government, the judiciary, and finance (Mosse, *Nationalism*, 138), in a preliminary move in their plot to take over the culture/the country/the world. Hence the effort, in many texts like Nordau's and Cesare Lombroso's, to train the general population to recognize the signs of degeneration; a vigilant national community would be able to spot the Jewish or homosexual infiltrators in its midst.

In a different vein, the amalgamation of Jewishness and "abnormal" sexuality would find its most elegant and ironic expression in the first decades of the twentieth century in the *apologia pro vita sua* of Proust's *Remembrance of Things Past*. Without ever quitting the vocabulary of explanation he inherited from the late nineteenth century's discourses on Jews and homosexuals, Proust offered perhaps the most thorough theorization of male homosexuality that had yet been undertaken by anyone in fictional form, an analysis in which homosexuality is insistently analogized to and linked with Jewishness. And André Gide approached the same project in a contemporaneous work composed in the form of a Platonic dialogue, *Corydon*. At one point, Gide's homosexual protagonist invokes Léon Blum's controversial book *Du mariage* in support of one of his arguments in favor of homosexuality. The obtuse narrator reviles the book as a typical Jewish attack on the morals and institutions of France; Corydon responds, "People have protested against this book . . . but no one has refuted it" (Gide, 103), suggesting that Jews and homosexuals are both victims of unfounded and irrational social prejudice. It seems, then, that by the early part of this century, homosexuals themselves had begun to analogize their sense of persecution to the oppression of Jews, perhaps playing on pro-Jewish sympathies roused by the Dreyfus affair in order to heighten awareness of the comparable injustices inflicted on the sexually marginal.

Gide and Proust were hardly, of course, the first homosexuals to engage in the debates about sexuality. Hellenism—the interest in Greek culture, art, and literature—had been mounting in Europe ever since the Enlightenment and had intensified in the 1870s with the rediscovery of Troy; and the image of classical Greece was always shadowed by the homoerotic. By the late nineteenth century, indeed, Greece was nearly as synonymous with sodomy as it is today, particularly for the educated classes, who could read classical languages. But this tradition harked back at least a century, to J. J. Winckelmann's 1764 work, *History of Ancient Art*.

Winckelmann, who was so well known as a homosexual that a contemporary French translation of his work openly refers to his murder at the hands of a casual lover, found the highest expression of human beauty in the Greeks' sculpted representations of the masculine form. He also proposed that there is an organic unity between the soil and climate of a country and its people's ethics and aesthetics. According to Winckelmann, the Mediterranean area, with its temperate climate and natural beauty, gave rise to the ideal human type and its aesthetic representations. Countries farther from Greece, the center of the world, produced human and natural anomalies.*

Understandably, generations of homosexuals shared in the enthusiasm for Hellenism. Many adapted Winckelmann's theories to support the argument that if a people's aesthetics and ethics were organically rooted in its soil, and Greek aesthetics were the apex of human artistic achievement, then the well-known problem of the Greeks' peculiar sexual ethics could not be overlooked or viewed as a deviation, but must also stem from and reflect the superiority of the culture as a whole. If the Europeans were the heirs of Greece (something to which most European nations laid claim) and aspired to emulate Greek aesthetics, they must also reckon with Greek morals.

John Addington Symonds was one of the first to make this argument explicit in *A Problem in Greek Ethics*, written in 1873 and privately printed in 1883. Forty years later, Gide's Corydon points out to the narrator of the text that they have both "been taught to venerate Greece, of which we are the heirs," and have learned that art always reflects the character of the people who produce it. "Are you trying to convince me," he asks the narrator,

> that this people, capable of offering the world such mirrors of wisdom, of graceful power and of happiness, did not know how to conduct its own affairs—did not know first of all how to apply this happy wisdom, this harmony to its very life and the ordering of its morals! Yet as soon as Greek morals are mentioned, they are deplored, and since they cannot be ignored, they are turned from in horror . . . we refuse to admit that they form an integral part of the whole, that they are indispensable to the functioning of the social organism, and that without them the fine flower we admire would be quite different, or would not be at all. (Gide, 106–7)

In Corydon's formula, in fact, homosexuality is so indispensable to the functioning of civilization that he can finally conclude, "I would almost go so far as to say that the only periods or regions

---

*See Winckelmann, *History of Ancient Art*, especially vol. 2, bk. 4, chaps. 1 and 2: "Ground and Causes of the Progress and Superiority of Greek Art Beyond That of Other Nations," and "The Essential of Art." The reference to Winckelmann's homosexuality is in the Preface to Winckelmann, *Histoire*.

without uranism are also the periods or regions without art" (Gide, 117).

In underlining the unity of art and homosexuality, Gide drew on the aestheticist movement of the previous century, which was one of the predominant currents of reaction against liberal bourgeois aesthetics and morals. By the late nineteenth century it was widely assumed that there was a connection between "artistic temperament" and homosexuality, and the milieu of the aestheticist avant-garde was hospitable to homosexuals like Oscar Wilde, Aubrey Beardsley, and Renée Vivien. Participating enthusiastically in the neo-Hellenic revival, these aesthetes made explicit the implicit homoeroticism that shadowed any invocation of Greek ethics and aesthetics. *L'art pour l'art*, or "art for art's sake," became the pre-text for "sex for sex's sake," the valorization of a "nonnatural," nonreproductive sexuality that was resistant to moral evaluation.

In the cult of beauty that informed a certain aesthetic ideology from Winckelmann onward, the two concepts became, indeed, inseparable. In the words of one homosexual German man, writing at the turn of the century, "Beauty knows only one law—its own. . . . [Homosexual men] love only 'Beauty,' beauty however and wherever it shows itself" (Caesaréon, 94). This homoerotic aestheticism defied the moral and aesthetic hegemony of the bourgeoisie, asserting sexual deviance as a mark of individual distinction in a monotonously democratized age and claiming the sensual as an end in itself.

In the following decades, modernist movements, even while sharply differentiating themselves from the dandified and effeminate posing of aestheticism, would retain aestheticism's contempt for bourgeois ethics and aesthetics, its debt to classical influences, and, consequently, its implicit homoeroticism. Eliot described the study of Greek culture as a kind of collective psychoanalysis of the European mind, claiming that "Neglect of Greek means for Europe *a relapse into unconsciousness*" (Eliot, "Commentary," 342; his emphasis). The homoerotic could, then, be read as modern Europe's *consciousness*, its civilized ego; "Greek morals" are, as Gide would have said, indispensable to the functioning of the European organism.

Joan DeJean has suggested in *Fictions of Sappho* that it was the figure of Sappho that came to symbolize modernity itself for the early moderns: " 'Homosexual passions among females'... become central to 'the *modus vivendi* of the modern world'.... In the age of the 'eternal feminine,' Sappho, and no longer those Symonds calls 'the heroic lovers,' was the logical center of a cult of sublimated homosexuality" (DeJean, 224). Many modernist texts bear this out: we might think of the way "the lesbian" becomes synonymous with "the modern" in a work like *The Rainbow*, or in the figure of Barnes's "Modern Girl" in *Ladies Almanack* (Kent, 93).

We will return to the subject of this aestheticist homoeroticism in the chapter on Barnes. But it is important to note that that tendency, and especially the focus on Sappho, voluptuous symbol of the "eternal feminine," represents only one strand of the genealogy of homoeroticism descended from neo-Hellenism, and appears to have had greater currency in the Latin countries than in Germany, for example. There, the cult of "the heroic lovers" thrived, and the challenge to liberal bourgeois aesthetics and morality took the form, in the late nineteenth and early twentieth centuries, of the rise of youth groups and other elements of the *Lebensreformbewegungen*, or "life reform movements." These movements also embraced concerns as diverse as clothing reform, nudism, vegetarianism, antialcoholism, and land reform (Mosse, *Nationalism*, 45, 50). In general, the reform movements shared in the neoromantic emphasis on the sensual and the mystical, rejecting liberalism's alienating dualism and rationalism. Though often antiliberal in sentiment, reform movements tended nonetheless to be a bourgeois phenomenon, the response of the middle classes—for whom socialism was too tied to the laboring classes, capitalism too Jewish, and the aristocracy morally corrupt—to the problems posed by industrial capitalism and urbanization (Steakley, 26–28).

The movements, while usually rejecting open expressions of sexuality, were informed by a barely subliminal homoeroticism.

The youth movement, for example, "held mystical rituals of ancient Germanic origin and venerated the Eros principle as a means of deepening male friendships" (Kedward, 198). In addition, at least two homosexual emancipation groups evolved directly from the reform movements. The *Wissenschaftlich-humanitäres Komitee*, or "Scientific-Humanitarian Committee," headed by Magnus Hirschfeld, a Jewish socialist, descended from the sexual reform movements; the group was profeminist and leftist in orientation, had women members, and espoused an ideal of egalitarian, erotic relationships. This group supported the medical theory that homosexuality was innate or "congenital"; same-sex object choice was viewed as a medical problem of inverted gender identity.

The other major homosexual group was the *Gemeinschaft der Eigenen*, usually translated as "Community of the Special," grouped around Adolf Brand and Benedict Friedländer, which evolved from the nudist movement. Brand was an anarchist, but the group moved at the end of the nineteenth century away from anarchism and toward an aestheticist or Hellenic model (Oosterhuis, 2–3). Exclusively male, antifeminist, and anti-Marxist, it also became progressively more nationalistic, anti-Semitic, authoritarian, and in its later stages, vehemently anti-Weimar (Steakley, 42–43). The philosophy of this group is worth discussing at greater length because of its bearing both on fascist erotics and on the erotic ethic that Yourcenar puts into play in works like *Le coup de grâce* (see Chapter 4).

Brand's group entirely rejected the medical model of homosexuality, espousing instead a theory of cultural homosexuality. Unlike the liberal reformist Hirschfeld, the members of the *Gemeinschaft* aimed not at political tolerance for a sexual minority, but at the "homosexualization" of society. Like other neo-Hellenists, the members of the *Gemeinschaft* believed that male romantic friendships had been the foundation of cultural achievements, patriotism, and military virtues in Greece and in pre-Christian Germany. The Germans were the heirs of Greece, and if the German Empire was to recapture the warlike disposition, heroic attitude, and aesthetic achievements of the Greeks, it would also have to encourage manly "friendship," nudism, and "every sport establishment that does not degrade people to machines in a revolting way, but rather elevates the pleasure of every individual and the joy of our whole people in bodily strength and beauty" (Oosterhuis, 119–20; Brand, "What We Want," 160).

The *Gemeinschaft*, then, espoused a politics of sexuality in many ways more radical than Hirschfeld's, while adhering to the reactionary values of nationalist militarism. Its members asserted that homosexual men made better soldiers, that antihomosexual prejudice was spread by Jews, and that nudism and homosexuality should be encouraged in the interest of "racial health and purity" (Steakley, 49; Mosse, *Nationalism*, 41–42; Oosterhuis, 4). The members of the *Gemeinschaft* were, furthermore, deeply antidemocratic, believing in the natural right to rule of a small, homosexual elite. Like the nineteenth-century aesthetes, the *Gemeinschaft* claimed their sexual deviance as a sign of distinction. But whereas someone like Oscar Wilde might have expressed the belief that the homosexual was more "sensitive," and thus a superior type, the *Gemeinschaft* believed that the homosexual was more "virile," and thus a superior type. Participating in the elite, aristocratic tradition of *pæderastia* raised the members of the *Gemeinschaft* above "bourgeois mediocrity and the materialism of the common people" (Oosterhuis, 185).

Democracy, "bourgeois mediocrity," and materialism were further associated with Enlightenment values belonging not to virile Germany, but to effeminate England and to Germany's historic enemy France; not to a community of men, but to women; not to the nation, but to the family. The members of the *Gemeinschaft* "were obsessed by the notion that female influence in culture and in politics was devastating for the vigor of civilization" (Oosterhuis, 187). Under the malevolent influence of bourgeois and proletarian movements like feminism and socialism—imported from England and France—German men were in danger of being forced back into "sexual slavery" and Germany risked becoming a weak, effeminate nation (Oosterhuis, 187).

Similar fears were expressed by Germans who were not homosexual; for example, Nietzsche and his vulgarizers opposed the concept of "Greece" to Christianity as well as to Judaism, finding in the classical model the image of a virile society that had been crushed by effeminate Judeo-Christian mores and by bourgeois democracy (Gilman, 169). Indeed, radical right-wing homosexuals like the *Gemeinschaft* had a good deal in common with other movements of reaction in Wilhelmine and Weimar Germany.

In 1925 a member of the *Gemeinschaft* described the ethos that bound together the youth movements, his own homosexual ideology, and fascist romanticism. What all these tendencies share, he argues, is their irrationalism, their affinity for a mysticism "that stands beyond the laws of church and morality, which arises from something instinctive":

> The rejection of the rational expresses itself, for example, in such diverse facts as the aversion to coercive institutions, in the fight against the norms of bourgeois morality, in turning away from every materialism that allegedly explains things "rationally" and likewise from logically constructed idealism, in the rejection of political machinery, such as formal democracy has made its own, in the emphasis on the sovereignty of one's own "I," in the attempt to remain in harmony with the great laws of nature (Tao), in the recognition of the significance of erotic elements as the principal natural connecting link between people. . . . The inclination toward the irrational is further attested through . . . the turning to the Gothic, to the native and Nordic romanticism, to so-called "folk art," to the "magical" mysticism of a Novalis. (Waldecke, 200)

The fascist romanticism that eventually evolved in Germany from the conjunction of conservative nationalism and radical socialism may have rejected overt homosexuality, but it espoused precisely the same aesthetic and ethical values as the *Gemeinschaft*. The *Hitler Jugend*, for example, which evolved from the youth movement, despised the "élitism and effeteness" of the earlier movement, yet shared its mythology, its style, and its ideals (Kedward, 198–99). The Storm Troopers and their leader Ernst Röhm, a notorious homosexual, had particularly close ties, both ideological and literal, to the *Gemeinschaft*. At least one friend of Röhm's published in *Der Eigene*, the group's journal. And in the late 1920s Brand pointed to the hypocrisy of the Nazi Party, which officially opposed homosexuality, writing that "Men such as Captain Röhm... are, to our knowledge, no rarity at all in the National Socialist Party. It rather teems there with homosexuals of all kinds. And the joy of man in man... blossoms around their campfires and is cultivated and fostered by them" (Brand, "Political Criminals," 236).

As soon as the Nazis took power, however, they launched a campaign against explicit expressions of male homosexuality. By 1934, "the period of struggle for power had ended, and with it any ambivalence about the prédominance of bourgeois morality" in the new Nazi Germany (Mosse, *Nationalism*, 159). On June 30, 1934, Hitler authorized the bloody purge known as "the night of the long knives," during which Röhm and numerous other members of the SA were murdered as the Nazis tried to solidify the image of respectability that had won them bourgeois support and helped bring them to power.

After the purge, the Nazi SS began to compile lists of known and suspected homosexuals, and a special task force was formed to combat male homosexuality. Significantly, the antihomosexual campaign focused obsessively on the possibility of seduction: "It is remarkable," notes one historian, "that the Nazis should have regarded all German males as susceptible to homosexual seduction to such a powerful degree. In fact, the consideration forced itself on them again and again that their own movement, which was based on male bonding, might evoke homosexuality" (Oosterhuis, 252). What German fascism was afraid of, it seems, was not same-sex relations per se, but a too-open manifestation of a kind of eroticism crucial to its own ideology and aesthetics.

While the Nazis forbade nudism and outlawed pornography, for example, they continued to permit the display of nude photos of athletes, and to model their ideal of physical beauty on Greek sculpture and a Winckelmannian aesthetic. After all, "the present-day German and the ancient Greeks were considered the twin pillars of the Aryan race" (Mosse, *Nationalism*, 171). We think immediately of the opening of Leni Riefenstahl's "Olympia," where the camera tracks the Olympic flame across a map from Greece to Germany, collapsing history into a synchronic narrative about the physical perfecting of the (male) Aryan form.

German fascist ideology and aesthetics make, in fact, what seem oddly contradictory uses of (homo)eroticism: creating a cult of virility that emphasizes male bonding while despising homosexual effeminacy; drawing on romantic and decadent motifs while rejecting decadentism; and tracing fascism's mythologized heritage to one of the most openly homosexual cultures in history while viciously persecuting openly homosexual people. But in all the different and sometimes contradictory uses fascism makes of the erotic, there is the tacit understanding that sexuality is in its essence political: "Fascism marks the intense politicization of sexuality and the body" (Gättens, 5–6). The erotic is not a private matter as it is in bourgeois liberal ideology, but plays an important role in social power relations.

The political use of the erotic is crucial to fascism's self-differentiation from both liberalism and Marxism. Fascism recognizes and exploits the determining role of mind-body dualism and the ethos of individualism in the formation of alienated liberal social relations; in the fascist view, "the cultivation of subjective interiority in liberal culture led only to failed eroticism" (Berman, *The Rise*, 207). In the words of French fascist Drieu La Rochelle, fascism is "the political movement that leads most frankly, most radically . . . towards the restoration of the body—health, dignity, plenitude, heroism—towards the defense of man against the big city and against the machine" (Drieu La Rochelle, 50). In fascist ideology, the alienated liberal individual is reconstituted in the figure of the Leader, who restores to the body politic its integrity, health, and authenticity; and his ecstatic, erotic fusion with the physically well disciplined masses overcomes atomization.

Fascism thus translated a commonly felt dissatisfaction with the superficiality and commercialism of capitalist culture into sexual metaphor. The idea of inauthentic, artificial, or commodified culture is frequently represented metaphorically in images of unnatural or commodified sexuality, particularly masturbation, homosexuality, and prostitution. For the Right, commodified sexuality stems from the loss of authentic cultural values, the *Verjudung* of society; and this "is where the strategies of fascist literary address emerge, calling individualism to account, pointing to its sexual misery, and generating images of a new collective of perpetual union. T. S. Eliot's *The Waste Land* stands as a paradigm" (Berman, *The Rise*, 207). This theme is also reiterated in Pound's association of usury with prostitution in the *Cantos*, and, to choose a much cruder example, in *Mein Kampf*, where Hitler aligns the degeneration of the body politic, urbanization, unnatural and commercialized sexuality, and Jews:

> Running parallel to the political, ethical and moral contamination of the people, there had been for many years a no less terrible poisoning of the health of the national body. Especially in the big cities, syphilis was beginning to spread more and more. . . . The cause lies primarily in our prostitution of love. Even if its result were not this frightful plague, it would nevertheless be profoundly injurious to the people [*das Volk*], since the moral devastations which accompany this degeneration suffice to destroy a people slowly but surely. This Jewification of our spiritual life and mammonisation of our mating instinct will sooner or later destroy our entire offspring, for the vigorous children born of natural feeling will be replaced by the miserable products of financial expediency. (Hitler, *Mein Kampf*, 224–25)\*

While the establishment of a technology of sex permitted the articulation of Hitler's reactionary system of discrimination, it also enabled the explicit theorizing of a politics of gender and sexuality by the Left. In the left analysis, inauthentic or commodified sexuality is a symptom of oppression, manifested in the authoritarian repression of eros. The urtext for this critical tradition is Engels's "Origins of Private Property, the Family and the State"; two of its most important proponents are Virginia Woolf and Wilhelm Reich, with whose work Woolf's has some remarkable correlations (see

\* In a few passages from works originally in languages other than English, I have taken the liberty of modifying the work of other translators to conform more closely to the language of composition. The interested reader will find both the original and the translation listed in the bibliography.

Chapter 5). Fictional works of the period, like Christa Winsloe's 1931 film "Mädchen in Uniform" and Isherwood's *Berlin Stories*, also make overt connections between the suppression of eros and fascist culture, or, alternatively, the celebration of eros and the resistance to fascism.*

The problem of "inauthentic" sexuality, we note, is only one aspect of the larger problem, endemic to capitalism, that we could call the sense of "reified consciousness"—the fear that not only has the body become an object of trade in human relations, but that every aspect of the dis-integrated personality of "atomized man" is susceptible to objectification and commercialization. The desire to define and promote "authenticity," in place of a culture characterized by the lack of genuine emotion, commercialized sexuality, and mass consumption, is shared by most social critics of the period, whether they are inspired by left or right ideologies. It is the proposed solutions that vary. According to Jeffrey Herf's tripartite schema in *Reactionary Modernism*, the Right attempts to sublate the consciousness of reification by abolishing the liberal concept of the individual with its concomitant notions of rational subjectivity and the duality of mind and body. The liberal center, in contrast, resigns itself to reification, while clinging to "remnants of individual autonomy"; and the Left perceives it as a result of capitalist commodity relations and believes that revolution will restore the integrated subject and authentic human relations (Herf, 88–89).

The three writers on whom this work focuses might be viewed, loosely speaking, as representatives of the three strategies Herf defines. For Barnes, liberal individualism is a trap that ensnares us in the unbearable knowledge of our own mortality, and only the submission of individual will to ineffable forces offers any hope of alleviating human suffering. Yourcenar, in contrast, reaffirms liberal

* It is striking that so much left-wing work on sexuality was produced during the interwar period by Germans and people who were living in Germany. It seems that it was easier for leftists like Reich, Isherwood, and Winsloe, who were immersed in the conflicts over sexuality in Weimar Berlin, to realize that sexuality was one of the forces fascism was already manipulating for its own uses, and to understand the necessity of responding with an equally politicized discourse of sexuality of their own.

individualism and authentic Western cultural values as the antidote to atomized society, defining fascism as the culmination of a mass culture that is incapable of distinguishing the unreal from the authentic. And Woolf views militarism and fascism as the inevitable consequences of the patriarchal, capitalist economic system and describes in *Three Guineas* her vision of the revolution of "Outsiders" that could end fascist patriarchy once and for all.

All three of the texts to which we now turn are, then, rooted in and enabled by some of the overarching ideological discourses of the late nineteenth and early twentieth centuries: the definition of national boundaries, the significations of the human body, and the relation of the Other(ed) body—Jewish, homosexual, female, proletarian, exiled—to the nation. Viewed in this light, these and other modernist texts cannot be neatly separated into fascist and antifascist, reactionary and progressive camps, according to whether they assimilate or reject the discourses of their Victorian heritage. We must instead consider the various ways in which they participate in these discourses, analyzing the different strategies they deploy in their negotiations and the different ends they attain in the process.

In asking what the relation is between fascist culture and modernity more generally, and how these women intellectuals reacted to both, I do not hope to arrive at a definitive analysis of the response of women to either modernity or fascism; it is impossible that there should be a single answer to these questions. Nor do I intend to formulate a new and better definition of fascism, for, as my remarks here suggest, I believe that even if such a thing were possible the very project would be suspect. Rather, my goal is to help map out a more exact cartography of the era, to try to trace more precisely the contours of the terrain on which both these rhetorical strategies, and our own responses to them, are arrayed.

CHAPTER 3

# "*The Learned Corruption of Language*": Nightwood's *Failed Flirtation with Fascism*

> What Decadence, in literature, really means is that learned corruption of language by which style ceases to be organic, and becomes, in the pursuit of some new expressiveness or beauty, deliberately abnormal.
>
> Arthur Symons,
> "A Note on George Meredith"

The relationship of Djuna Barnes's 1936 novel *Nightwood* to fascism is sufficiently ambiguous and complex to have been suppressed by a first generation of critics. Kenneth Burke, for example, insists that although he chooses to discuss it in the "Hitlerite" terminology of "folk" and "blood," the book has absolutely nothing to do with fascism and is "'innocent' of political organization" (K. Burke, 252). Barnes's biographer Andrew Field reports that in later years Barnes herself vehemently disliked the idea that people might associate the novel with "the spirit of Nazism" (Field, 15). The force of the denial speaks to the persistence with which fascism seems to surface in the text, the difficulty of suppressing *Nightwood*'s "potent 'political unconscious.'" Recognizing this, later generations of critics have begun to try to situate the novel in its political and historical contexts. Field suggested in 1983 that Barnes's portrait of a world in intensely still crisis and on the verge of disintegration corresponds remarkably well to the social and political age in which it was written. If one understands the spirit of the Thirties at all, it is quite clear that . . . *Nightwood* does not speak only to the question of lesbianism or the private life of Djuna Barnes but also to its time. The Elizabethan passion is there, and so is the mood of a time when Bakelite radios first said terrible things to the world. The sudden appeal of Catholicism to many writers and intellectuals of the period is also there. This contextual atmosphere of *Nightwood* has not been sufficiently noticed. (Field, 214)

Jane Marcus has produced perhaps the most important work of criticism to date to take up this challenge, claiming that *Nightwood*'s emphasis on abjection implicitly opposes an Aryan ethic of "uprightness," and that the text itself can be read as "a kind of feminist-anarchist call for freedom from fascism" (Marcus, "Laughing," 223, 221). Marcus's characterization of fascism is, however, rather reductive, which renders her conclusions suspect. A closer investigation into *Nightwood*'s ideological and aesthetic affiliations suggests, in fact, that they tie the novel to central elements of Italian, French, and German fascist thought.

There are conjunctions between the Decadence (and aestheticism more generally), a particular strain of romantic Catholicism, and fascism that can be traced from the mid-nineteenth century through the 1930s; all three philosophies or ideologies can, for example, be viewed as responses to human suffering and mortality that reject rationalism or positivism, whether liberal or Marxist in inspiration. Thus *Nightwood*, clearly informed by both aestheticism and Catholicism, cannot be said to have a purely oppositional relation to fascism, and indeed, the novel mimics many of fascism's favorite tropes. My intention here is to try to demonstrate not that Barnes was a fascist sympathizer in any literal sense, but rather that her fascination with such themes and images needs to be taken seriously as we deepen our understanding of her work.

The aesthetic and ideological tradition that bears the greatest relevance to the relationship of Barnes's work to fascism is the Decadence, and the aestheticist movement in the broader sense, of approximately the mid- to late 1800s: the tradition Mario Praz calls the "Anglo-French Byzantium" (Praz, 279).* The influence of decadent aesthetics on *Nightwood* and Barnes's other work has been frequently remarked upon, by her contemporaries as well as more recent critics. Aestheticism, as we saw in the previous chapter, was part of the nineteenth-century wave of neoromantic reaction to the bourgeois rationalism and positivism that we characterize as "Victorianism" in England. The artists associated with aestheticism manifested their profound revulsion against "Victorian utility, rationality, and realism, or the reduction of human relations to utility and the market and the representation of this in bourgeois literature" (Gagnier, 3). Distinguishing themselves both from realism and from the romantic cult of nature, these neoromantics insisted on the value of form, external appearance, and artifice and assumed a position of moral neutrality with regard to the content of the work of art. This notion of *l'art pour l'art*, the refusal to admit ethical or political considerations into the aesthetic domain, functioned "to negate the means-end rationality of everyday middle-class life by theorizing art as an autonomous 'useless' realm" (Gagnier, 3).

As a philosophy of art and life, aestheticism and its morbid progeny, the Decadence, offered a sharp challenge to what were perceived as the optimistic positivism and sentimentality of bourgeois Victorianism. Gautier's inflammatory introduction to *Mademoiselle de Maupin*, which Praz labeled "the Bible of the Decadence," was "intended to frighten the bourgeoisie and spit at both

---

*Establishing precise dates for aesthetic and ideological trends is of course always troublesome; the tradition Praz and I refer to can be dated to at least as early as 1835, with the publication of *Mademoiselle de Maupin*. I also do a certain violence to the distinctions between periods of the nineteenth century, and English and French literature, by collapsing them into a single aesthetic phenomenon. Naturally Parnassianism, the pre-Raphaelite movement, symbolism, and so on all had distinctive and often conflicting philosophies. It is nonetheless fair to describe a consistency between, for example, Baudelaire's work of the 1840s and 1850s and Oscar Wilde's of the 1890s. Perhaps more pertinent, they are associated in the imagination of later generations; the "neodecadent" Brian Howard, for example, formed a club at Eton after World War I whose honorary members included "Whistler, Beardsley, Swinburne, Mallarmé, Samain, Savage, Wilde, Symons, Verlaine, Gautier, Ricketts, Pryde, Housman, Tree, Beerbohm, and Meredith" (Martin Green, 140–41).

respectability and revolt" (Fletcher, 3), an accurate description of the polemical stance of the aesthetes and decadents in general. Their rebuttal of Victorian mores focused on the problems of evil, pain, mortality, and the significance of corporeal suffering and fragility. For both bourgeois conservative and radical left thought of the day, the evils attending human experience could be characterized, quite literally, as diseases of the social body and hence as potentially curable by modern science. The most naive expressions of this belief seemed at times to imply that no malaise was beyond human control and cure.

For aestheticism, such confidence constituted a willful denial of the essential neediness and frailty of the human frame. Gautier had suggested this in his well-known maxim, "There is nothing really beautiful except that which is useless; everything useful is ugly, for it is the expression of some need, and the needs of man are ignoble and disgusting, like his poor infirm nature" (Gautier, 22). The apparently frivolous posturing of the dandy reveals itself in this light as a profound and poignant acknowledgment of mortality; the aesthete who rejoices in the beauty of the human body can never forget its ephemerality. Dorian Gray, the decadent protagonist par excellence, is never a more sympathetic figure than when he frankly admits, "I am jealous of everything whose beauty does not die. . . . Death is the only thing that ever terrifies me. I hate it" (Wilde, 50, 250). Haunted by their sense of human transience, the aesthetes felt that "only an art purified of irrelevant intrusions of morality and social-political ideas could resist time" (Beckson, xx).

Their art functioned in part as a memento mori to a culture doggedly determined to sentimentalize suffering and to rationalize it by attributing it either to social injustice or to those diseased Others who were spreading their degeneration throughout the social body. For aestheticism, the innumerable random tragedies and accompanying psychic anguish of the mortal condition were the proper subject of art. It is for this reason that Huysmans's protagonist des Esseintes admires Baudelaire:

> In a period when literature attributed man's unhappiness almost exclusively to the misfortunes of unrequited love or the jealousies engendered by adulterous love, he had ignored these childish ailments

and sounded instead those deeper, deadlier, longer-lasting wounds that are inflicted by satiety, disillusion, and contempt upon souls tortured by the present, disgusted by the past, terrified and dismayed by the future. (Huysmans, *Against Nature*, 147–48)

The decadents used the prevailing rhetoric of degeneration, with its focus on corporeal decay, as a way of thematizing this insistence on suffering. Their vision of death was, to be sure, a highly aestheticized and sensual one: "The very adoption of a rhetoric of sickness, be it Baudelairean or Lombrosian, is a thematization and valorization of the corporeal" (Spackman, *Genealogies*, 106). But the body that the Decadence valorized, while beautiful, was usually either dying or dead; and its fate was not specific, as in Lombroso or Nordau, to a few diseased individuals, but was the destiny of humankind. Accepting the terms of hegemonic organicist discourses, but inverting their premises, the decadents argued that the decay they represented was in fact a universal condition; from this position they challenged the pretensions of an age that seemed at times to hope it could transcend mortality:

> A contagious rhetoric spreads from the body to the already-made topos of the body politic. The very epithet "decadent," uttered first by critics encamped on an island of normalcy, is filtered through a positivistic progressive ideology that can define itself only against a negative regressive pole.... "Le Décadent" collapses the opposition to an identity, denies the existence of an isle of health and of the clear-eyed ones who claim to reside there. There is only decadence, only sickness, and only those who welcome it can represent "progress." (Spackman, *Genealogies*, 5)

One of the most important manifestations of corporeal decadence, and one of the central tropes of decadent art and literature, was, of course, deviant sexuality, especially (though not exclusively) homosexuality. As we have seen, in a certain aesthetic ethic descended from Winckelmann, *l'art pour l'art* was thoroughly imbricated with *le sexe pour le sexe*. Though this association was in place well before Wilde's time, it had never before been so publicly represented as it was at his trial: "As the prosecutors pushed the connections between the art world and domestic and sexual deviation, aestheticism came to represent a secret, private realm of art and sexuality impervious to middle-class conformity. In other words, aestheticism came to mean the irrational in both productive (art) and reproductive (sexuality) realms: a clear affront to bourgeois utility and rationality in these realms" (Gagnier, 5). Male homosexuals like Wilde had, perhaps, a particular interest in delineating an aesthetic ethic of male beauty and masculine romantic friendship; less "decadent" homosexual writers like J. A. Symonds also celebrated the cult of "the heroic lovers." For writers particularly fascinated by decadence per se, however—especially for those who were themselves more or less heterosexual—*female* homosexuality became the perfect figure for *l'art pour l'art*. Voluptuous (that is, aesthetic) yet sterile (that is, nonutilitarian), Sapphism represented what Baudelaire had called, in another context, "the immoderate taste for form" (Baudelaire, "L'École Païenne," 423).

At the turn of the century, the decadent discourse on sexuality had undergone a crucial transformation when a number of women writers in Europe, notably Natalie Barney and Renée Vivien, began writing "fictions of Sappho" from the perspective of the desiring female subject. As men writers had adopted lesbianism as a leitmotif of the discourse of aestheticism, lesbian writers in turn adopted the aesthetics of the Decadence. Temperamentally the ebullient Barney had little in common with the decadents, but both her work (especially her aphorisms) and her aesthetic philosophy of turning her own life into a work of art are in many ways reminiscent of Wilde, in particular. And Vivien was undoubtedly a daughter of the decadents, carrying their association of lesbianism with the aesthetic so far as to use it to validate her own artistic production, suggesting "that the 'unnatural' longing of the decadents' Sappho turns the lesbian into a prototypical artist, for her obsession with a beauty that does not exist in nature is part of a satanically ambitious effort against nature to attain the aesthetic par excellence" (Gubar, "Sapphistries," 49).

Like the organicist discourses they inherited, the "decadent lesbians" emphasized the sterility of lesbian sexuality. Vivien and Barney's preoccupation with sterility recalls the fundamental anguish underlying the decadent's proud perversion: the cycle of sexual reproduction is a reminder of human transience, and fertility recalls the horror of mutability. We hear a distant echo of des Esseintes's bitter "What madness to breed children!" in Barney's assertion that Sapphic "love has the sterility of immutable things.... It will outlive those fertile loves that multiply in generations on the earth and then are no more" (Huysmans, *Against Nature*, 170; Barney, *Dialogues*, 21, 19). Controverting the conventional view that procreation assures an individual's continuation in future generations, Barney suggests instead that, once removed from the cycle of reproduction, the homosexual is protected from (the reminder of) her own mortality.

This attitude may also be interpreted in part as a feminist gesture, unlinking an autonomous female sexual pleasure from the attendant obligations of marriage and maternity on which Victorian notions of womanhood insisted. "For Vivien," one critic suggests, "Sapphism, precisely because it is what the decadents called 'barren,' provides access not to the future of the human species but to the present of the female of the species" (Gubar, "Sapphistries," 50). Such a gesture constitutes a total defiance of the Victorian sex/gender system, as had the Decadence. Like Gautier and Baudelaire before them, Vivien and Barney explicitly (and in Barney's case rather gleefully) named lesbianism as a threat to bourgeois morality, the family, the Church, and ultimately the State. Following the decadent tradition of adopting and perverting Christian rhetoric and iconography, Barney presented Sapphism as a cult that both mimics and supersedes Christianity, writing to a lover, "If you love me, you will forget your family and your husband and your country and your children and you will come live with me" (Barney, *Dialogues*, n.p.). DeJean writes that

> Barney inaugurates the Sapphic fiction of "Sapho 1900" by assaulting her reader with a definition of Sapphism as a totalizing "cult" experience, a pseudoreligious experience that requires those who would be believers to sacrifice everything else to it, to give up all aspects of a traditional "normal" life, to leave the ranks of their families' genealogies, on whose uninterrupted unfolding the state depends for its security.... Furthermore, Barney flaunts the unspoken threat of Sapphism, its potential contribution to depopulation.... Barney offers a "cunning perversion" of the standard defense of *pederastia*: the goal of male homoerotic pedagogy had traditionally been presented as the initiation of

the young male to civic virtue; she proclaims its female counterpart to be the initiation of the young female to the perversion of all public values. (DeJean, 280–81)

Barney and Vivien were, of course, the forerunners of the generation of women-writers-in-exile to which Barnes belongs. Vivien died tragically and young, but Barney lived to supervise the flowering of a community of women that took up and transformed the aestheticist tradition. In his study of the late manifestations of decadence, Martin Green writes that "American culture has been unkinder to dandies and aesthetes than almost any other, but just for that reason there has always been a highly self-conscious colony of American dandies in exile" (Martin Green, 94). Strangely, Green entirely overlooks the fact that the pre-eminent figures who come to mind as "dandies in exile" in his sense are the women expatriates of the 1920s and 1930s. Barney, Barnes, Romaine Brooks, H.D., Janet Flanner, Gertrude Stein, Dolly Wilde, and their friends were perhaps the first generation of women with the means to aestheticize and represent themselves with the same wit and gender-bending irony that the male dandies of the nineteenth century had displayed, and their art often employs the same figures and explores the same themes as their male predecessors'.

Some interpret the female expatriates' adoption of decadent aesthetics and figures of lesbianism as a symptom—or cause—of their internalized misogyny and homophobia, even going so far as to blame Vivien's death on her overidentification with the Decadence.* But women writers living and writing a sexuality that had rarely been represented in any literature not explicitly pornographic were bound to look to men's writings to ground their own sexual and textual histories. They had little else to refer (themselves) to besides fragments of Sappho and a medical discourse that was far more oppressive and normalizing than the images of lesbians in Baudelaire, Gautier, or Swinburne—images that, if distorted by men's fetishes and fears, are also powerful and sensuous. It has been persuasively argued that, indeed, "H.D. and others 'used' the Decadents to fashion a feminist poetic of female desire,"

---

* See Benstock, "Expatriate," 200n11; and Faderman, 363.

finding, in the "effeminate" perversity that Eliot, Hulme, Pound, and Yeats repudiated so violently, an empowering model of sexual and gender transgression (Laity, 462–63). A deliberate assertion of abnormality can, after all, constitute a radical challenge to hegemonic, and repressive, definitions of normalcy.

Furthermore, we must not overlook the fundamental seriousness of the metaphysical problems with which decadence is engaged. The sexually marginal "women of the Left Bank" were concerned with the same problems: with mortality, the problem of evil, the significance of art, the relation of aesthetics to the body, and the relation of the individual body to the body politic. And of all these women, none realized and elaborated on the philosophy of decadence to the extent that Djuna Barnes did.

Barnes is most obviously indebted to the Decadence for elements of her style. Her early short stories, drawings, and journalism show the strongest decadent influence, with their preciosity, artifice, and "extreme stylization" (Kannenstine, 24), their images of vampires and "the Oriental" and dead flowers, and of course the marked derivation from Aubrey Beardsley in the technique of the drawings. Certain passages of the early work especially "echo the art-for-art's sake detachment of *The Yellow Book*, the mode of the decadents that would render aesthetic all emotions, appearances, and matters of life, including death" (Kannenstine, 10). But in fact all of the varied genres and styles Barnes explores exemplify the definition Arthur Symons formulated of decadence in 1897: "that learned corruption of language by which style ceases to be organic, and becomes, in the pursuit of some new expressiveness or beauty, deliberately abnormal" (A. Symons, 149). Barnes herself characterized her style as a kind of realism,* which recalls Adorno's comment that "modern art is as abstract as the real relations among men"; in the pursuit of ways of expressing grotesque realities, her style becomes grotesque and "abnormal."

* See, for example, her 1919 interview with Guido Bruno (a piece whose title, "Fleurs du mal à la Mode de New York," underlines her decadent heritage); when Bruno accuses her of being morbid, she retorts, "This life I write and draw and portray is life as it is, and therefore you call it morbid" (Barnes, *I Could Never Be Lonely*, 386).

In this sense, style is for Barnes, as for the decadents, a means of expressing, rather than masking, the central preoccupation she shares with them, an emphasis on suffering and death.

> The attitude is perfectly serious, though it deeply involves the frivolous. . . . Suffering becomes tolerable, even purifying, if it is done prettily. "Going down" is bearable if it is within an aesthetic context. The result of such an attempt, not to deny, but to ward off the necessary anguish of mortality is an extraordinary emphasis upon surface and manner, an unnatural stress upon superficiality, upon unnecessity. (Kannenstine, 9)

In an essay on Barnes's early plays, Joan Retallack similarly implies that the aestheticizing impulse in Barnes, beyond simply "purifying" suffering, forestalls mortality itself by circumventing the demands of a realist narrative that would mimic the passage of time. Claiming that Barnes is "condemned to surfaces," Retallack suggests that her difficulties with narrative reflect an inability to cope with temporality: "The surface is the true object of desire—to linger there, exploring its baroque intricacies while avoiding inevitabilities, catastrophes associated with forays which bring on the future tense" (Retallack, 51). While *Nightwood*'s narrative structure, unlike that of the early plays Retallack analyzes, is quite coherent and even symmetrical, it is also fiendishly intricate, anticipating itself, circling back again and again to the same chronological moment, deferring and baffling temporal resolution and the realization of meaning. Both an aestheticized style and an antirealist narrative structure, then, can express the desire to evade finality.

The same impulse drives Barnes's use of the trope of sterility. As it often does for aestheticism, homosexuality in Barnes's work represents the *chose en soi*, the value of the moment; temporality and sexuality are inextricably linked. "Methinks," says Patience Scalpel of the lesbian coterie in *Ladies Almanack*, "they love the striking Hour, nor would breed the Moments that go to it" (Barnes, *Almanack*, 13). Seizing on one of the aspects of homosexuality most threatening to dominant organicist discourses, its non(re)productiveness, Barnes inverts it and raises it, not only to an aesthetic principle but perhaps even to a claim for lesbianism as a privileged attitude in the face of the "universal maladies" of loss, suffering, and death. For organicist thought from Nordau to Himmler, homosexuality represents pure decline, without the hope of renewal and regeneration. For Barnes, however, as for Barney or Huysmans, regeneration is not a hope but a threat; sterility is, in the shadow of this persuasion, at least a mixed blessing.

The theme of sterility, as insistent in *Nightwood* as in many fin-de-siècle works, extends from the literal sterility of the sexual relationship between Robin Vote and Nora Flood to numerous other images of sterility, castration, impotence, abortion, and decline. Barnes, like other writers preoccupied with decadence and degeneration, depicts a decaying aristocracy, alluding in particular to Ludwig II.* References to "figureheads" evoke people who, like Mademoiselle Basquette, are missing their lower half, their genitals. Doctor Matthew O'Connor is both an obstetrician and an abortionist, interrupting the cycle of regeneration as well as occasionally assisting it. Count Altamonte is impotent; the second Guido Volkbein, sickly and otherworldly, will be the last of the (very short) lineage his father and grandfather are so obsessed with establishing. And his is only one of the incomplete or interrupted lineages in *Nightwood* — interrupted usually by the absence of mothers, in a world where women especially struggle to escape their role in reproducing humanity and thus human pain. The novel opens with the death of Felix Volkbein's mother, Hedvig, in childbirth. Nora refers to her father and *his* mother, but never to her own; Robin has no relatives save the husband and son she abandons, and is described in the draft of *Nightwood* as an "orphan" (Barnes, *Nightwood* TS, 50). Felix and Robin's son, Guido, has in the end only the representation of a Mother, the medallion of the Virgin he wears.

---

* For a discussion of this theme in French texts see Praz, 361–62. The most interesting passage in *Nightwood* on Ludwig II is only to be found in the unpublished draft in Barnes's papers at the University of Maryland. In the draft, Matthew O'Connor tells a story about the king that acknowledges his homosexuality while questioning the normalizing diagnosis of his psychopathology, thus imitating the decadent gesture of questioning the concept of "normalcy" and claiming decay as a universal human condition (Barnes, *Nightwood* TS, 28–31).

The Madonna is the focus of Guido's and all the characters' fantasies of immaculate love, an eternal intimacy without threat of loss, their quest for a reincorporation into the maternal body that would turn time backward in its course. "How more tidy had it been," muses the doctor, "to have been born old and have aged into a child, brought finally to the brink, not of the grave, but of the womb; in our age bred up into infants searching for a womb to crawl into, not be made to walk loth the gingerly dust of death, but to find a moist, gillflirted way" (Barnes, *Nightwood*, 98–99). Robin and Nora battle to contain one another, to get inside each other, to control each other's sexuality by figuring each other as mother or as child. And Robin wins: "You almost caught hold of her," Matthew tells Nora, "but she put you cleverly away by making you the Madonna" (Barnes, *Nightwood*, 146). Nora, as the Madonna, is not allowed to have sexual or any other human needs or weaknesses; for what is the Madonna but the mother-without-body, whose sexuality is suppressed, who is without corruptibility—the eternal progenitrix abstracted from the cycle of regeneration, the transcendent and disembodied metamother? In Her pure abstraction, She both represents and evades maternity.

The Virgin Mary is thus associated with the other simulacrum of procreation in the text, the doll. (The doll may well be another sign of decadent influence in Barnes's text, since it seems likely that she borrowed the image from Pierre Louÿs's *Chansons de Bilitis*, where Bilitis gives Mnasidika a wax doll of which she says, "C'est notre enfant" [Louÿs, 102].) "We give death to a child when we give it a doll," says Nora to the doctor. When Robin gives Nora a doll "it is the life they cannot have," the mimetic "effigy" of their nonreproductive sexual love. But it is also the "shroud," the symbol of productive sexuality and hence the reminder of transience. Female children are given dolls to socialize them to be mothers, to perpetuate the reproductive cycle, to acknowledge their own mutability. The doll Robin gives to Nora is a reminder not only of what they cannot have, but of what they have escaped.

Lesbians, then, are assimilated to both dolls and the Virgin Mary, all "exonerated of their earthly condition" (Barnes, *Night-

*wood*, 44). At Jenny Petherbridge's fateful party the night of the opera, the fortune-telling Marchesa de Spada asserts that, of all the assembled company, only Robin is exempt from the cycle of regeneration: "The Marchesa remarked that everyone in the room had been going on from interminable sources since the world began and would continue to reappear, but that there was one person who had come to the end of her existence and would return no more." Matthew says to Nora, "The doll and the immature have something right about them, the doll because it resembles but does not contain life, and the third sex because it contains life but resembles the doll" (Barnes, *Nightwood*, 70, 148). Robin, in her cataleptic inertia, is especially close to the object status of the doll. Part of her power is that, in her "middle condition" between male and female, beast and human, inanimate and waking, she is beyond (the consciousness of) "the world of becoming":

> Part of Robin's allure . . . is that, by turning herself into an object, she transcends the world of becoming as effectively as the saint. . . . In *Nightwood*, where childbirth only results in death, the invert's sterility is as precious as the saint's chastity, for both evade the horror of generativity and successiveness. Taking all punishment, resembling without containing life, the transvestite-doll becomes a fetish with magical powers. A remnant of childhood play-acting, the transvestite-doll sustains our trace memories of an androgynous (pregenital?) time when we evaded the trap of gender. (Gubar, "Blessings," 499)

This interpretation of lesbianism's privileged status is reinforced by consideration of a passage from *Ladies Almanack*. Inverting the psychoanalytic reduction of homosexuality to a narcissistic and immature evasion of sexual difference, Barnes implies that (male) heterosexuality is the fear of the confrontation with the self, and the subsequent recognition of the self's impermanence; for heterosexual men, love can only be a denial of separation and loss. Lesbianism, in contrast, acknowledges the "universal malady" and yet continues to find ways to hope, embracing loss and the prospect of death with resignation and courage.

> Love in Man is Fear of Fear. Love in Woman is Hope without Hope. Man fears all that can be taken from him, a Woman's Love includes

that, and then Lies down beside it. A Man's love is built to fit Nature. Woman's is a Kiss in the Mirror. It is a Farewell to the Creator, without disturbing him, the supreme Tenderness toward Oblivion, Battle after Retreat, Challenge when the Sword is broken. (Barnes, *Almanack*, 23)

Like aestheticism, we note, Barnes opposes lesbianism to "Nature," valorizing artifice over realism as a way of transcending the limitations of (human) nature. Her "decadence," and particularly her insistence on a decadent lesbianism, must be understood in this light, as a rejection of a liberal or Marxist positivism that she found totally inadequate to solve the problem of suffering and mortality, as did many of her contemporaries who turned to fascism. Barnes's decadence is a question of philosophy as well as of style, and it runs deep in all her work, even the high-spirited *Almanack*. And while decadence is neither equivalent to nor totally assimilable by fascism, it is generally even less digestible to left or liberal ideologies. As we investigate Barnes's relationship to fascism, then, those critics who want to claim her for the Left* must consider the fact that Marxist criticism has often been deeply hostile to Barnes and the tradition in which she follows.

While a few writers in that tradition, like Ruskin, Morris, and Wilde, have tried to theorize a synthesis of socialist principles and decadent aesthetics, more orthodox Marxist thinkers have generally found aestheticism unpalatable. A Marxist critique is just as likely as a conservative one to reject decadence in the name of "health."

> Health as a "logical" opposite of sickness appears in the criticism condemning decadence, where it stands for alternative practice, be it the realist novel (Lukács), the classicism of Giosuè Carducci (Croce), or the novels of Harriet Beecher Stowe (Nordau). Lukács is most straightforward in the essay "Healthy or Sick Art?" . . . Decadents are decadent not because they depict illness and decay but because they do not recognize the existence of health, of the social sphere that would reunite the alienated writer to the progressive forces of history. Sickness, then, is a reactionary mode of insertion into the class struggle. (Spackman, *Genealogies*, 6)

* As well as the work already cited by Jane Marcus, see, for example, Benstock, "Paris Lesbianism," 333.

*Nightwood* inspired precisely this reaction in 1937 from a Marxist critic who denounced Barnes's decadence, her lack of "genuine values." In a scathing review in *New Masses*, Philip Rahv implies that it is not the topic of homosexuality per se that he finds offensive, but the fact that for Barnes homosexuality is not an individual problem to be realistically analyzed but a *trope*, a figure for universal metaphysical concerns that "transcend reality." In effect, modernism itself is on trial in Rahv's critique, for its elitism, its antirealism, and what he views as its inherent decadence; as we saw in Chapter 1, modernism could be viewed as the descendant of an aestheticist tradition of both privilege and homoeroticism, and thus, in the eyes of some, as inimical as aestheticism to democratic, "healthy" (heterosexual) criticism.

> But the trouble with Miss Barnes is that she has not really written about perversion; she has merely exploited perversion to create an atmosphere of general mystification and psychic disorder that will permit her to transcend reality and make plausible a certain modernist attitude whose essence is a tragic pose and a learned metaphysical sneer. . . . It is not the doom of a world reeling to its destruction that Miss Barnes expresses, but those minute shudders of decadence developed in certain small in-grown cliques of intellectuals and their patrons [sic] cliques in which the reciprocal workings of social decay and sexual perversion have destroyed all response to genuine values and actual things. (Rahv, 33)

This view cannot simply be dismissed as the reaction of one peevish male leftist, for the concerns it expresses are integral to a historical materialist critique. The philosophy of the decadents, and Barnes, denies the origins of suffering in material conditions, ascribing it instead to that which it is entirely beyond the power of historical, political, or scientific progress to rectify. Their attitude is fundamentally ahistorical, making of decay a culturally and historically universal malady. In Spackman's description of the Decadence, "The rationality it calls into question is that of positivism and all ideologies of 'progress.' . . . Sickness provides them with the alibi they need for an alterity that positivism finds criminal" (Spackman, *Genealogies*, 215–16). Barnes's metaphysics is so entirely outside the logic of Rahv's worldview that he can only assert, against all the text's own claims for itself, that the suffering of *Nightwood*'s characters is purely individual, "neurasthenic," specific to the historical conditions of "certain small in-grown cliques of intellectuals": criminal.

According to some, the seemingly paradoxical relation of decadence to a more "futurist" or "virile" energy and to nationalism was already in place at the fin de siècle: "The apparent paradox of the Aesthete who is also an Activist is not uncommon in the period; though some wrote of ennui, lassitude, disillusionment, and disengagement, at the same time they might praise the virtue of energy, the glory of nationalism, or the mystique of manhood" (Beckson, xxxivn23). The most notable precedent for the association of decadent aesthetics with an affinity for fascism is probably the life and work of Gabriele D'Annunzio. As early as 1925, Osbert Sitwell could claim that "Fascism is the child of Fiume," referring to D'Annunzio's attempt to turn the conquered Adriatic city into a model corporativist state, in which the arts would flourish and a poet—D'Annunzio himself—would lead (Sitwell, 219).

Numerous analysts besides Sitwell have seen in *l'art pour l'art*'s insistence on "the immunity of aesthetics to ethics" (Spackman, *Genealogies*, 194) the Achilles' heel that allows aestheticism to become, with little struggle, the aestheticization of politics. The best-known analysis of the link between decadence and fascism is, of course, Benjamin's "Work of Art in the Age of Mechanical Reproduction," published in the same year as *Nightwood*, in which he proclaims that fascism is "the consummation of *'l'art pour l'art'* " (W. Benjamin, "Mechanical," 242). In Benjamin's analysis, "the categories of the traditional auratic work are transferred from the aesthetic sphere, where mechanical reproduction has rendered them obsolete, and transplanted into politics"; the aesthetic object becomes technology or violence, the artist becomes the fascist leader, and the crowd becomes the viewer or consumer of the spectacle of, for example, war (Berman, "Wandering Z," xix). Ethical or political evaluation of these newly conceived objets d'art is, naturally, excluded. Just as *l'art pour l'art* furnished the decadents with the ideology of *le sexe pour le sexe*, it becomes the pre-text for what we might call "*la guerre pour la guerre*" in the work of a writer like Jünger:

> The very purposelessness of the spectacle of destruction, its quality as something done for its own sake alone, these features of war are what Jünger celebrated in his language of will and beauty. For this "inner experience" of the war, wholly divorced from the questions of war aims or of the relation between sacrifices and political ends, meant a deliverance from middle-class society, from individual isolation, and from the emotions of pity and compassion. (Herf, 77)

Fascism is also indebted to the irrationalist tradition to which aestheticism belongs. For Zeev Sternhell, fascism descends directly from fin-de-siècle neoromanticism in its antirationalist appeal to instinct and emotion; it represents the spirit of the fin de siècle adapted to mass society (Sternhell, "Fascist Ideology," 349). Herf writes:

> Weimar's right-wing intellectuals claimed to be in touch with "life" or "experience" and thereby to be endowed with a political position beyond any rational justification. To conservative revolutionaries, no accusation was more damaging than to describe an idea or institution — positivism, liberalism, Marxism, science, parliament, reason — as *lebensfeindlich* (hostile to life). They, of course, viewed themselves as representatives of all that was vital, cosmic, elementary, passionate, willful, and organic, of the intuitive and living rather than of the rational and dead. (Herf, 26–27)

Herf also mentions the "contributions of European theorists of decadence such as Wilde and Baudelaire" to the effort to reconcile the machine with irrationalist romanticism, and writes, "By elevating the idea of beauty over normative standards, linking this concept of beauty to an elitist notion of the will, and finally interpreting technology as the embodiment of will and beauty, Weimar's right-wing intellectuals contributed to an irrationalist and nihilist embrace of technology" (Herf, 30). Fascism, in this view, is interpreted as the effort to reconcile the aestheticist spirit of irrationalism with technological modernity. Where capitalism commodifies the art work, and Marxism subordinates art to polemical criteria, fascism holds out the promise that the aestheticized life of the dandy can become available to the masses, through the aestheticization of every aspect of modernity.

Barnes herself seems to acknowledge German fascism's romantic roots, when she has Doctor Matthew O'Connor in *Nightwood* say, "I shall rest myself some day by the brim of Saxon-les-Bains and drink it dry, or go to pieces in Hamburg at the gambling table, or end up like Madame de Staël—with an affinity for Germany" (Barnes, *Nightwood*, 126). In the context of the 1930s, the doctor's allusion inevitably evokes both *De l'Allemagne* and romanticism's fascist heirs—and associates them both, furthermore, with his own homosexual sensibility.

For the neodecadents of the 1930s fascism was not, however, the only alternative to Marxist or liberal positivism. Another ideology rejected modernity while making the same romantic appeal to instinct, the beauty of form, and the quest for transcendence: the dogma that shadowed aestheticism in the nineteenth century and, in the 1930s, offered many intellectuals a spiritual option that fulfilled some of fascism's metaphysical promises. Catholicism, like dandyism, would seem indigestible to fascism, but it can be argued that a certain romantic or mystical Catholicism addresses many of the same metaphysical problems that fascism does: to the point, indeed, that—particularly in the Latin countries—Catholicism seems to have been viewed by some as a complement, rather than an alternative, to fascism.

This conjunction was not without precedent: in the middle of the previous century, an alliance among decadence, Catholicism, and political reaction had already announced itself in France with the wave of dandy converts that began with Barbey d'Aurevilly and swept up, among others, Huysmans, Verlaine, and Léon Bloy. There is a certain logical association between an aestheticist view of the frailty of human nature, the Christian doctrine of original sin, and the rejection of radical politics; as one critic writes, as a "believer in original sin, Baudelaire had contempt for humanitarian ideals and the nineteenth-century faith in progress" (Beckson, xxv). Barbey d'Aurevilly himself said of his conversion, "I settled on Catholicism. It is a convenient balcony from which I can spit down on democracy" (qtd. in Schnurer, 39). The famous choice with which Barbey d'Aurevilly presented Huysmans—the mouth of a pistol or the foot of the cross—he first offered to Baudelaire; he claims Baudelaire chose the cross, and wonders whether Huysmans will do the same (Barbey d'Aurevilly, 281–82). Huysmans, of course, did eventually become a devout Catholic, as does des Esseintes at the end of *Against Nature*. Martin Green suggests that Catholicism offers aestheticism a way of coming to maturity:

> Culturally speaking, Catholicism has often been a means whereby dandyism has been reconciled to reality; the repudiation of Protestantism has been a symbolic repudiation of philistinism and "squareness," and the acceptance of Rome and ritual has made dandyism seem a mode of paradoxical seriousness. But there have been two divergent strategies for Catholics to follow in developing a post-dandy ideology. One is the black romanticism of Huysmans; the other, the bright and cheerful clarity of Chesterton. (Martin Green, 138–39)

It is, obviously, the specific form of Catholicism manifested in Huysmans's "black romanticism" with which we are concerned here, and his comments on religion in *Against Nature* provide great insight into the appeal of his kind of romantic Catholicism to an aestheticist sensibility. Catholicism, like aestheticism, acknowledges the profound reality of human suffering and mortality. Huysmans associates the romantic doctrines of Schopenhauer with those of the Church, admiring in both, as he says in his preface, their pessimism and admission of "the horror of life," but finding a solution only in the Church (Huysmans, *A Rebours*, 12). Other passages of *Against Nature* remind us, however, that if Catholicism promises a more perfect transcendence than art, its rituals are nonetheless informed by a lush appreciation of the material world. The *glissement* between the sensual and the sacred is very short. Des Esseintes furnishes his bedroom as "a facsimile of a monastery cell," feeling that a bedroom should either be "a place . . . for nocturnal delectation" or "a sort of oratory" (Huysmans, *Against Nature*, 74–75). (We note that Djuna Barnes furnished the apartment she shared with Thelma Wood, particularly the bedroom, with liturgical ornaments, crosses, "ecclesiastical pillows," and paintings of saints and other religious themes [Field, 151]; Nora and Robin collect "cherubim from Vienna" and "ecclesiastical hangings from Rome" [Barnes, *Nightwood*, 55].) Huysmans also associates the smell of incense and the Church's rich ornamentation with art and with decadence. It is the Church, he claims, that has preserved culture from barbarism (in Green's interpretation, "Protestantism") (Huysmans, *Against Nature*, 88). And des Esseintes makes the same claims for Christianity that the decadent tradition makes for homosexuality, especially lesbianism: it represents the thirst for the unattainable desire, an ideal beauty. He traces his own tastes back to a Jesuitical upbringing: "Thus his penchant for artificiality and his love of eccentricity could surely be explained as the results of sophistical studies, super-terrestrial subtleties, semi-theological speculations; fundamentally, they were ardent aspirations towards an ideal, towards an unknown universe, towards a distant beatitude, as utterly desirable as that promised by the Scriptures" (Huysmans, *Against Nature*, 88–89).

Oscar Wilde drew the same connections between aestheticism, Catholicism, and, implicitly, homosexuality, emphasizing the passion for form; Dorian Gray flirts with Catholicism because "the Roman *ritual* had always a great attraction for him" (Wilde, 163; my emphasis).

For D'Annunzio's generation, "Roman ritual" became associated not only with the romantic and the sensual, but with the style and rituals of fascism as well. Praz traces the complex genealogy of that conjunction when he describes the style of *The Child of Pleasure* as "aesthetic Hellenism *à la* Gautier . . . with the music of Wagner (*Tristan*), aesthetic backgrounds, and pseudo-mysticism" (Praz, 376). In *The Triumph of Death*, Giorgio contemplates the choice between suicide and Catholicism, characterizing conversion as a new form of sensuality and describing the quasi-erotic fascination of what Foucault calls the "confessional imperative." D'Annunzio's own trajectory from aestheticism to Catholicism to an affinity for fascism is not unique; we could also consider, for example, the careers of Ezra Pound or of Antony, Viscount Knebworth, who was a "powerful dandy" and "interested in Fascism and Roman Catholicism," and whom Virginia Woolf points to in *Three Guineas* as an example of the British fascist (Martin Green, 123; Woolf, *Three Guineas*, 7). The Italian fascist regime also deliberately adopted and updated Catholic ritual, iconography, and traditions, employing a "secularized rhetoric of the sacred" to link Italy's Catholic and imperial past to its fascist and modernized future (Schnapp, "Epic," 21).*

One way of interpreting these curious convergences is to view both fascism and Catholicism as ideologies that fulfill the aesthete's craving for form, spectacle, and the unattainable ideal. From the aesthete's perspective, Marxism seems concerned only with the material conditions of humanity, dismissing our metaphysical needs and fears; liberalism, in contrast, relying on an abstract view of human nature as the essentially rational, takes no account at all of the corporeal. But fascism and Catholicism seem to promise the aesthete a kind of transcendence *through* the immanent, the material and subjective, while offering what Eliot calls "an escape from personality" (Eliot, "Tradition," 43), from the burden of aestheticism's focus on the self.

Aestheticism glorifies (male) individuality. For the aesthetes, "the artist is a 'law unto himself,' born to follow his own impulses; if he does not harmonize with society, then so much the worse for society. Sensibility consequently substitutes for morality: the subjectively good and beautiful become the end of life" (Fletcher, 10). Baudelaire, for example, described "dandyism" as "an institution beyond the laws.... It is first and foremost the burning need to create for oneself a personal originality.... a kind of cult of the self" (Baudelaire, "The Painter," 26–28). This insistence on the value of the subjective and the sensual is, as I suggested in Chapter 2,

---

*See also Casillo, "Fascists," 102; and Adamson, 362. Examples of this kind of rhetoric in Italian fascist texts, in which fascism is overlaid with Christian symbolism, described as a faith and/or explicitly compared to Catholicism, are almost too numerous to be cited. Representative passages can be found in Camillo Pellizzi's "Idea e fede del fascismo" in his *Problemi e realtà del fascismo*, and in a section of Giovanni Gentile's *Che cosa è il fascismo* titled "Il fascismo è religione," where he draws an extended comparison between fascism and Catholicism (Gentile, 38).

equally a precondition for aestheticism's challenge to oppressive hegemonic moral and aesthetic standards, for fascism's rejection of liberal humanism, and for the project of homosexual emancipation. It fails, however, to address the need for fusion, the desire to transcend the limitations of self. The fascist finds this transcendence in the *Männerbund*, the community of soldiers, and the Catholic in communion with God and the community of believers.

*Nightwood* is infused with a Catholic sensibility that few readers since Eliot, it would seem, have fully appreciated. Some critics have seen in Eliot's introduction the religious red herring that sent Barnes's readers off on the wrong track for the next 40 years (see, e.g., Gerstenberger, 131), and his curiously ambivalent praise of the novel undoubtedly reveals as much about his own Anglo-Catholic leanings as it does about the book. Nonetheless, I believe that in one respect at least Eliot's reading is accurate and strongly supported by the text. Eliot describes two alternative positivist ideologies—a normative conservatism, which he terms "Puritanism," and a progressive radicalism—and correctly finds them both inadequate to encompass *Nightwood*'s insistence on the universal malady.

> In the Puritan morality that I remember, it was tacitly assumed that if one was thrifty, enterprising, intelligent, practical and prudent in not violating social conventions, one ought to have a happy and "successful" life. Failure was due to some weakness or perversity peculiar to the individual; but the decent man need have no nightmares. It is now rather more common to assume that all individual misery is the fault of "society," and is remediable by alterations from without. Fundamentally the two philosophies, however different they may appear in operation, are the same. It seems to me that all of us, so far as we attach ourselves to created objects and surrender our wills to temporal ends, are eaten by the same worm. (Eliot, "Introduction," xv)

Matthew O'Connor cannot, of course, be equated either with the narrator or with the author of *Nightwood*; however, to the extent that he *is* representative of Tiresias, his pronouncements on the other characters and on the text can be assigned a certain prophetic and narrative authority. And for Matthew, "pride" is indeed "the inveterate sin" and individual neuroses a mere cover-up for a universal condition of suffering. "I'm not neurasthenic," he tells Felix; "I haven't that much respect for people—the basis, by the way, of all neurasthenia" (Barnes, *Nightwood*, 33). Neurasthenia, the catch-all nineteenth-century malady that gave rise to its own cure, psychoanalysis, is the neurotic culmination of post-Enlightenment Western society's obsession with individual subjectivity. Barnes implicitly disdains the "respect" that the liberal or Enlightenment notion of the subject accords to personal suffering: "The intricacies of personal history interest Miss Barnes only as examples of the wrong road. To her mind neurasthenia covers up the universal horror with the individual malady, and that is why she has O'Connor reject it out of hand as a kind of arrogance which gives the individual too much leeway for rationalization" (Pochoda, 189).

Nora's Puritan heritage, in contrast, encourages a belief in individual solutions: "By temperament Nora was an early Christian; she believed the word. There is a gap in 'world pain' through which the singular falls continually and forever." (Barnes, *Nightwood*, 51). The doctor says of Nora that she is "A religious woman . . . without the joy and safety of the Catholic faith, which at a pinch covers up the spots on the wall when the family portraits take a slide" (Barnes, *Nightwood*, 60). He berates Nora for her self-absorption, which he, "as good a Catholic as they make," recognizes as delusion and arrogance:

> Do you think there is no lament in this world, but your own? Is there not a forbearing saint somewhere? Is there no bread that does not come proffered with bitter butter? I, as good a Catholic as they make, have embraced every confection of hope, and yet I know well, for all our outcry and struggle, we shall be for the next generation not the massive dung fallen from the dinosaur, but the little speck left of a humming-bird. . . . A broken heart have you! I have falling arches, flying dandruff, a floating kidney, shattered nerves *and* a broken heart! But do I scream that an eagle has me by the balls or has dropped his oyster on my head? Am I going forward screaming that it hurts, that my mind goes back, or holding my guts as if they were a coil of knives? Yet you are screaming and drawing your lip and putting your hand out and turning round and round! . . . Are you the only person with a bare foot pressed down on a rake? Oh, you poor blind cow! (Barnes, *Nightwood*, 154–55)

Protestantism—with its focus on the individual interpretation of the Word, its rationalism and its perviousness to social and political pressures—stands, in Matthew's worldview, for logocentric individualism. In contrast, Catholicism allows the believer "your own meditations *and* a legend," offering the faithful a way to merge into a tradition that transcends historical particularities (Barnes, *Nightwood*, 21; her emphasis).

Like fascism, Catholicism in Barnes's text represents the force of myth, of instinct; it fills in the (visual) space abandoned by the "family portraits" with its own mythologized images. Barnes's contemporary May Sinclair, analogizing the poetics of imagism to the Catholic's belief in transubstantiation, wrote, "The Victorian poets are Protestant. For them the bread and wine are symbols of reality, the body and the blood. . . . The sacrament is incomplete. The Imagists are Catholic. . . . For them the bread and wine are the body and blood" (Sinclair, 456). According to this formulation the Catholic, like the fascist, would seek an unmediated relation to blood, valorizing the instinctive, the authentic. "What do you listen to in the Protestant church?" Matthew asks.

> To the words of a man who has been chosen for his eloquence—and not too eloquent either, mark you, or he gets the bum's rush from the pulpit, for fear that in the end he will use his golden tongue for political ends. For a golden tongue is never satisfied until it has wagged itself over the destiny of a nation, and this the church is wise enough to know.
> But turn to the Catholic church, go into mass at any moment—what do you walk in upon? Something that's already in your blood. You know the story that the priest is telling as he moves from one side of the altar to the other. (Barnes, *Nightwood*, 20)

The doctor's description of the mass is peculiarly reminiscent of the appeal that fascism made to the *Volk*'s instinctive feeling for blood and soil. His Catholicism is also, as Joseph Frank points out, "deeply rooted in his emotional nature," his homosexuality; and we saw earlier that Matthew implicitly positions himself between the romantic tradition and fascism when he speculates that he might "end up like Madame de Staël—with an affinity for Germany." Again we find that the knot that ties together romanticism, decadence, Catholicism, and fascism is the combination of a certain aesthetic orientation, homoeroticism, and a deeply pessimistic "understanding of sin and evil." And in the worldview that emerges from this admixture, the recognition of that evil, and the renunciation of individuality, are the only possible means of escaping suffering, the "worm" that eats all those attached to personal, material, and temporal ends (see Frank, 41, 47).

Matthew himself, it is suggested, is closer than Nora, if not than Robin, to renouncing individuality and achieving a kind of (a)historical universality. When Nora goes to visit Matthew in his room, she finds him in his gown, the "natural" and universal garment. "Is not the gown the natural raiment of extremity?" she asks herself. "What nation, what religion, what ghost, what dream, has not worn it—infants, angels, priests, the dead; why should not the doctor, in the grave dilemma of his alchemy, wear his dress?" (Barnes, *Nightwood*, 80). The gown signals the juncture of male and female, birth and death; the doctor, in putting on his gown, begins to approach undifferentiated anonymity (Pochoda, 186). By the end of the novel's penultimate chapter, "Go Down, Matthew," he may be close to achieving the stance of self-effacing indifference Eliot embraces in "Ash Wednesday" when he strives to pray for humility and the ability "not to care" (Frank, 47). Certainly Matthew has given up his own frenetically aestheticizing logocentrism: "He has moved, as he should, toward quiescence and wordlessness; as Wittgenstein remarks, what you cannot say, you cannot whistle either. If, as the doctor says, there will be nothing but wrath and weeping, at least he has gotten beyond hope and beyond words to the despair which purifies and terrifies" (Pochoda, 188).

It is somewhat problematic, of course, to read the doctor's final pronouncement as *Nightwood*'s definitive "moral," since such a reading fails to account for the novel's last chapter, necessarily characterizing it as a formal error on Barnes's part—Eliot's original impression—or as evidence of the author/narrator's willful refusal to renounce her own stylistic singularity (Gerstenberger, 137). The text's Catholic pessimism seems at this point to be in conflict with its aestheticism. Many have read Matthew's reproach to Nora to "put the pen away" as Barnes's ironic commentary on her own writing process; in this reading, the author, and her characters, "are damned by their willful singularity, by the excrescence of style which sits between them and their recognition of the universal malady of guilt" (Pochoda, 184–85). The doctor's lecture to Nora implicitly condemns the aesthete's impulse to make art out of pain as self-indulgence, which keeps her not only from recognizing guilt but from attaining bliss: "Can't you be quiet now? . . . Can't you be done now, can't you give up? Now be still, now that you know what the world is about, knowing it's about nothing? . . . Is there such extraordinary need of misery to make beauty? Let go Hell; and your fall will be broken by the roof of Heaven" (Barnes, *Nightwood*, 124). But if *Nightwood*'s characters forswear speech, the narrator refuses to "be still," stepping in where the doctor leaves off to reassert her narrative control. We will return to this point later, when we consider the implications of the final chapter for fascist aesthetics.

For the moment, I wish to argue that the "Catholic" narrative/ ideological position, described above, which is associated with the doctor—a position of considerable if not ultimate narrative authority in *Nightwood*—can rather easily be aligned with certain predominant impulses in fascist writing. May Sinclair's analogy between imagist poetics and Catholic ritual points us toward the fascist's desire for a mimetic aesthetics, for example; we will see below that an emphasis on Nature and mimesis is a marker of fascist literature, one manifestation of the quest for authenticity inspired by the reifying effects of modernity.

In Chapter 1, I cited Jeffrey Herf's description of right-wing, centrist, and leftist responses to the reified consciousness created by the modern age. The response of the Right, we recall, is to attempt to sublate it through acceptance (Herf, 88–89). Herf's characterization of the style of reactionary modernism associated with Jünger strongly recalls *Nightwood*'s ethical or ideological stance in some respects:

> Unlike the romantic Marxists, the cultural revolution Jünger advocated endowed the eclipse of individuality with a halo of heroism. Re-

actionary modernists agreed with exponents of the "tragic vision" that suprahistorical forces lay behind external appearances of modern culture and that these forces were the genuinely decisive ones. They also agreed that individuals were powerless to change or oppose these forces. Where they differed was in justifying acceptance of these supposedly omnipotent forces. In this regard, Jünger's discourse of will, nature, and sacrifice is important, for it comprises a collection of metaphors and symbols that urge acquiescence to one's own powerlessness. (Herf, 89)

As we have seen, Matthew repeatedly urges acceptance of the "eclipse of individuality," "acquiescence to one's own powerlessness." This acquiescence is not heroic for Barnes in the sense that it is for Jünger; and yet the doctor is a heroic figure in his way. The buzzwords of liberal humanism—rationalism, individual freedom, progress—are, for fascist thought and for Barnes, derisory and illusory. For fascism, irrationalism represents the liberation of and from the self, as does, for Matthew, the instinctive adherence to Catholicism. Fascist thought, like Huysman's "black romanticism" and Matthew's Catholicism, asserts the inadequacy of external changes to affect the subject; the emphasis is instead on transforming the subject from the inside out, through the individual's submission to "suprahistorical forces," whether these are defined as the nation, God, or simply the acknowledgment of suffering as the ultimate reality.

We might ask whether Barnes's trans- or a-historicism does not also resemble a certain fascist view of history, which collapses historical epochs together in the image of a transhistorical Aryan nation. While it is difficult to tie differing accounts of history too tightly to particular political tendencies, in general it can be argued that both fascist and conservative ideologies eschew the liberal and Marxist emphasis on progress, and focus instead on a cyclic or static conception of history. Spengler and the fascist legal theorist Carl Schmitt both describe German history as cyclical; Herf says of Schmitt, "He rejected a linear conception of historical evolution that he imputed to liberalism and Marxism and stressed in its place the coexistence of different historical epochs in German society" (Herf, 119). Again, we are reminded of Riefenstahl's "Olympia," which traces the progress of the *Geist* represented by the Olympic flame from Greece to Germany, substituting visual synchronicity for diachronic historical progress.

Barnes also rejects historical contingency and "a linear conception of historical evolution," appealing throughout her text to the eternal, the racial, the transhistorical. As Elizabeth Pochoda points out, the cryptic line *"Wir setzen an dieser Stelle über den Fluss"* invokes crossing the Styx to Hell and Dante's *Inferno*: "This is a trip like Dante's where all history is present at once so that the distinctions between man and man, and between time and time, can be obliterated in an awareness of the universal malady." The image of the circus, too, functions, like Barnes's style and narrative structure, to evade temporal—that is, historical—progress: "the ring itself contains all time at once—there is movement but no progression" (Pochoda, 188). And Barnes's aphoristic language frequently seems directed toward a community that shares with her a set of values and cultural references that transcend historical immediacy: "Nora had the face of *all people* who love the people"; "*one of those* panicky little women"; "what is this love *we* have for the invert, boy or girl?" (Barnes, *Nightwood*, 51, 65, 136; my emphasis).

The most important correlation between *Nightwood* and the various ideological traditions we have been discussing emerges when we realize that for fascism, the emphasis on the supercession of individual subjectivity by a fusion with a transhistorical community functions to overcome the intolerable threat of individual mortality.

> The collective which supersedes the bourgeois subject is not simply the national community of the present but the unbroken presence of past generations as well. The end of atomistic individuality, at least in its fascist version, therefore holds out an additional ideological promise: the victory over death. The erotic union in which isolation is overcome produces no new generations; indeed the literature of race and blood is marked by a ubiquitous fear of reproduction, most certainly linked to a profound misogyny. But this literature offers the hope of redeeming the past generations, retrieving them from an other-world of forgetfulness. Hence the monumental character of fascist modernism, holding onto images of ancestors, in contrast to the commitment to progress in the ideology of liberal individuation. (Berman, *The Rise*, 210)

There is an odd conspiracy between the misogyny of fascism, expressed in the German "literature of race and blood" or in Italian futurist texts,* and the Sapphic modernists' rejection of maternity; both recoil from the physical process of reproduction, and not infrequently renounce bourgeois, liberal subjectivity in response to their preoccupation with mortality. They represent this reaction in quite different ways, of course. In futurism, for example, the conflict between the individual and technological modernity is ultimately resolved by the annihilation of the (liberal) subject and the identification of humans with machines. In *Nightwood*, in contrast, the boundaries between humans and animals, or humans and reified works of art, waver and dissolve in the figures of Robin and Nikka the Nigger. In both cases, what is called radically into question is the notion of rational subjectivity on which liberalism and Marxism insist. *Nightwood*, like many fascist texts, treads the ground where the borders of that subjectivity disintegrate; like fascism, it occupies the territory of the irrational.

It is important to recognize that Barnes's interest in what we might call the psychology of the irrational is fundamentally different both from the representation of psychic interiority with which Woolf experiments and from Yourcenar's explorations of individual masculine psyches in her later works. Barnes rarely "gets inside" her characters as individuals; we are hardly ever told how they feel or what they think. It is not individual psychologies but psyche per se, psychology as a collective or racial phenomenon that occupies her. This is particularly evident in her characterization of Robin.

Robin has been identified with the id and instinct (Nadeau, 160); another critic writes that "Robin Vote, the 'somnambule' of the novel, lives in contact with a world of primitive darkness, the subterranean realm of the unconscious" (Henke, 333). (The epithet "La Somnambule," incidentally, refers to Bellini's *La somnambula*, in which the heroine's spirit makes her walk in her sleep and she

---

* See Alice Kaplan's discussion of Marinetti's horror of "the putrid complicity of the uterus of woman," expressed in Mafarka the futurist's immaculate conception of a machine/son (Kaplan, 82).

has no rational control over her actions. Bellini's story "was written to prove the existence of the soul to atheists and rationalists" [Marcus, "Laughing," 241].) But Robin is not simply an "irrational" woman, governed by unconscious impulses; the hypnotic fascination she exercises over the other characters suggests that, in a wider sense, she figures the universal drive toward a "world of primitive darkness" that is not (yet) governed by the law of the father. Robin may even be said to stand in for the function of the unconscious; she is a container for the repressed, instinctual, or pre-rational impulses of the other characters, "the infected carrier of the past," representing the chaotic, prehistoric moment of narcissistic fulfillment whose loss they all mourn. "The Baronin had an undefinable disorder," says Felix, "a sort of 'odour of memory,' like a person who has come from some place that we have forgotten and would give our life to recall" (Barnes, *Nightwood*, 118).

That "place" can be identified with the womb or space of fusion with the maternal. We have already noted Robin's correlation with the Virgin; more broadly, she is aligned not only with the Mother of God but with the maternal or semiotic register as well. Associated with animals, plants, music, and inanimate objects, Robin is virtually extra-verbal; she speaks only ten or so times in the text, and a number of her short utterances are no more than profanities. Outside of history and rationality, the symbolic order, it is "as if the hide of time had been stripped from her, and with it, all transactions with knowledge." Even her eyes are "timeless," like wild beasts' (Barnes, *Nightwood*, 134, 37). Robin inhabits a prelapsarian world.

When the doctor roars, "It's my mother without argument I want!" he voices the obsessive desire of all of *Nightwood*'s lovers and orphans, of the text itself, to find a way back to that unmediated space (Barnes, *Nightwood*, 149). Images of oral sadism and partial objects in *Nightwood* inspire a Kleinian analysis of the relation to the mother, of the primitive rage and desire provoked by separation from her. The text is filled with images of amputation and disembodiment, from the "Roman fragments" in Hedvig and Guido's home to Mademoiselle Basquette. The specter of World

War I, which shadows the entire text and particularly the doctor's monologues, conjures up scenes of amputees and shell-shock victims, the eternally incomplete. The very subtitle Barnes originally gave to *Nightwood*, "An Anatomy of Night," recalls dissection.

This sense of separation and loss is figured in and recuperated by lesbianism. The recurrent trope of "going down" identifies oral sexuality with a return to the womb/grave. (One critic points out that both birth and death "represent forms of permanent separation, but when they are conflated they represent the (narcissistic) denial of separation" [Lee, 213].) Lesbian sexuality in *Nightwood* is not so much a question of identification with the loved one as of the desire to *incorporate* her, to ingest her, to fuse with the erotic, prehistoric object: "we feel that we could eat her, she who is eaten death returning, for only then do we put our face close to the blood on the lips of our forefathers" (Barnes, *Nightwood*, 37). Barnes thus again turns the particular instance of homosexuality into the figure for universal loss, grief, and desire: we love "inverts," says the doctor, because "they go far back in our lost distance where what we never had stands waiting; it was inevitable that we should come upon them, for our miscalculated longing has created them" (Barnes, *Nightwood*, 137).

The yearning for the lost maternal object, expressed in writing, inevitably creates a tension between what I am characterizing here as semiotic and symbolic registers. *Nightwood*'s formal structure consists in part of repetitive elements, recurrent tropes that superimpose patterns on the byzantine narrative. The text is organized by references to music and to color; by the chanting rhythms of the doctor's monologues; by reiterated words and phrases (particularly repeated jokes, like the doctor's prophecies that Felix will take to drink). *Nightwood* is a text in love with the semiotic. And yet, of course, as text it operates, perforce and by definition, through the symbolic or verbal register, represented especially by the doctor—whose verbal pyrotechnics are arrested only once before the denouement of "Go Down, Matthew," in the carriage on the night at the opera. Matthew gets into a carriage with Jenny, Robin, a young Englishwoman Robin is flirting with, and a little girl who lives with Jenny but seems infatuated with Robin. Mad with jealousy, Jenny attacks Robin. In the narrator's version of the incident, the child begins crying out and Matthew is silent; later, when *he* tells the story to Nora, he says that he screamed. In either version it is clear that, confronted with the primordial violence of the erotic scene between women and between woman and child, the doctor, impotent representative of phallic and verbal authority, has, for once, nothing to *say*. The text is torn between its desire for the erotic/maternal object and its need to represent it.

Fascist thought, too, is torn between semiotic and symbolic registers. Studies of the "authoritarian personality" of the fascist have noted his "unwavering rigidity" and unquestioning submission to the (law of the) Führer/father (see Jay, *Dialectical*, 240). And yet, building on Adorno's analysis of the "magical" and "archaic" orality of the fascist leader, Alice Kaplan has also identified a "fascist semiotic," the register "governed by rhythm and repetition" and subject to *maternal* authority (Adorno, "Freudian Theory," 132; Kaplan, 9–10). She points to the desire, reiterated in para-fascist texts from Sorel's to Jünger's to Pound's, for immediacy, wholeness, fusion, a desire seemingly at odds with a rigid sense of hierarchy and boundary: "Against the distance between the state and the people, [fascists] hoped for immediacy; against alienation and fragmentation, they hoped for unity of experience" (Kaplan, 3).

For the dis-integrated subject, however, fascism can represent both devotion to the mother and fealty to the father: "Hitler . . . can be mother in a utopian moment, father in an authoritarian one." This psychological conflict is acted out in fascist texts as a "confusion about boundaries between self and other" (Kaplan, 22, 6). In their introduction to Theweleit's *Male Fantasies*, Jessica Benjamin and Anson Rabinbach argue that the fascist male attempts to resolve this tension by gendering the poles of repulsion and attraction: "His desire for fusion is above all directed to other men exactly like himself, his soldier-brother-mirror; his fear of fusion is directed toward all that is female, and his world banishes women as much as possible" (Benjamin and Rabinbach, xxii).

Thus, for Spengler and Pound, certainly, formlessness and indifferentiation are identified with nature, mud, and the maternal, representing a chaos that needs to be mastered and organized by technology, for example, or by the masculine authority associated with the sun in the *Cantos*. At the same time, Jünger can describe combat as a merging with an undifferentiated liquid element that is identified not with the feminine, but presumably with his fellow soldiers; in the "ecstasy" of war, "man is like the raging storm, the thundering sea and the roaring thunder. He has melted into everything. . . . And if the dark waves close above him, he has long been oblivious to the transition. It is as if a wave slipped back into the flowing sea" (Jünger, *Kampf*, 54).

For a cruder example of this confusion of ego boundaries we might turn to *Mein Kampf*; Wilhelm Reich notes that Hitler often refers to miscegenation as "incest," while insisting that there is no blood relation between the races. Reich sees in this only proof of Hitler's "irrationality," in the conventional sense of illogicity (Reich, 78); I would argue that it points instead to the irrational as the persistent instability of self/Other boundaries. Hitler's ideology says the Other is too far away; but the word he uses suggests that his real fear is that the Other is, in fact, too close.

One writer confronts head-on the insecurities provoked by the tension between the symbolic and semiotic orders, and the consequent volatility of identity we find in many fascist texts. In Céline's texts, the integrity and boundaries of the body itself come into question, as Céline "takes swipes" at the body, disembowels it, and analyzes its excrements, dispelling any hope that the body might prove to be a last refuge of ontological stability (Kaplan, 109–10). Kaplan's reading of Céline makes it clear that Céline's fantastic deconstructions of the human body (and the French language) are derived, like Barnes's, from the decadents' valorization of sickness; he shares with them, and her, a focus on the decaying body and its privileged relation to truth. For Kaplan, the focus on bodily degeneration in Céline distinguishes him from authoritarian fascism: "Unlike a conventional fascist ideologue who posits a whole, healthy body, an authoritarian voice-body alliance, Céline is constantly digging away at the body in [his] texts" (Kaplan, 109).

At the same time, however, Céline seeks to reintegrate text with voice, which is another and perhaps profounder way of attempting to reconstitute the self, or more accurately, to transcend autonomous selfhood entirely by reincorporating it into the mother/tongue. "In striving to capture the rhythmic drive and vocal immediacy of vernacular French," notes one critic, "Céline crafted a language whose populist appeal was immensely useful to France's more resolute Fascists and contributed much to their utopian celebration of 'phonocentric' art forms" (Scullion, 181). What Céline called his "great attack on the Word," his celebration of the voice, appeals not to authoritarianism but to fascist populism; calling on the force of the "oceanic" or "utopic" moment of the irrational, he fuses reactionary populism with the avant-garde.

> What Céline is offering the fascist right . . . is a chance to differentiate itself from that lucid, classical Maurrasian right, from right-wing aristocracy and right-wing lucidity. With Céline, the right can reject the aristocracy for "the people" and still stay on the right. . . . It can be earthy; it can speak with the voices of the people; and, at the same time, it can ally itself with forces of regeneration in French prose: it can be culturally avant-garde. Losing Maurras, it loses its stuffiness. Being a racist à la Céline is not the same as being a blue-blooded snob. It has the very different cachet of desperate revolt, the heroic edge of a lifesaving measure taken against a deadly parasite. Céline's fascism, read in the novels of the 1930s, lies in his populist combination of the ethnographic and diagnostic gesture: the discovery of the low life, the production of the germ. (Kaplan, 120)

The "combination of the ethnographic and diagnostic gesture" points us back to organicist discourses and medical models; Céline, we remember, was a doctor, and his depictions of the decaying body illustrate his diagnosis of a decaying body politic. Barnes, too, adopts the medical model that conflates race and pathology, miming in *Nightwood* fascism's obsession with bodies—their typologies, differences, significations. Kannenstine relates Barnes's concept of "blood" (in what Kenneth Burke tellingly calls a "folkish" sense, while denying any connection to a fascist conception of the *Volk*) "to the theme of the primitive as well as to preconsciousness" (Kannenstine, 125). That is, Barnes's invocations of "blood," as her allusions to "racial memory" make clear, refer not just to psychological ontogeny but to phylogeny, the experiences of racially differentiated collectivities.

Barnes, in fact, in recapitulating widely prevalent tropes of organicist discourse, frequently overlaps with fascism's favorite stereotypes. Many of the aphorisms in the text, especially the doctor's, concern racial differences: "All right, Jews meddle and [the Irish] lie, that's the difference, the fine difference" (Barnes, *Nightwood*, 31). Barnes associates homosexuals and Jews: the homosexual and the Jew are both marked physically, according to the prevailing stereotypes of the time. Robin has "the body of a boy"; Guido has a "sweeping Cabalistic line of nose" and "thick eyeballs." Homosexuality is repeatedly identified with physical and metaphysical sterility. Hedvig, the text's representative Aryan, dies giving birth to a mixed-race child; her death can be interpreted as the result of her contamination by Jewish blood. The son of Felix the half-breed and Robin the invert is, inevitably, a sickly idiot. Barnes also makes use of the stereotype of the Jew as the principle of mediation, who "participates in the two conditions"; Felix is always "tailored in part for the evening and in part for the day." If this were not enough, he even works in a bank.

Barnes undoubtedly understood what her symbols, particularly the image of the Jew, meant to the (fascist) age. If, as Russell Berman has suggested, anti-Semitism is the logical outcome of an ideology caught—as *Nightwood* is—between semiotic and symbolic registers, an ideology that, like Catholic aestheticism, valorizes the unmediated, instinctive seduction of the image, then we might expect Barnes as aestheticist and Catholic to participate in this rejection of the Jew as the figure of the Law and rationalism:

> To the extent that fascism signifies a specific unresolved tension between imaginary and symbolic orders, the Jew was by no means an arbitrary victim. . . . Cipher of the law and the book, he bears the brunt of the aestheticist preservation of the image impervious to conceptual scrutiny and outside the venue of any legal rationality. Perpetual patriarch, he draws on himself the wrath of the matriarchal moment of vitalist desire in the presymbolic "oceanic feeling" of fascism. . . . The people of the book, prohibited by the decalogue from a cult of graven images, operate in a linguistic realm of perpetual mediation that en-

dangers the auratic uniqueness of visual representation and the corporeal presence of the eucharist.... As the carrier of the law, the Jew represents the state and conceptual rationality, from the strictures of which only a recovery of genuine origins, preserved in the prelinguistic imaginary, can emancipate the nation.... Extermination is implicated in a retreat from patriarchal law... that is a constituent of the autonomous identity, so enviously detested by fascism. (Berman, "Wandering Z," xx–xxii)

Berman's analysis seems instead to indicate to us, however, Barnes's point of departure from fascism. If *Nightwood*, like fascism, manifests "a specific unresolved tension between imaginary and symbolic orders"; if *Nightwood*'s inhabitants enviously detest the autonomous identity, always searching for their origins and a return to "the matriarchal moment of vitalist desire"; nonetheless, Barnes ends up, albeit regretfully, in "a linguistic realm of perpetual mediation." If fascism represents an ultimate allegiance to the Father, into which individuals are seduced by the appeal of the semiotic register—the omnipresence of the voice, the erotic thrill of rhythm and repetition, the oceanic fusion of the crowd—then *Nightwood* expresses the hopeless longing for a return to the maternal, which can only be signified within the symbolic order—in Barnes's "learned corruption of language."

Barnes's language, in defiance of a central aesthetic principle of fascism, has "ceased to be organic." Her artifice, that antagonism to "Nature" which makes her so inimical to Marxist criticism, is, equally, a rejection of the fascist literary ideal of mimesis. For Italian fascists, this ideal was often expressed in a "hypermimetic model of representation, the aesthetic counterpart to fascism's politics of activism and antiparliamentarianism" (Schnapp, "Epic," 23). Berman notes the centrality of the notion of "Nature" to other fascist texts: "Perhaps more than any other motif, the desire for a nature as guarantor of unchanging order—and as the alternative to the metropolis as the locus of individuality and democracy—marks the various fascist literary imaginations: the German literature of blood and soil, Pound's invocations of the natural order of ancient China, and above all the cult of nature in Hamsun (Berman, "Wandering Z," xvii).

Pound's is a particularly interesting case to examine in this context, since he articulated and drew his political ideology from an aesthetics nearly antithetical to Barnes's. Pound, like Spengler, or Theweleit's fascist male, fears de-differentiation and "mud," the loss of authenticity and individuality in the flattening-out processes of capitalist democracy. He values precision, clarity, and order in politics, and poetry. For him the Chinese ideogram seems to fulfill his dream of a mimetic poetry; it expresses, he feels, the unmediated relation of the signifier to the signified, the sign arising directly from the thing it represents. He rejects ornamentation and conventional meter, which creates unnecessary space in the poetic line that has to be filled up by an excess of signs. "Excess" in poetry, like "usury" in Pound's economic philosophy, impedes the free circulation of the (monetary or poetic) sign. As Marinetti did with his "words-in-freedom" technique, Pound attempts to strip away syntax in order to allow the sign to function as pure pulsation.

Barnes's style, in contrast, relies on simile, metaphor, and metonymy—signs that point only to other signs. Far from being mimetic, the Barnesian sign "seems to respond to the subject at hand by aiming in the opposite direction," as Donna Gerstenberger says of the doctor's narrative technique (Gerstenberger, 133). Barnes traps signs in dense webs of syntax and encrusts them with ornamentation. It is true, as I have said, that *Nightwood* is a text crisscrossed by traces of the semiotic; it is also true that, as if in recognition of the futility of the quest for fusion—of lovers, of the infant with the mother, of the signifier with the signified—Barnes exploits the possibilities of the symbolic with the abandon of the damned.

This is, in *Nightwood*, a gesture made in regret and even despair. As Catharine Stimpson writes, "Like Nora Flood, before Nora's discovery of the night, Barnes wished she had been a Christian in Christianity's first days. She might then have freshly, purely believed in Logos, the Word that generates, orders, and regenerates, the Word that was with God in the beginning." Nonetheless, Stimpson continues, Barnes recognizes that in the postlapsarian world, "the powers of language have gone astray in multiple, twisted ways"; her "ransacking" of literary genres can be interpreted as an exploration of this fall from purity (Stimpson, 371). Her verbal experimentation constitutes an anatomy of the modes of mediation.

We can return now to the point I raised earlier, when I observed that *Nightwood*'s final chapter, in which Nora and her dog find Robin in the chapel on Nora's American estate, poses a problem for a reading of the novel that would take Matthew's last pronouncement as the text's "moral." The narrator does not forswear speech at the same point as the doctor, which might seem to indicate a stubbornly optimistic faith on her part in the regenerative powers of the Word, à la *The Waste Land*, or, alternatively, a perverse refusal to relinquish linguistic mastery even if it condemns her to hell. Other possibilities are suggested, however, by the fact that the style of "The Possessed" departs radically both from the doctor's and from the narrative technique of the opening chapter, when the narrator also speaks directly.

In "The Possessed" Barnes comes as close to a mimetic style as she ever will, allowing herself only three modest similes and describing the final encounter between Nora, Robin, and the dog in comparatively brief declarative sentences. The change of tone in this last chapter could be interpreted as Barnes's rejection of her own aestheticism; viewed from one angle, we can see the culmination of *Nightwood* in "The Possessed" as Barnes's final acquiescence (albeit several pages late) to the doctor's Catholicism, her refusal of aestheticism's claim to transcend moral considerations. *Nightwood* "has gone so far in implicating its own beauties in the general malady that art cannot be said to arrest horror. Like the tattoos of Nikka the Nigger, its beauties are built on its barbarities" (Pochoda, 190). But viewed from another angle, "The Possessed" can also be read as Barnes's ironic rebuttal of fascism's utopian fantasies of a return to an unmediated (poetic) space. As it approaches mimesis, the text goes down, like Robin, not into semiotic bliss but into animalism and then silence. The only unmediated language, Barnes implies, is the howl of the dog; the text that attempts to achieve such a language will self-destruct.

It would be both facile and dangerous to found assertions about *Nightwood*'s ideological content—not to say Barnes's own politics—entirely on what we could term the novel's antifascist style. The claim that a highly figurative and mediated literary style is inherently antifascist has been made about, for example, both Céline and D'Annunzio, of whom Spackman writes that he brought to Italian literature "the awareness that language is not a transparent neutral vehicle for the transmission of thought" (Spackman, *Genealogies*, 9). But if a more mediated style is always antifascist, and a more "organic" style inherently fascist, then Hemingway, for instance, would have to be considered more of a fascist than Yeats, contrary to what we know about their personal political commitments: and while it is also problematic to derive our interpretations of texts from their authors' political biographies, the incongruity of the example at least suggests that there are no simple correspondences to be drawn here between the form and content of either texts or lives.

*Nightwood*'s aesthetic, however, also reflects an ethic that, like the novel's style, calls into question fascism's utopian visions of the body politic's future, as well as its mythological revisions of the past. Just as there is no organic, unmediated, "healthy" sign in *Nightwood*, there are also no healthy human beings, with an unmediated relation to blood, culture, or history. The Jew in *Nightwood* is certainly the icon for the predicaments of modernity (Frank, 36), but he is responsible neither for causing nor for curing them; they are, indeed, incurable. There is no doubt that the text compels the reader's identification (which Eliot knew readers would resist anyway), just as in decadent texts, "The distance that separates the naturalistic narrator from his pathological subjects is replaced by an identification with pathology and degeneracy" (Spackman, *Genealogies*, 131). But there is little evidence that, as Jane Marcus claims, this identification unites the reader with the marginalized in opposition to the absent "blond Aryan beast" lurking outside the text (Marcus, "Laughing," 230). It is true that Barnes refers to "the people of the underworld"; but who else is there in *Nightwood*? There is no "outside" to Barnes's text/world; her stance is, again, that of the decadents, who deny "the existence of an isle of health and of the clear-eyed ones who claim to reside there." If *Nightwood* is antifascist, it is so not because it opposes the absent Aryan Superman, but because it denies that he exists, or ever could.

*Nightwood*'s assault on history, although it has some important correlations with certain fascist versions of history, also ultimately undermines fascism's self-legitimating revision of its own historical origins, and indeed all claims to historical or narrative "authenticity." Furthermore, it mocks the fascist's assertion that war and violence offer the (male) individual a way to fuse with the forces of history. The opening scene, for example, inverts Mussolini's famous dictum that war is to men what childbirth is to women by parodically metaphorizing childbirth as a scene of military spectacle and then letting Hedvig disappear from the (hi)story. War is not a substitute for childbirth, it is implied; giving birth, rather, is war, a war in which there is little glory and the victims leave nothing to posterity.

It is possible, in fact, to interpret all of *Nightwood*'s statements about history as a conflict between "masculine" (and fascist) and "feminine" values. While Felix's "reverence for culture is a reverence for military and economic power," for teleology, culture, and a history "from which [Guido and Felix] are categorically excluded," Robin represents that which cannot "be accommodated or tainted by historical time," a woman attracted to women who escape from culture (Lee, 210–11). Felix's earnest respect for the past is, it is important to note, not simply conservative; his vision, like the fascist's, looks forward as well: "To pay homage to our past is the only gesture that also includes the future," he tells Matthew (Barnes, *Nightwood*, 39). But Robin is indifferent to Felix's vision and resistant to the role he—like Mussolini—has designated for her in it, as the perpetuator of the race and thus of history; she eventually forces him to the uneasy half-consciousness of the falsity of his own narrative:

> Felix, with tightly held monocle, walked beside Robin, talking to her, drawing her attention to this and that, wrecking himself and his peace of mind in an effort to acquaint her with the destiny for which he had chosen her—that she might bear sons who would recognize and honour the past. For without such love, the past as he understood it,

would die away from the world. She was not listening and he said in an angry mood, though he said it calmly, "I am deceiving you!" And he wondered what he meant, and why she did not hear. (Barnes, *Nightwood*, 45)

A fascist conception of history that proposes the synchronic unity of the Aryan nation with its Hellenic past, and whose teleo-logic culminates in the phantasm of the Third Reich, would, then, be just as objectionable to Barnes as more linear historical narratives. The interpolation of a passage from *Ladies Almanack* helps to reinforce the point that for Barnes, all history is masculine, and—whether presented as mythology, Gospel, or fairy-tale—inadequate:

> Was there a whisper of Ellen or Mary, of Rachel or Gretchen, of Tao or Hedda or Bellorinabella y Bellorella, or Tancred of Injen in the Old Winds, or of Wives whispering a thing to a Wife? What's in a name before Christ? Were all Giants' doings a Man's, and no mountain-top moultings of a Goblin well-papped to the Heel? To say nothing and less of Myths Tongue-tied with Girl-talk. . . . No Time without God, no end without Christ! (Barnes, *Almanack*, 70)

In her reading of *The Antiphon*, Julie Abraham proposes a strong motivation for Barnes's antipathy to history. She makes the point that in Barnes's version of developmental psychology, "history" is installed at the point of the daughter's Oedipal struggle, in which she learns that her father has sexual access to her mother and she never will: "Unlike the Freudian daughter, this girl-child does not agree to transfer her desire from her mother to her father. Unlike the Freudian son, waiting until adulthood will not change her situation, will not provide her with a wife/mother of her own. 'History' begins with the heterosexual 'facts of life.' So history, whether explicitly identified with the father or not, is the first and ultimate antagonist" (Abraham, 265). Robin's refusal of history, her allegiance to the maternal or semiotic principle, can, then, be read in part as a refusal to acknowledge the father's sexual prerogative and her own sexual inferiority. In *The Antiphon* that refusal gains a defiant intensity, for it is in *The Antiphon* that Barnes comes closest to telling the story she tried over and over to tell all her life, of a daughter's sexual victimization by her father, with the tacit complicity of her mother.*

In this, her last major work, published in 1957 and set "during the war of 1939," Barnes finally draws an explicit connection between patriarchy and fascism. *The Antiphon* intercalates references to "myopic conquerors / With pebbled monocles and rowel'd heels" (Barnes, *Antiphon*, 15) into the progressive revelation of the late Titus Hobbs's dictatorial brutality to his wife Augusta, mistresses, and children. Defending herself against her brother's charge that she "condoned" Titus's behavior, Augusta both evokes the fascist conception of the family and the role of women, and places it in the larger context of all ideologies that subordinate women's lives and sexualities to the demands of men and the State: "Don't come at me too! I was a victim: / I've done my duty to the state—in children. . . . In my day we did not leave our husbands" (Barnes, *Antiphon*, 73). In Louise DeSalvo's words, "the norm in a patriarchal family is brutality and victimization. In setting her play during 1939, Barnes suggests that the events of that year were not an aberration in the history of the human race; rather, Hitler's behavior is reinterpreted . . . as normal behavior for a well-socialized male" (DeSalvo, 311).

It would seem that Barnes did not arrive at a fully articulated analysis of fascism as a patriarchal ideology until after World War II. *Nightwood* addresses the same metaphysical problems that fascism did in the 1920s and 1930s, and uses the same images and tropes that fascism used. It illustrates faithfully the connections fascism forged among those perceived to disrupt national/patriarchal boundaries, to be transient or without lineage in a society held together by its lines of demarcation. It is a text preoccupied with the significance of history and the problem of mediation, as was fascist thought. It occupies the same terrain that fascism tried to manipulate, that of the

---

*One version of that story exists in an early draft of *Nightwood*, and passages that would have made the story much more explicit were edited out of *The Antiphon*. See the essays by Lynda Curry and Louise DeSalvo in *Silence and Power*.

irrational. And it shares fascism's corporealization of racial difference. It is only with regret, and because Barnes shared what one critic calls Céline's "eternal pessimism running counter to fascism's thrill-seeking pursuit of direct political action and to its grandiose schemes of refashioning human existence" (Scullion, 194), that Barnes finally dismisses fascism's utopian fantasies of immediacy and fusion with the mother/tongue, at the end of *Nightwood*. And it was not until she wrote *The Antiphon*, when she considered the interconnections of authoritarianism, the psychopathology of the patriarchal, heterosexual family unit, and the (sexual) violence of Nazism, that the on-again, off-again flirtation with fascism evident in *Nightwood* appears, finally, to have broken down into irrevocable loathing.

I conclude this chapter with a caveat. The same attack on history, narrative finality, and truth claims that makes *Nightwood* exasperating to Marxism, and ultimately unassimilable by fascism, also makes the text very difficult to recuperate for feminist readings that would foreground its sexual politics as the key to a definitive interpretation of Barnes's life/work. Recent feminist criticism tends "to read the novel in both the cultural and obligatory countercultural terms of Barnes's lesbianism and her biographical misfortunes in love," implying that *Nightwood*'s tragic vision simply expresses Barnes's resentment of the patriarchy, or of Thelma Wood. But, as Gerstenberger has pointed out, "What may have been true about Barnes's own life is not necessarily true of the novel, which gives the lie through its narrative form to the idea that any language claims or cultural visions, patriarchal or other, can provide a grounding for 'truth' or 'knowledge.' The claims of *Nightwood*'s narrative are too radical to admit meaning to such a reading" (Gerstenberger, 131–32).

Just as *Nightwood*'s relationship to fascism is unstable, its resistance to any totalizing "cultural vision" or interpretation, including my own, is both wily and forceful. Like fascism itself, *Nightwood* seems to pose a fascinating, seductive, and perilous challenge to those of us who approach it again and again, armed with every critical weapon at our disposal, only to find that it slips through our hermeneutic nets. We might ask whether the academic debates about *Nightwood* do not simultaneously mask and reveal the uneasy awareness that it is a dangerous book to read. Its complexity piques our professional pride, egging us to try once more to arrive at *the* definitive critical reading; its beauty makes us eager to claim it, to gather it protectively into our particular critical fold. It makes us afraid to ask difficult questions of it: for example, just how it feels about fascism. But, to paraphrase Barnes, the indeterminability that has made one the bête noire of critical theory for 60 years makes the other the property of no critic. In saying this, however, I have no intention of being drawn into the aestheticist fallacy; though our investigations into *Nightwood* and (its relation to) fascism are unlikely to provide any definitive readings, we continue them so that we will not, in refusing to politicize art, find ourselves helpless when confronted with the aestheticization of politics.

CHAPTER 4

## *Neither Right nor Left: Marguerite Yourcenar and the Crisis of Liberalism*

> And, finally, groups have never thirsted after truth. They demand illusions, and cannot do without them. They constantly give what is unreal precedence over what is real; they are almost as strongly influenced by what is untrue as by what is true.
>
> Sigmund Freud, "Group Psychology and the Analysis of the Ego"

I turn now to a reading of the work of Marguerite Yourcenar, in particular her 1934 novel *Denier du rêve*, set in Rome in the year XI of Mussolini's dictatorship.\* In the first edition of this novel, Yourcenar attempted to challenge Italian fascism's claim to represent a radically new solution to the failures of modernity, by assimilating it to the reified culture of capitalism that it aspired to transcend. Contesting the fascist regime's assertion that it had inaugurated a new age of unmediated political and cultural authenticity, and recuperated Italy's imperial past in a newly aestheticized political present, Yourcenar depicted fascist

---

\*The first edition of *Denier du rêve* was published by Bernard Grasset in 1934; the second by Plon in 1959; the "definitive version" by Gallimard in 1971. The English translation, titled *A Coin in Nine Hands*, is of the last version. Because the 1959 and 1971 texts are substantially the same, differing largely in Yourcenar's addition of a preface to the Gallimard edition (an afterword in the translation), they will be referred to collectively as "the second version" of the novel. My translation of the first edition is based on Dori Katz's translation of the second.

Rome as a scene of alienation and commodification. She particularly attacked fascism's pretensions to provide access to the "natural" or "real," often characterized in fascist texts as a realm of experience that is unmediated, virile, and antibourgeois.

Yourcenar's critique of Italian fascism, however, relies on many of the same ideologemes as Italian and other forms of fascism — particularly the reactionary elitism, distinct from radical fascism but related to it, of French and German conservatives like Spengler, Barrès, and Maurras. John R. Harrison has named the representatives of this conservative tendency in the Anglo-American literary tradition the "reactionaries"; they include Eliot, Lewis, and Yeats. Like them, Yourcenar in her work of the 1920s and 1930s disdains urbanization, industrialization, and mass culture as symptoms of the decline of European civilization, favoring instead an idealized vision of preindustrial agrarian or village economies, harmonious peasant-landowner class relations, and classical "high" culture.

After the war, Yourcenar came to adopt an ethos of liberal humanism, the philosophy that clearly informs the revision of *Denier du rêve* undertaken in 1959. Yourcenar's postwar liberalism aligns her with the Crocean analysis of fascism adopted by theorists like Hannah Arendt during the Cold War, in which fascism and communism are interpreted as twin forms of totalitarianism, both equally alien to the liberal, democratic, Western tradition. The shortcomings of such an understanding of fascism have been highlighted in the large body of work on fascist culture, and it is not my intention to reiterate those arguments here. Rather, I ask whether the concepts of humanism, culture, and Western identity expressed in the postwar writing of Yourcenar and Arendt do not in themselves replicate certain tendencies of both conservatism and radical fascism, notably their ethnocentrism.

Such a reading of political tendencies in Yourcenar's work encounters one problem that a similar reading of *Nightwood* does not. Unlike Barnes, Yourcenar left an enormous body of commentary on her own work, including *Denier*, that specifically addresses its political implications and that endeavors to forestall interpretations that might uncover fascist significations in her texts. The ever-present difficulty of distinguishing the views of a historical figure from the positions assumed by her texts is further complicated in Yourcenar's case by the fact that so many of her texts claim to be a transparent revelation of authorial intention; they forbid the reader to imagine that there could *be* textual positions that diverge from the views of the historical figure, or, indeed, that Yourcenar's innumerable prefaces, postfaces, author's notes, autobiographies, and interviews could themselves be scanned, as texts, for signs of contradiction or inconsistency. Yet it is only one of many such inconsistencies that Yourcenar often describes the author as an indifferent voyager through or vessel for the text, while also suggesting, by the very proliferation of her self-commentaries, that author and text are one, and that that one is the author. The challenge, then, in reading Yourcenar, is to read her (as text) against the grain of her own claims (as author), and to read her authorial claims as texts themselves. And the challenge of reading her relation to fascism is to understand how a writer who explicitly disavows fascism could be, before and even after the war, so reliant on concepts, motifs, and tropes that also inform fascist ideologies and writings.

Yourcenar may seem like a curious choice of subject for a book treating Sapphic Modernism, since neither she nor her work is in any obvious way either Sapphic or modernist. Almost all of her works touch on male homosexuality in one guise or another, but references to female homosexuality are rare. She had a warm friendship with Natalie Barney, but claimed that she did not frequent her salon or the other circles of lesbian writers in Paris; and she always maintained a rigorous discretion about her own personal life, preferring to leave her relationships with Grace Frick and other women in, as she said, "the shadows that suit the essential things in life so well" (Yourcenar, *Open Eyes*, 193n1). Furthermore, she was not connected to surrealism or other avant-garde literary movements in France or elsewhere, and in fact before the war she explicitly rejected literary experimentalism. While she worked in a variety of genres, her style usually shows the influence of a classical formation; her limpid, formal prose and severely elegant poetry seem to owe more to Racine and La Fontaine than to the work of contemporaries like Breton or Céline. And most of her important and well-known texts were produced after World War II. In what sense, then, can she be considered part of the phenomenon I have identified as Sapphic Modernism? To begin with, it would be a mistake to treat Yourcenar, as some critics have done, as an Academician lost in ancient Rome or the Renaissance and divorced from the concerns of the twentieth century. From the moment of her birth she was, as she describes herself, a "girl-child, already fixed by the space-time coordinates of the Christian era and twentieth century Europe" (Yourcenar, *Dear Departed*, 3). Even Yourcenar's historical novels demonstrate the influence of her own time and culture as well as her skill at recreating the historical "coordinates" of other places and times. According to Yourcenar, *Mémoires d'Hadrien* (1951), while set in the second century A.D., could only have been written in the optimistic period just after World War II; *L'Œuvre au noir* (1968), set in sixteenth-century Flanders, mirrors the bleaker mood of the 1950s and 1960s (Yourcenar, *Open Eyes*, 133).

Three aspects of Yourcenar's œuvre in particular reveal how influenced she was by the ideological concerns of the twentieth century, and how much her work has in common with many modernist texts. The first is her interest in the ideas of nationality, nationalism, and expatriation. Yourcenar's own national identification was always ambiguous. Even before she became a permanent expatriate and adopted U.S. citizenship, her mixed Belgian-Flemish-French heritage and a peripatetic childhood in Europe influenced her interest in the intersections and gaps between cultural and national identity. The protagonists of her best-known works, although they ostensibly live during eras predating the establishment of nation-states, experience conflicts in their cultural identity that clearly reflect Yourcenar's preoccupation with the problems of nationalism and nationality. Hadrian, a Roman born in what is now Spain and who thinks of himself as Greek, struggles with the conflicts between his identification with the Roman Empire and his respect for other cultures. It is possible to read *Mémoires d'Hadrien* as a direct response and challenge to the nationalistic hatreds that exploded in

World War II; one critic has described the text as "a profoundly antimilitaristic novel, a monument . . . to the need to preserve civilization, Yourcenar's homage to the emperor who tries to break the bond between nationalism and xenophobia, between the empire and the narrow definition of its civilizing mission as the automatic impulse to replace Other (barbarian) with Same (Neo-Greek or Roman)" (DeJean, 297–98). Yet Yourcenar's antinationalism, which grew more fervent as she grew older, was, as we shall see, both antidote and complement to a sense of European cultural identity that could express itself in overt ethnocentrism.

The second element of Yourcenar's work aligning her with many contemporaries is her view that European culture was firmly rooted in antiquity. She disdained the undiscriminating neo-Hellenism of the late 1800s,* but she was herself strongly influenced by the classics; her father began teaching her Greek and Latin while she was still a child. By her early twenties she was thoroughly immersed in Greek philosophies, a passion that became more nuanced but no less ardent as she aged: "When I was about twenty I believed . . . that the Greek response to human questions was the best if not the only one. I realized later that there is no single Greek response but a series of responses which derive from the Greeks and among which one must choose" (Yourcenar, *Dear Departed*, 232). The archaeological discoveries of the previous century sparked a particular interest in Antinoüs and then Hadrian; in writing *Mémoires d'Hadrien*, she said, she wanted to "redo, from the inside, what the archaeologists of the 19th century did from the outside" (Yourcenar, *Hadrien*, 327). Virtually all of her early works also reflect a classical influence, notably *La nouvelle Eurydice* (1931), *Pindare* (1932), and *Feux* (1936), a collection of prose poems that includes "Sappho ou le suicide," one of the only references in her work to the Greek poet, and her only prolonged treatment of female homosexuality.

Yourcenar's Hellenism was, not surprisingly, indissociable from her interest in homosexuality. It is her emphasis on sexuality that

---

* See her essay "A quelqu'un qui me demandait si la pensée grecque vaut encore pour nous," 14–15.

marks her most clearly as a writer of the (Sapphic) modernists' generation. In the 1920s, when Yourcenar wrote *Alexis ou le traité du vain combat*, she was largely concerned with describing an erotic ethic derived from the Greeks and with challenging the medical model of homosexuality. She was obviously influenced in this project by Gide, whose *Corydon* had been published five years before *Alexis* and from whom she borrowed her title, and, more distantly, by Proust.

Yourcenar's vehement distaste for medical models and terminology lasted to the end of her life; she always refused to use the word "homosexuality," which she found "too medical," preferring instead to speak of "sensual choices" (Savigneau, 72, 229). Her rejection of a reductive and repressive medical model expanded into an analysis of the politics of sexuality, of sexuality as "an especially dense transfer point for relations of power" (Foucault, 103), for the transmission of knowledge, and for knowledge-as-power. In *Le coup de grâce*, published in 1939 and set during the Balkan conflicts after the Bolshevik Revolution, the erotic triangle of Eric von Lhomond and Conrad and Sophie de Reval both reflects and informs the political conflicts among the three. Eric and Conrad's relationship is strongly reminiscent of a fascist model of fraternal homoeroticism; in Yourcenar's preface to the work she says that the relationship "corresponds to a certain ideal of austerity, a dream of heroic comradeship ... [Eric's] very sense of the erotic is one aspect of his discipline" (Yourcenar, *Coup de grâce*, 132). One critic has also noted the similarity between Jünger's depictions of male homoerotic military communities and Eric and Conrad's " 'männerbündlerische' ideal of friendship," the misogynist fascist vision of an "earthly Paradise in which woman has no place" (Garmann, 88). In the end, Eric executes Sophie both because she is a Bolshevik and because she loves him; the power struggle reflected in their political antagonism is figured in the power struggles of their erotic relation.

The interlaced themes of sexuality, knowledge, and power run through all of Yourcenar's best-known works. In *Mémoires d'Hadrien*, Hadrian dreams of founding a philosophy based on the erotic, and his relationship with Antinoüs, in conformity with the master/disciple model of *pæderastia*, fuses eroticism with the quest for knowledge: "For Hadrian, as for Zeno, eroticism is the basis of a pedagogy of initiation, from which emerges the figure of the perfect Disciple without whom Knowledge could not be perfect" (Madou, 52). After Antinoüs's death, Hadrian establishes a city dedicated to his cult: the erotic is the very foundation of the polis. In *L'Œuvre au noir*, Yourcenar's analysis of sexuality is filtered through the lens of the religious ideology of sixteenth-century Europe. Zeno's homosexual experiences, which represent and reflect his association with a Greek tradition beginning to flower again in Europe, help prove his apostasy to a Church for which humanism is heresy. Furthermore, the incident that provokes the final political cataclysm in the novel, with its fatal consequences for Zeno, is the discovery of a secret religious cult dedicated to mystical erotic practices. The narrative foregrounds the deployment of sexuality in a culture in which the experiences of the body were investigated and regulated with fanatical care by religious authorities who viewed unsanctioned expressions of eros as a threat to political order.

For Yourcenar, a "tolerance" for, or lack of distinction among, different sensual tastes is an essential part of a Western Enlightenment tradition directly inherited, in her view, from the ancients. She invariably associates the repression of sexual expression with irrationalism, religious fundamentalism, and the Middle Ages (see, e.g., Yourcenar, *Open Eyes*, 142–44). As she matured, she came to focus less on the idea of the repression of discourse and instead to describe a discourse about repression; by the 1970s she had developed a sophisticated theory of sexuality that bears notable similarities to the work of Foucault, and this later work on sexuality can justly be described as postmodern. But in the 1920s and 1930s it is fair to infer that she was still most strongly influenced by the tradition of sexual liberalism that had blossomed in nineteenth-century Germany and influenced many of the "sexual radicals" of the period, from Gide and the Sapphic Modernists to Reich.

Yourcenar's interest in nationality and nationalism, her Hellenism, and her sensitivity to the political significations of sexuality would situate her in the modernist era even if she had no other connections to modernism. She was, however, less isolated from predominant currents of modernist thought, including fascist modernisms, than either she or her critics have usually allowed. Her reading matter even as a very young girl was not restricted to the classics and seventeenth-century writers but included Nietzsche, Thomas Mann, Barrès, D'Annunzio, and Henry de Montherlant; she met or corresponded with, among others, Colette, Janet Flanner, Jünger, and Woolf, whose novel *The Waves* she translated in 1937. Yourcenar's work of the 1920s and 1930s is obviously informed by contemporary events and texts; its style is also less distinctive than that of Yourcenar's mature writing and owes more to the influence of her peers and immediate predecessors. In *Alexis*, she takes the stripped-down form of the *récit* from Gide and Schlumberger; then, heading in the opposite direction, she experiments with the ornate and rather precious style of *Feux*, attributing it to the influence of Barrès and Suarès (Yourcenar, *Open Eyes*, 29). Interestingly, *Feux* also recalls the aestheticist tendencies of Barnes's early writings; lines like "She was afraid of everything: of ghosts, of men, of the number thirteen, and of the green eyes of cats" could have been taken from any of Barnes's short stories (Yourcenar, *Feux*, 200).

Though Yourcenar is not a central figure of Sapphic Modernism, then, it seems fair nonetheless to consider her a fellow traveler of the writers grouped under that rubric. And two of her texts, *Denier du rêve* and *Le coup de grâce*, place her squarely in the center of the political and cultural conflicts of the interwar period. *Le coup de grâce* has attracted a good deal more critical attention than *Denier* (it has even been turned into a movie), and its treatment of political and erotic conflict between anti- and pro-Bolshevik forces during the Baltic Wars has been widely read as a metaphor for the political conflicts of the 1930s.\* But curiously, the few critical treatments of *Denier*, which is explicitly about fascism, have largely ignored ideological considerations and focused on formal questions instead. The novel is, however, an interesting and important document in the history of European intellectual response to fascism. Not only is its subject contemporary political events in Europe, but Yource-

\* See, for example, Judith Johnston, "Marguerite Yourcenar's Sexual Politics in Fiction, 1939"; and Saul Friedländer, *Reflets du nazisme*, 27–30.

nar's analysis of fascist culture, as we shall see, bears strong resemblances to other contemporary cultural critiques—including that of fascist modernity itself.

Before we turn to a reading of that text, it would be useful to consider another of Yourcenar's less-known early works for what it tells us about her intellectual and ideological leanings during the period when she was working on *Denier*. Her "Diagnostic de l'Europe," written in 1928 and published a year later, is an analysis—an anatomy—of the decadence of Europe, vibrant with echoes of the conservative *Kulturkritik* articulated by figures like Nordau, Barrès, and Spengler.* Yourcenar's critique of European culture draws on the racial and sexual stereotypes typical of organicist thought; she writes that Europe is the brain of a world of which Asia is the heart and Africa the womb. The best of the Western tradition, its virile intelligence, has given way to irrationalism, effeminacy, and sentimentality and is degenerating to the level of these "barbaric" cultures.

In this essay Yourcenar maintains that European cultural decline has been provoked by the influence of romanticism on the "firm" spirit of the Europe of Goethe and da Vinci; Rousseau, Chateaubriand, Gide, and Claudel have all contributed to a cult of sentiment and subjectivity in which Yourcenar finds a certain "tragic beauty," while regretting its consequences. Culture, no longer the prerogative of a refined if neurasthenic elite, has become vulgarized by mass education and mass culture; cinema and mass-produced media spread false and corrupt illusions to an unsophisticated proletariat: "Today's prodigious vulgarizing effort—always hasty, often clumsy—made in books and in newspapers affords a vast, inexperienced majority the illusion of universal knowledge." Film, in particular, has encouraged agitation, hypersensitivity, and an aesthetic consciousness that is impressionistic rather than thoughtful and synthetic (Yourcenar, "European Diagnosis," 445, 446, 448).

The cultural avant-garde fares even worse in Yourcenar's analy-

---

*For an interesting reading of this piece and *Denier du rêve*, see François Wasserfallen, "D'un art protoromanesque à un art romanesque."

sis than mass culture; even writers she rather admired are diagnosed as neurasthenics: "The style of Proust subdivided in the extreme, confusing by dint of its abundance, ceaselessly foundering in thoughts that are submitted to rather than directed, and the style of Breton, spasmodic and dry, full of thrusts and tensions, alternate like nervous prostration and excitement" (Yourcenar, "European Diagnosis," 447–48). The piece culminates in an attack on surrealism, primitivism, free verse, and other modernist forms, couched in the same medical terminology as Nordau's *Degeneration*. Yourcenar accuses modernist artists, who should be the "guardians of thought's hereditary disciplines," of abandoning the traditional, universal forms "crafted and tuned by the centuries" in favor of decadent and barbaric thrill-seeking:

> Modern aesthetics of thought, like those prevailing in the linear arts, whether out of a disdain for virtuosity or, perhaps, on account of fatigue, are lapsing back, as liberation follows liberation, into the troubling conventions of dying civilizations: sharply delineated colors, clumsy drawing, summary forms. . . . The turbulence of life, exotic travels, the shocks transmitted to the brain by jolting sequences of cinematic images, and sensual obsessions or financial worries are fraying to shreds the nerves of an elite that no longer trusts in the future. . . . And, punctuating the clamorous, fitful expressions of this amazing mortal agony, Afro-American music, a sudden burst of passion, is transporting to a barbaric world a world that is itself becoming barbaric again. (Yourcenar, "European Diagnosis," 448–49)

Yourcenar's commentary on this manuscript, probably added after the 1970s, retracts her attack on contemporary artists but does not refer to the racism and conservatism of the piece; perhaps, in her later years, she was embarrassed by the severity of her youthful judgments. Certainly she came to appreciate, and sometimes to enjoy, some avant-garde and "low" or popular cultural forms like Negro spirituals. Her apparent belief that Europe has a monopoly on intelligence, civilization, and culture was also modified later by her thorough study of Asian philosophies and aesthetic productions. But however much her attitudes later changed, "European Diagnosis" is an important representation of one aspect of Yourcenar's ideological views during the interwar years.

The most significant thing to remark about this piece is that Yourcenar's critique of European decadence, mass culture, and the avant-garde is extremely similar to the views on culture associated with the more conservative strains of French and German fascisms, except that it is not anti-Semitic; in many regards it probably would have been approved by Alfred Rosenberg. The notable difference is that Yourcenar specifically rejects fascist irrationalism as well as the fascist glorification of hygiene and the body, viewing fascism as just another of the illusory and absurd doctrines to which a culture that has lost its intellectual acuity haplessly subscribes:

> While the spirit, given over to capricious sensations, ceases even to coordinate them, the mind, desperately seeking an ethic, reaches only to the level of mental gymnastics [*l'hygiène sportive*]. In both cases the body, in reaction, triumphs. . . . The body, and the spirit too: between the body and the innermost spirit, between instinct and the unconscious, reason is dying. . . . On all sides, the artisans of thought are doing their best to take the rust off old formulas or forge new ones; all of them equally intransigent concepts, which end up resembling one another in the realm of the absurd. Nationalism, internationalism, Bolchevism [*sic*], fascism, pacifism, the Asiatic dream of nonresistance to force, which is no more than an admission of being powerless to appropriate that force, a brutal materialism that glorifies might substituted for right, and is no more than an admission of being powerless to determine what is right. These concepts wend their way in the world, where they are distorted with a singular rapidity: the most contrary doctrines, in a moment of lucidity, end up finding themselves identical. (Yourcenar, "European Diagnosis," 446–47)

This, I argue, is the analysis that Yourcenar puts into play in *Denier*: a critique of culture that closely resembles that of certain fascisms, while rejecting the solutions proposed both by fascism and by the antifascist Left as illusory and irrational. Both the fascist ideal of a heroic, aesthetic, cultural politics and the revolutionary struggle for a classless society are hollow, futile, and ultimately pernicious. "There is no solid ground," Yourcenar writes in "European Diagnosis," "beneath these builders of smoke, these analysts of fog" (Yourcenar, "European Diagnosis," 445); a few years later, this line could have served as the epigraph for *Denier du rêve*.

The original edition of *Denier* appeared in 1934. Yourcenar had spent a good deal of time in Italy in the previous decade, had witnessed the March on Rome, and had, by her own account, friends in anarchist and resistant circles. She rewrote the novel in 1959; turned it into a play, *Rendre à César*, in the early 1960s; and published the "definitive version" of the text in 1971. Given what her biographer describes as her "incurable penchant for self-commentary" (Savigneau, 71), it is not surprising that she added an afterword to the 1971 edition that orients our reading of the text, proposing certain interpretations and discouraging others. She particularly insists on the ideological consistency of the multiple versions of the text: even though the first version was written "before the expedition into Ethiopia, before the regime's participation in the Spanish Civil War, before the alliance with and quick subjugation to Hitler, before the promulgation of racial laws . . . before the years of confusion, disaster, but also heroic partisan resistance during World War II," Yourcenar claims that "the political climate of the story" was left unchanged and that the novel remained "precisely dated" in the year XI of the fascist regime. Furthermore, she claims that the original *Denier* was "one of the first French novels (maybe the very first) to confront the hollow reality behind the bloated façade of Fascism" (Yourcenar, *Coin*, 172–73).

At least one of Yourcenar's friends who knew her before the war contested her reading of her own text, arguing that the first *Denier* "was absolutely not anti-Mussolini" and that in fact Yourcenar got along quite well in fascist Italy (Savigneau, 94). Since this particular friend, André Fraigneau, was a right-wing Frenchman who became a collaborator, it is permissible to take his assertions with a grain of salt; but we must also ask whether it was actually possible to rewrite a book about fascism after the war with exactly the same perspective one had had in 1934. What we find in the original version of the novel is in fact neither evidence of Yourcenar's complicity with Italian fascism, nor the unequivocal rejection of fascism expressed in the rewrite.

In both versions, Yourcenar gives us the portrait of an atomized society, of individuals alienated from themselves and each other, and of a commodified mass culture. In other words, while both versions of the novel certainly challenge fascism's claim to represent the "real," both offer a diagnosis of the *maux de siècle* that is similar to cultural critiques circulating in both fascist and, mutatis mutandis, leftist ideologies of the period. The rewrite, however, which resembles Arendt's response to fascism in works like *Origins of Totalitarianism* and *Eichmann in Jerusalem*, clearly valorizes the rational, free-willed individual subject and the restoration of an "authentic" Western culture as antidotes to barbarism. It is less obvious in the first version what, if any, nonfascist remedies are available for the cultural malaise it describes; the first *Denier* tends to recapitulate fascist themes and images without producing any alternative to them.

The loose plot of *Denier* follows the peregrinations of a ten-lira coin that passes from person to person in Rome in the course of 24 hours. Most of the characters use the coin to buy something that will prop up their illusions about themselves or others (Farrell and Farrell, 30–31): Paolo Farina buys the pretense of love from Lina Chiari, the prostitute; Lina, ravaged by cancer, buys a lipstick from shopkeeper Giulio Lovisi that will restore the image of her former health and beauty; Giulio buys votive candles for the Virgin, hoping that they will serve "to maintain the fiction of a hope" (Yourcenar, *Denier* 1934, 58). In later years, Yourcenar would interpret the coin as a symptom of the characters' alienation from one another; all their relations are mediated by money. The commodified relations among the characters in *Denier* are, for Yourcenar, symptomatic of the general rationalization of human relations under capitalism, to which she assimilates Italian fascism. In an interview she says:

> I can't imagine believing that you can call it even with someone just because you've paid him a salary (or received a salary from him); or, *as they do in cities*, just because you've paid him a few cents for something, or a few dollars for your dinner. (Incidentally, this is the basic idea of *A Coin in Nine Hands*: a coin passes from hand to hand, but each person who comes into possession of it remains alone.) (Yourcenar, *Open Eyes*, 191; my emphasis)

She goes on in this passage to contrast the impersonal and mediated economy of a city with the village life that she enjoyed on Mt. Desert Island in Maine. As it is for cultural conservatives like Barrès, Maurras, or Spengler, the city—in *Denier*, Rome—is for Yourcenar the site of alienation, anonymity, and an exchange economy; the rural village privileges use-value, craftsmanship, and personal relations that transcend the artificial barriers of class (Yourcenar, *Open Eyes*, 191–93).

The urban crowds of *Denier* are constantly threatened with becoming "the postpsychological de-individualized social atoms" which, in Adorno's analysis, form "the fascist collectivities"; Freud, following Le Bon, described in 1921 their irrationality and susceptibility to the Ideal, in the passage cited at the beginning of this chapter (Adorno, "Freudian Theory," 136; Freud, 173). Alienated from themselves and others, they are easily swayed by illusions of wholeness, belonging, order. The principal characters in the novel emerge from the crowd, struggling to achieve individuation and identity. But, although the characters cross paths repeatedly, they never recognize each other and rarely recognize themselves; they are all on the verge of sinking back into the dehumanized, alienated mass that Yourcenar refers to as "plankton" and "opium smokers." Yourcenar, unlike communism or radical fascism, cannot conceive of a "good crowd." There is no equivalent in her texts for the revolutionary proletariat or the disciplined, aestheticized, fascist masses: no difference between the crowd, the masses, Freud's "group," or the mob. For Yourcenar, the crowd is always and only irrational, seduced by inauthenticity, and alienated.

Given Yourcenar's acute sensitivity to sexual politics, it is not surprising that in her representation alienation is particularly evident in the realm of sexuality, in the relations of the characters to their own and others' bodies. Although the first *Denier* is one of the only works in which Yourcenar does not focus on homosexuality, sexuality in a broader sense remains the arena in which the other important themes of the text are played out. In particular, the commodification of sexuality in prostitution is, as in so many texts of this period, a heavily overdetermined symbol of modern alienation and decay. Lina, the prostitute, is so estranged from her body that she fails to recognize her own reflection in a shop window. When her breast is invaded by a cancer that she considers an alien being, her appointment with the doctor, Alessandro Sarte, is described by analogy to an encounter with a client purchasing her sexual services; the money that is the intermediary between her, her body, and her clients is implicitly compared to the disease that becomes the intermediary between her, her body, and the doctor.

Yourcenar focuses her critique of alienation and inauthenticity, in sexuality and culture, in one of the novel's central scenes, which takes place in a movie theater. The choice of venue is significant; for Yourcenar, as for other cultural critics both left and right, the cinema, as site of the loss of both individual and aesthetic autonomy, is emblematic of mass modernity itself. Film and the film industry played, of course, an important role in fascism's cultural critique and in the development of a totalitarian fascist culture. For Jünger, for example, the goal of film was "the integration of the viewers into an unbroken totality" (Berman, *The Rise*, 220). Indeed, under National Socialism, public screenings of films—and not only propaganda films—were supposed to help create a crowd that would be unanimous in its enthusiasm for fascist spectacle.* In her analysis of French fascisms, Alice Kaplan focuses on the use of the image to create in crowds a sense of group identity that would transcend differences in the service of the aesthetic:

> A familiar Bergsonian vocabulary of pure energy and life force is used to transcend mere political differences in the interests of fascist aestheticism. At the center of the new aesthetic is the group. . . . Crowds watching films learn from the screen to know themselves as a crowd; moviegoing becomes a group rite, or a place where strangers gather to dream together. The crowd comes to know itself as film. (Kaplan, 154–55)

It has been repeatedly commented that Nazi rallies, marches, speeches, and other public events were conceived of and organized

---

*Goebbels was so concerned with guaranteeing a unanimous reaction to film that he was deeply disturbed by the "problem" of people who laughed at inopportune moments during movies, and envisaged means of controlling this phenomenon (Rentschler, "The Ministry of Emotion").

as theatrical or filmic spectacles. Commenting on the *Große Deutsche Kunstausstellung*, a major nationalist art exhibition, the *Völkischer Beobachter* proclaimed, "Today we sat as spectators in the theater of our own time and saw greatness" (qtd. in Barron, 18). Most notably, the Nuremberg rally was staged according to the requirements of Riefenstahl's *Triumph of the Will*, and certain speeches were delivered again because the first takes were unsuccessful. National Socialism did not simply use film to propagate a political message; it also represented itself as film.

Italian fascism was slower to acknowledge film as a medium for transmitting, or as a figure for, State power. Even in this case, however, film was clearly understood as a challenge, perhaps as a potential danger, to fascism's powers of cultural assimilation; its importance to conceptions of modernity is also manifest in the anxiety or mistrust the medium could provoke. The normative model for Italian fascist culture was based on physical presence and immediacy, and the normative venue for the transmission of culture was the outdoor Roman amphitheater. New technologies like film and radio, while they appealed to Italian fascism's futurist bent, also represented a worrisome layer of mediation between the leader and the crowd. Once Mussolini's regime began to use film more extensively, therefore, in the mid-1930s, it was assimilated to a model of theatrical performance, with traveling vans projecting films in outdoor spaces.

By 1936, Pope Pius XI found it necessary to issue an encyclical on "motion picture entertainments," the *Vigilanti Cura*, which noted the cinema's influence on the masses and cautioned against immorality in film (De Grazia, 143–44). Right-wing cultural critics also worried that film had been commercialized and corrupted by the movie industry, controlled, naturally, by Hollywood Jews, who had used film to "jewify" culture, to render it artificial and inauthentic, substituting a false cult of stars for the authentic expression of the personality of the race or nation. Rosenberg, for instance, complained in 1925 that Jews dominated the Western dramatic arts and especially film, which could, if only it were properly used (presumably by fascists), "cause millions of hearts to beat in a single direction." Instead of actors, according to Rosenberg, Jewish management created "stars"; instead of an art form, film was in their hands an industry and "a means of infecting the *Volk*." The performing arts in the West were thus degraded, under Jewish influence, "into mass-hypnosis and sensual excitement" (Rosenberg, *Selected Writings*, 172–73, 167).

Left criticism, of course, also analyzed fascism as a kind of "mass hypnosis" transmitted through mass media. In the left analysis, fascist culture overlaps mass culture to the point of becoming identical with it. Fascist culture, responding to the alienation and loss of individuality endemic to mass society, creates the reified "Personality" of the Leader, a "blank" onto which the crowd can project its own desires. Although Benjamin is guardedly optimistic about the revolutionary potential of film, he also believes that it has been co-opted by the film industry, which commodifies "personality" (W. Benjamin, "Mechanical," 231). Adorno and others, like Isherwood, are more skeptical of the emancipatory possibilities of mass media, pointing out that fascist propaganda relies on the techniques of commercial advertising to "brainwash" the infantile, irrational crowd:

> Through a process of "freezing," which can be observed throughout the techniques employed in modern mass culture, the surviving appeals [of fascist agitators] have been standardized, similarly to the advertising slogans which proved to be most valuable in the promotion of business. This standardization, in turn, falls in line with stereotypical thinking, that is to say, with the "stereopathy" of those susceptible to this propaganda and their infantile wish for endless unaltered repetition. (Adorno, "Freudian Theory," 133)\*

In fascist/mass culture love, art, sex, freedom, and human beings themselves become reified elements, infinitely substitutable for every

---

\* In his fiction, Isherwood produces a very similar analysis of the debasement of the German language in mass/fascist culture, through the mass circulation in advertising and propaganda of words stripped of semantic function: "The murder reporters and the jazz-writers had inflated the German language beyond recall. The vocabulary of newspaper invective (traitor, Versailles-lackey, murder-swine, Marx-crook, Hitler-swamp, Red-pest) had come to resemble, through excessive use, the formal phraseology of politeness employed by the Chinese. The word *Liebe*, soaring from the Goethe standard, was no longer worth a whore's kiss" (Isherwood, *Berlin Stories*, 86).

other element, in the same way that movie stars are interchangeable in standardized film roles.

Yourcenar articulates a similar critique of fascist/mass culture in *Denier*'s movie theater scene, attacking Italian fascism's claim to have broken with the reified culture of capitalism; in *Denier*, all the world's a (fascist) stage. The movie star Angiola, daughter of a Sicilian and a "vulgar" Algerian Jewess, goes out to watch one of her own films at the Cinema Mondo—the theater of the world. The relation between commodified culture and alienation is evoked the moment that Angiola buys her ticket "from the cashier who serves as intermediary between us and the shadows"\* (Yourcenar, *Denier* 1934, 157–58). Money, identified with the cashier/pimp, mediates between Angiola and her "idol," her commodified double, the actress Angiola Fidès; she has to purchase access to her self. In the theater, "Angiola leaned forward on her elbows to watch Angiola Fidès" (Yourcenar, *Denier* 1934, 155). But, looking for her self, her personality, she finds instead a Personality. The narrator says ironically of Angiola Fidès that "no role could disguise her real personality" (Yourcenar, *Denier* 1934, 162); Angiola, however, has no "real personality." Angiola Fidès's name is the guarantee of her fidelity (to herself), the identity of the Personality and the person. But the two are not identical, are indeed deeply estranged. Angiola Fidès is only a fetishized mechanical reproduction of Angiola; in the illusory world of fascist/mass culture, however, Angiola is assumed to be a reproduction of Fidès.

In the dark, a stranger—Alessandro Sarte—enters Angiola's loge and, never recognizing her, makes love with her during a love scene in the movie. The picture of the lovers kissing on the screen reflects the real lovers' alienation, threatening to disintegrate into indifferent, de-individualized atoms, like the members of fascist/mass society: "If they grew any larger, these faces would disintegrate into the movements of atoms, as indifferent to this kiss as we can be to the immeasurable loves of the stars" (Yourcenar, *Denier* 1934, 172).

\*The original text reads, "la caissière qui sert d'entremetteuse entre les ombres et nous." The word "entremetteur" not only comprises the sense of mediation, but also has the specific meaning of "procurer" or "pimp."

After their encounter, Alessandro and Angiola exchange a stilted good-bye in English, both of them disappointed by the difference between their meaningless and unreal sexual relation and the illusory but convincing emotion communicated by the film actors.

As one critic has noted, for Italian characters in a French novel to communicate in English represents "the height of alienation" (Van der Starre, 72–73); the foreign words measure their inability to apprehend reality, semantic or otherwise. Alessandro thinks to himself that Angiola is just another woman doing her best to imitate Angiola Fidès without succeeding, because she is incapable of expressing or inspiring the authentic passion that he attributes to the actress who mimes it so well.

> Like all women who try to model their face and their soul after Hollywood, she was doing her best to look like Angiola Fidès. But her beautiful, banal features were infinitely less expressive than those of the admirable Jewish actress who had just occupied the screen. An Angiola Fidès able to mimic passion so well must also be able to feel and to inspire it. On the other hand, this easy pick-up was the type of woman one didn't want cluttering up one's life. (Yourcenar, *Denier* 1934, 172)

While Alessandro imagines that Angiola apes the real Angiola Fidès, Angiola knows that, simulacrum of a simulacrum, she "can only ape her own life" (Yourcenar, *Denier* 1934, 176).

It is clearly significant that in the original text Angiola, the emblem of inauthenticity and imitation, is a Jew—and not even a Roman Jew, but of mixed Sicilian-Algerian blood. Interestingly, in the rewrite it is not Angiola whose Jewishness is emphasized, but her wealthy middle-aged impresario and lover, whose name is changed from "Sir Julius Round" to "Sir Julius Stein." Yourcenar retained, however, a reference to Sir Julius's "exploitation of the world." Possibly she wished to deflect attention from what seemed, especially after the war, too ideologically loaded an image of the Jew, by transferring it to a more minor character—although the exploitative Jewish movie producer / financier is surely, if anything, an even more recognizable stereotype than the Jewish actress.

A more important effect of the change is that in the revised edition the inauthenticity of the film medium, and of the actress herself, is tacitly attributed to the jewifying influence of the producer. At the end of this novel Angiola, stripped of her actress's makeup as she sleeps, regains an "innocent beauty" (Yourcenar, *Coin*, 158). The second *Denier*, with its focus on the integrated individual as an antidote to atomization and massification, allows for the recovery of an essential and authentic self. In the first novel, however, this scene is lacking. Angiola, the half-breed Jew, has already "put aside the real Angiola" by the age of sixteen (Yourcenar, *Denier* 1934, 79) and can never recuperate innocence or authenticity. Only the painter Clément Roux preserves the memory of the beautiful young girl he once saw on a Sicilian beach, and he fails to identify her with "that tart Angiola Fidès" (Yourcenar, *Denier* 1934, 215). There is no redemption from the falsity of mass modernity, here identified both with miscegenation, Jewishness, and prostitution (as it is in fascist cultural critiques) and with fascism itself.

Especially in the first edition of the novel, Yourcenar reinforces the stereotypical association of the Jew with inauthenticity, mechanical reproduction, and imitativeness by underlining Angiola's literal and metaphoric sterility. Her relationship with her sister Rosalia is tinged with suggestions of incest, recalling the fin-de-siècle preoccupation with both incest and lesbianism as figures of sterile and degenerative love. Angiola's self-absorption is also described in terms that recall the narcissistic model of lesbianism: "Angiola was . . . free tonight to abandon herself completely to the woman who made her heart pound"—that is, Angiola Fidès (Yourcenar, *Denier* 1934, 156). And her relationship with Sir Julius is sterile, like her other affairs: "Angiola cannot manage to integrate her passions with the continuity that alone makes them real, organic as a heart: the loves of her real life are aborted one after the other, like her only child" (Yourcenar, *Denier* 1934, 176).

Angiola is not, it is true, the only character in the text associated with sterility; sterility and degeneration are in fact recurrent tropes in both versions of *Denier*, as they are in *Nightwood*. Lina the prostitute has had either syphilis or an abortion; Marcella's mother, wife and mother of revolutionaries, is arrested for performing abortions; Mimi, the daughter of the partisan Carlo, is, like *Nightwood*'s Guido, a sickly cripple; Marcella has had to renounce her desire for children to devote herself to the partisan cause. In fact, the only characters in *Denier* who succeed in reproducing are Catholics, members of the laboring classes and adherents of fascism: Giulio, Oreste Marinunzi, Mother Dida, and her aptly named husband, Fruttuoso. Yourcenar not only takes up fascism's emphasis on the sterility of modern culture, but seems to suggest that the antidote to sterility is a return to the fascist values of "blood and soil." It is only in the light of her later works, in which indiscriminate procreation is associated with the devaluation of human and natural resources in industrialized mass society, that we can understand this gesture as partly ironic; I will return to this point later.

Italian fascism is explicitly invoked at several points in the movie theater scene. When Alessandro first enters the loge, "the film of his life was running backwards" and he remembers the fascist rally he has just attended as a kind of nightmarish film clip. Reality, "the present," is contrasted with "*l'actualité*," the news, which, in spite of fascism's claims to represent historical immediacy and authoritative presence, is always already "a week old" (Yourcenar, *Denier* 1934, 168–69). In the Cinema Mondo, the feature film is preceded by a newsreel:

> The dictator inaugurated a Roman art exhibit; the Jews, guilty of their race, crossed the Polish border; here, the cannons thundered in the Mongolian desert. Angiola closed her eyes, letting pass these residues of gestures, half-digested by Time, which for another few weeks would be scattered around the world, detached from their causes, before rotting like dead leaves. She hadn't come to see these banal film shorts produced at great expense by the firm of Universe and God. (Yourcenar, *Denier* 1934, 158–59)

The news is presented according to the conventions of realism, but here political and historical events, "*l'actualité*," are reduced to the same level of "nonactuality" as Angiola Fidès's adventure film; fascist spectacle is revealed as pure banality, the insubstantial and transient production of a commercialized universe, rather than the realization of the glorious forces of history. This was not an uncommon contemporary criticism of fascism; but it is important to note that if Yourcenar's critique coincides here with a neo-Marxist analysis like that of the Frankfurt School, it can hardly be considered materialist. Like Barnes's, Yourcenar's pessimism is ahistorical; the "material conditions of history" have no more substance in the cinema of the world than the fascist dream of a newly imperial, aestheticized polis suggested by the "Roman art exhibit."

Yourcenar writes in the afterword to the 1971 edition of *Denier* that that version, conditioned by the horror of World War II, is "more bitter" than the first edition (Yourcenar, *Coin*, 174). She is wrong: the first edition is far more bitter, presenting all of fascist/mass culture as equally unreal and banal, and offering only a suggestion of the valorization of individuality that will be so much more pronounced in the later version. Both editions are prefaced by an epigraph from Montaigne (*"C'est priser sa vie justement ce qu'elle est, de l'abandonner pour un songe"*) that suggests that nonfascist realities are worth no more than the fascist dream. In the second *Denier*, however, the realism of the text offers an antidote to the inauthenticity of the culture it depicts; it offers, that is, an image of a nonfascist reality expressed in physical, psychological, and historical detail.

Fascism claimed to privilege a materiality—a "reality"—associated with blood, community, soil, and the body, while also transcending the basely material in its rhetoric of heroism, myth, and Spirit. As we have seen, this ideological emphasis on the "real" could be expressed in an aesthetic of hypermimeticism; in various forms of "fascist socialist realism"; or in officially approved Nazi *Volkskunst*. The second version of *Denier du rêve* challenges all of these aesthetic ideals, enacting instead a "liberal realism" that restores interiority and integrity to its subjects and promotes a version of the "real" that relies on the shared metanarratives of Western culture. As one critic writes, "in the 1959 novel the symbolic dimension is weaker than in the 1934 version; it has given way to historical realism and a more profound psychological portrayal of the characters" (Restori, 123).

We do find in the first *Denier*, as well, traces of the philosophy of individualism that Yourcenar would later oppose to what she viewed as fascism's idealism. For instance, in the first edition, as in the second, it is at the moment where Marcella is on the verge of killing "Caesar" that she recognizes the reality of the individual called Benito Mussolini, and misses her shot: "Instead of a ruler in uniform, facing the people, fascinating the crowd, she had before her only a man in evening dress, getting into his automobile" (Yourcenar, *Denier* 1934, 153). The reality of the individual man redeems the unreality of Mussolini as an Ideal. For the most part, however, the original version of the novel is marked by a feeling of dreaminess and a lack of concrete detail that puts all the characters and events on the same plane, not of heightened reality as in the rewrite, but of the same unreality of which it accuses fascism.

Not only does the first edition fail to *enact* a remedy to fascism, it avoids explicitly proposing one, and political alternatives to fascism—in the novel, revolutionary socialism and anarchism—are treated, like fascism, as illusory. In contrast to the second edition, most of the political commentary is attributed to one of the characters, rather than to the narrative voice; and questionable political views are shared by leftists and fascists alike. Alessandro, for example, who supports Mussolini out of expediency rather than conviction, learns that his anarchist wife Marcella intends to try to assassinate the dictator and argues with her, "I know quite well that he's not a man, to you, he's an idea . . . Being an idea is what makes him great . . . That's what he is for millions of people." And she responds, "At the moment I shoot, I will be an idea too" (Yourcenar, *Denier* 1934, 130; her ellipses). The idea that the individual, meaningless in her- or himself, achieves glory by incarnating the Idea(l) is of course central to fascist ideology,* but here it is attributed equally to both the fascist and the anarchist. The police informer Massimo argues that idealism, whether of the Right or

---

* In one representative passage from *Der Kampf als inneres Erlebnis*, Jünger reflects that most soldiers "are really material, material that the Idea immolates for its own greatest purposes, without their knowing it. That is the essential meaning of their lives, the greatness of which they are unable to understand, and that is the source of their sufferings" (Jünger, *Kampf*, 87).

the Left, is meaningless, one of the misperceptions of reality afflicting everyone in fascist/mass culture. For Massimo, it is the opposition of the Left as much as the adulation of the Right that creates the "reality" of the dictator; he says to Marcella, "That man (that puppet of flesh), you're going to swell him with your hatred, like the others, the thousands of others, who puff him up with their fervor. Him, that man who doesn't exist . . ." (Yourcenar, *Denier* 1934, 138).

This mistrust of the idealism of both Left and Right occasionally emerges in the narration of the first *Denier*, as well as in Massimo's dialogue. Mussolini is described as the "god" of the crowd; the imprisoned revolutionary Carlo Stevo is also described as Marcella's god (Yourcenar, *Denier* 1934, 152, 105). After Marcella's assassination attempt fails and she is killed, she and the young fascist she has shot by accident are described as "two victims of different gods" (Yourcenar, *Denier* 1934, 181). The idea that all idealisms are equally murderous is a good deal more attenuated in the second edition, where the resistants are more obviously heroic. By the time Yourcenar rewrote the novel, she clearly felt that the moral stakes in the conflict between Left and Right had changed, and her sympathy for the resistants of World War II made her sketch the leftists in the second *Denier* in more flattering terms, muting the idea that their ideals were as false as the fascists'.

If the differences between Left and Right are ironed out in the original *Denier*'s flattened and ahistorical perspective, so are the differences between individuals, between past and present, and between myth and history—in rather the same way that fascism subsumes historical or individual particularities into totalizing narratives about History, Spirit, or Race. In the first *Denier*, motivations and character, rather than being informed by either political actuality or individual circumstances, are attributed to vague forces like "destiny." The characters are repeatedly associated with mythological figures, and with statues; Marcella, for example, is called "Phèdre" and "Némésis" and is compared to marble or a statue. She even hides behind a statue to shoot at Mussolini (Restori, 125), flattened against its back so that she seems to merge with the marble. These effects de-individualize the characters and lend both characters and events a static quality, undercutting the intention Yourcenar claimed later to have had, to point out an immediate historical danger (Van der Starre, 66–67).

Yourcenar implicitly criticizes fascism's attempt to associate Mussolini's regime with imperial Rome, while herself relying on imperial, classical, or mythological figures. In one suggestive scene, for example, Clément Roux thinks with disgust of the cats that have been exterminated during the archaeological digs at Trajan's Forum, "this work which, in the name of a more ancient past, destroyed a more recent one" (Yourcenar, *Denier* 1934, 199–200). The painter's reflections on the sanctity of animal life make it clear that he considers the attempt to uncover Rome's imperial past literally murderous; the slaughter of the cats is the representation, in miniature, of the violence unleashed by Mussolini's imperialist regime. Yet Yourcenar's references to Rome as *"la Ville,"* as well as her invocations of classical legend, also recall myths of the Eternal City and link ancient and fascist Rome. In her 1971 afterword, furthermore, she explicitly claims that intention, saying, "The tendency toward myth or allegory was somewhat similar in the two versions; it attempted to meld into one picture the Rome of the year XI of the Fascist era and the City where the eternal human story is set and unraveled" (Yourcenar, *Coin*, 170). And in 1980 Yourcenar again characterizes her use of mythology in the novel as a deliberate strategy:

> But in *A Coin in Nine Hands* there is something else: a strong desire to draw a parallel between the characters of the novel and the figures of Greek mythology—the characters are seen as avatars of legend.... This was to make the reader feel the grandeur of their actions, not unlike the grandeur that one finds in ancient legend and myth, and in the year 1933 legend and myth were quite prevalent in Rome's "modern" center. (Yourcenar, *Open Eyes*, 60)

She then retreats slightly from this assertion, however, tacitly acknowledging the inadequacy of her approach by asserting that in the 1920s and 1930s she saw clearly what was happening in fascist Italy but was unsure "what little *facts* to use to express it" (Yourcenar, *Open Eyes*, 61; my emphasis). Her words also suggest that by the time she rewrote the novel she sensed that mythology, at least in her un-ironic use of it, was not an appropriate weapon against what she perceived as fascism's own illusory myth-making, and that realism was a more suitable tactic: "All of these parallels [with mythology] are maintained in the second edition, though in a much less pronounced way, because the *realistic* level of the novel is given greater prominence" (Yourcenar, *Open Eyes*, 61; my emphasis). In 1934, while clearly skeptical of fascism's pretensions to have a privileged access to reality, she was unsure what, if any, alternatives were available. Assimilating all of the novel's characters and events to the mythological, the "unreal" or oneiric, she undermines her own attempt to formulate a topical political critique.

Other points in this 1980 interview suggest that, even years later, Yourcenar was still unable entirely to divorce her criticism of fascism from the categories of fascist thought. In *Denier*, for example, Yourcenar implicitly contrasts the "natural" or "real" with the fascist "dream," challenging fascism's fantasies of mimesis not by dismissing them as unattainable, like Barnes, but by associating fascist aesthetics with decadent aestheticism and its love of artifice. She would seem, then, to be enacting the same maneuver as Benjamin by contrasting the real—politicized art, like socialist realism or the second *Denier*—with the artificial: aestheticized politics. She reveals, however, to what extent her critique of the aestheticization of politics relies itself on purely aesthetic criteria when she says during the interview:

> Fascism seemed grotesque to me; I had seen the march on Rome: gentlemen of "good family" sweating under their black shirts, and beating up people who didn't agree with them. *It wasn't pretty.* [*Cela ne m'avait pas paru beau.*] What's more [*De plus*], I was never taken in by the claims of unanimous support. It's never true that a whole country is in step with the government. (Yourcenar, *Open Eyes*, 61; my emphasis)

The first argument against fascism that occurs to her fifty years later, then, is an aesthetic argument; her resistance to fascism's coercive, totalitarian aspect is an afterthought, something *"de plus."* Yourcenar even recognizes that the sentiment evoked by fascism is akin to her own passion for the aesthetics of ritual and ceremony, while distinguishing fascism as a base version of such emotions: "Ceremonies... in which people feel a sense of togetherness, that's *beau-*

*tiful*, like a more fervent form of life. Provided, of course, that it doesn't degenerate into a sort of mass chauvinism [*chauvinisme de foule*], whether it be Catholic, communist, fascist, racist, or whatever, in which fervor quickly gives way to arrogance and hatred" (Yourcenar, *Open Eyes*, 21; my emphasis).

Yourcenar's equation of "Catholic," "communist," and "fascist" crowds points again to her rejection of "the crowd" per se and to her attempt to escape the closed, binary terms of fascist/antifascist discourse by defining a centrist position that rejects "extremisms" of Left and Right. Significantly, in both versions of *Denier du rêve*, the treacherous Massimo is of Slavic origin. (Later commentary indicates that he is meant to be a White Russian, a reactionary, but this is not at all clear in the 1934 text.) Our assumptions about his rightist political leanings intersect confusingly with the image of the Soviet Union evoked by the vague references to his nationality, enforcing the suspicion that for Yourcenar the "Red menace" is always the twinned counterpart to fascist barbarism, whatever she claimed after the war about her admiration for the leftist partisans. She admits, furthermore, that she mistrusted contemporary French writers who were engaged on the Left in the 1930s; she thought that Malraux and other left writers were simply engaging in rhetorical posturing, and describes her attitude at the time as "One of indifference" (Yourcenar, *Open Eyes*, 90).

A declaration of indifference, in the European political climate of the 1930s, amounts almost inevitably to a position, if not of radical reaction, then of conservatism. Interviewer Matthieu Galey makes this very point when, during a discussion of *Le coup de grâce*, he responds to Yourcenar's remark that Eric von Lhomond "dismisses ideology" by saying, "I'm sure I won't be telling you anything you don't already know if I remind you that a person who describes him or herself as apolitical generally stands politically on the right" (Yourcenar, *Open Eyes*, 89). Yourcenar's response is both evasive and revealing:

> Let me think a moment about that statement, which strikes me as too cut and dried to accept on its face. . . . What your proposition proves is simply that, for the time being, left-wing ideology is dominant over right-wing ideology, or at any rate is attempting to assert its domi-

nance. Any minority appears apolitical to the surrounding majority. Mussolini, for example, surely looked upon any writer who did not subscribe to his imperial policy as an "apolitical" person with anarchist tendencies. (Yourcenar, *Open Eyes*, 89)

What Galey suggested was that "a person," Eric von Lhomond or Marguerite Yourcenar, who defined him- or herself as apolitical was probably on the Right. But what Yourcenar seems to defend herself against instead is an accusation that she is apolitical—the premise she had originally introduced herself in reference to Eric—by intimating that she is, instead, part of that right-wing minority that appears apolitical to a dominant leftist ideology. Begging Galey's question, she appears, inadvertently, to answer another.

It is surely noteworthy that Yourcenar's lapsus, evasion, or simple illogicity occurs in the context of a discussion of the European politics of the 1930s and especially the politically loaded *Coup de grâce*, and that she evokes Mussolini's name. For the older, U.S.-based Yourcenar had developed a consistent philosophy of liberalism—she was a registered Democrat—and though that position is problematic in ways we will discuss later, it was unlikely to appear controversial to a French interviewer in 1980. It is the European political context of the 1920s and 1930s, and the need to explain textual positions she adopted during those years, that provokes Yourcenar's defensiveness, her lack of clarity, and her tacit admission that to assign her to the Right during this period would not be entirely unjust.

But which Right? The Yourcenar of this period rejects not only left and right modernisms, but post-1850 modernity itself almost entirely; her value system is firmly rooted in the Enlightenment and consequently, in her view, in the classical tradition. It could be said, indeed, and only partly facetiously, that the only period of the entire postclassical era with which Yourcenar is ideologically comfortable is the century 1750–1850; for her, the pre-Enlightenment period represents feudal barbarism and the industrial period a return to barbarism in the forms of mass culture.

Yourcenar's allegiance to certain Enlightenment values undoubtedly puts her at odds, then, with important aspects of radical fascism or National Socialism; her embrace of Reason, individual rights, and sexual liberalism, for instance, and her rejection of romanticism as well as any progressive or positive vision of technology, are inimical to radical fascism's blend of irrationalism, authoritarianism, and fascination with the aesthetics of industry and technology. By 1940, when Yourcenar writes a rebuttal of a pro-Nazi piece by Anne Lindbergh, it is clear that she opposes Nazism because she (correctly) views it as a rejection of the Enlightenment. For her, fascist Germany represents not the power of the future but an outdated feudalism that is dragging the "civilized" countries down with it:

> Not only do the countries where civil liberties had borne their sweetest fruits—Holland, Belgium, the Baltic states and certain of the Scandinavian states—find themselves reduced to their old situation as vassal provinces, but victorious Germany herself, denying her own 18th century and a large part of her 19th, now has no more up-to-date ideal than to resemble pre-Christian Germania as closely as possible. If this is the direction being taken by the Forces of the Future, symbolized by the tanks of the three dictators, then a few more turns of the wheel, and humanity is going to find itself back in the middle of the Stone Age. (Yourcenar, "Forces du passé," 58–59)

Even in this explicitly antifascist piece, we note, Yourcenar acknowledges the "beauty" of fascist images ("And certainly, no one contests the fact that there is beauty in the passionate exaltation of a young Nazi, and in his total sacrifice to his beloved leader"), while arguing that the perhaps admirable ideals of the Nazis are insufficient compensation for their ill-advised hero worship, their violence, and their hostility to civilization: " 'One cannot save civilization by war,' says Anne Lindbergh quite rightly; neither can one save it by allowing oneself to be so easily seduced by that which is its opposite" (Yourcenar, "Forces du passé," 61).

At the same time that Yourcenar rejects fascist irrationalism, however, her emphasis on "traditional" Western aesthetic values (remember her scathing attack on modernist poetics in "European Diagnosis"), her racism and especially anti-Semitism, her antipathy toward modernization, and her covert but distinct disdain for the masses do tend to align her with the elitist conservatism of figures like Spengler, Maurras, and Barrès. Like them, she responds to industrialization, urbanization, the development of technologies of mass destruction, and the collapse of cultural identities in World War I not with the apocalyptic verve of the futurists or the authoritarian triumphalism of National Socialism, but with a gloomy sense of decline and nostalgia for an idealized agrarian, aristocratic past.

"Democracy," we note, is not one of the Enlightenment values for which Yourcenar tended to express great enthusiasm. The kind of aesthetic elitism she evinces in "European Diagnosis" can be closely allied with antidemocratic sentiment, as Harrison points out in *The Reactionaries*: "Contempt for the taste and judgment of the public can easily become contempt for the public itself, particularly when that public is becoming more numerous and self-assertive" (Harrison, 25). And after all, the period of history that Yourcenar seems to favor, that century between 1750 and 1850, was an era when the franchise was restricted to male landowners, and great estates like her own aristocratic family's preserved both the land and intimate but hierarchical relations among gentry, servants, and peasantry.

Indeed, at Yourcenar's most conservative moments, as in "European Diagnosis" or *Le coup de grâce*, she approaches the reactionary ethos of the Junkers, the Prussian landed aristocracy whose type she represents in Eric von Lhomond. Yourcenar never embraces Junker militarism, nor Maurras's and Barrès's strident nationalism and later glorification of "the mob"; and her pessimism certainly never reaches Jünger's, or Barnes's, nihilistic depths.* But her sympathy with some of their most conservative positions reminds us that for many liberal centrists of the 1930s fascism seemed not so much intrinsically *wrong* as wrong-headed, offering solutions that were at once too extreme and inadequate to address the crises of modernity.

* For a discussion of the relation between elitism, conservative pessimism, and fascism, see Arendt, *Origins*, 112, 328. Yourcenar's later admiration for the archreactionary—some would say neofascist—Japanese writer Mishima suggests that, even in her apparently more liberal maturity, the combination of aesthetic elitism, authoritarian politics, and devotion to a homoerotic *Männerbund* never lost its appeal for her.

Both the second version of *Denier du rêve* and Yourcenar's other postwar works reflect the ever-deepening liberal humanism that eventually becomes her response to both fascism and Stalinism. After the war, Yourcenar's increasing commitment to Enlightenment values of religious and racial tolerance, and freedom of individual expression in art and sexuality, softens the judgmental severity expressed in "European Diagnosis" and infuses her best works with a tone of genuine compassion and respect for the varieties of human experience. That same commitment to the Enlightenment, however, forecloses the possibility of investigating the ideological ties between fascism and the humanist tradition Yourcenar embraces. As a renewed emphasis on the rational, free-willed individual and on a Western culture rooted in the Greco-Roman tradition comes to stand in her work as the alternative to the various barbarisms of collectivist ideologies, those ideologies become, by definition, aberrations in the progress of Western civilization: parentheses in history.

It is interesting in this context to read Yourcenar in conjunction with Arendt. While Arendt's work can hardly be subsumed wholesale under the rubric of "liberal humanism," there are nonetheless many similarities between her work and Yourcenar's, and Arendt's greater polemical explictness helps to illumine some of the more obscure aspects of Yourcenar's texts. For Arendt, as well, fascism is an aberration in Western culture, distinct even from the horror of imperialism that preceded it, as well as from the rest of Western history:

> We can hardly avoid looking at this close and yet distant past [i.e., the period of imperialism] with the too-wise eyes of those who know the end of the story in advance, who know it led to an almost complete break in the continuous flow of Western history as we had known it for more than two thousand years. But we must also admit a certain nostalgia for what can still be called a "golden age of security," for an age, that is, when even horrors were still marked by a certain moderation and controlled by respectability, and therefore could be related to the general appearance of sanity. In other words, no matter how close to us this past is, we are perfectly aware that our experience of concentration camps and death factories is as remote from its general atmos-

phere as it is from any other period in Western history. (Arendt, *Origins*, 123)

What this analysis fails to recognize, of course, is the possibility that both imperialism and fascism are phenomena integral to "Western civilization," an unsurprising (if not inevitable) product of some of the "Western values" Arendt and Yourcenar espouse. Even Yourcenar's postwar humanism continues, then, to be double-edged, ambivalent in its relation to conservative fascist thought; she, like Arendt, produces a committed critique of imperialism and fascism that simultaneously reproduces certain reactionary themes and values.

One of the most subtle manifestations of conservative and elitist tendencies in Arendt's and Yourcenar's work is the fact that their focus on the individual, their desire to recuperate a notion of rational, integrated subjectivity from fascist irrationalism and Stalinist collectivism, also borders at times on a certain antagonism, not simply to the evils of mass society but to the masses. In their view, totalitarianism is not only a way of organizing mass society; it is also inevitably produced by mass society. I have already proposed that for Yourcenar, the crowd or the masses are always antipathetic. There is also a trace of this antagonism in Arendt's *Eichmann in Jerusalem*. With its focus on "the person of the defendant, a man of flesh and blood with an individual history, with an always unique set of qualities, peculiarities, behavior patterns, and circumstances," *Eichmann* attempts, like the second version of *Denier*, to enact the antidote to massification that it prescribes: it returns to Eichmann the individuality of which totalitarianism has stripped him (Arendt, *Eichmann*, 285). National Socialism has made Eichmann a "post-psychological de-individualized social atom." The only relations between these alienated atoms in mass/totalitarian society are paranoid: everybody they ever come in contact with may denounce them or be put in danger by the fact of having known them (Arendt, *Origins*, 323). The fascist culture represented in *Denier* is not yet totalitarian in this sense, for it is not yet entirely organized or rationalized; there still exists the possibility of human connection and intimacy. Yet the most apparently intimate relationships, between

Massimo, Carlo, and Marcella, become the occasion for Massimo's treacherous betrayal of the partisans, suggesting that Arendt's paranoid society is close at hand, and that Eichmann's fate awaits the characters in *Denier*:

> [Eichmann is] the individual who, in bureaucratic society, surrenders individuality and thereby the ability to think, to make moral decisions, and to recognize the humanity of other individuals.... His banality is not a quality necessarily shared by everyone but rather the lack of quality and the lack of character that mark human behavior in societies where the valorization of conformism displaces individual autonomy. (Berman, "Wandering Z," xvii)

In support of her claim that massification inevitably creates people like Eichmann, Arendt argues in the epilogue to *Eichmann* that the new form of crime she attributes to National Socialism is more likely to be repeated in the future, because of "the frightening coincidence of the modern population explosion with the discovery of technical devices that, through automation, will make large sections of the population 'superfluous.' " (Arendt, *Eichmann*, 273) It is striking how closely this statement resembles many of Yourcenar's pronouncements on the evils of overpopulation, as when she says of people in the nineteenth century that "they were not afflicted with the overcrowding that causes world wars, devalues the individual, and rots the species" (Yourcenar, *Dear Departed*, 82). For Arendt, "the impoverishment of politics in modern mass society [is] a consequence of quantitative expansion beyond the dimensions of the idealized polis" (Berman, "Wandering Z," xviii). For Yourcenar, too, the "banality of evil" would seem an inevitable consequence of overpopulation, which she conflates with the population *density* of urban areas; the "idealized polis" she contrasts with fascist/mass society is, as I have suggested, rural village life in Maine.

Now, there are unquestionably many ills attendant on global overpopulation, and both Yourcenar and Arendt have as their stated aim a laudable desire to uphold human dignity in a world of widespread degradation and horror. What is perhaps more dubious is, first, their conclusion that horror in this century has been directly consequent upon population growth, and, second, the models they propose as alternatives to mass society. In particular, Yourcenar's antagonism toward mass, industrial, urban society inclines her to adopt positions which, though by no means exclusive to fascism, are certainly closer to conservative fascist ideas than to left or even liberal ones. We recall Herf's claim that the liberal center resigns itself to reified consciousness while attempting to rescue "remnants of individual autonomy" (Herf, 88–89). The figures Yourcenar chooses to represent her notion of individual autonomy are often, revealingly, either aristocrats or peasants: Hadrian, a Roman emperor; the simple and uncultivated Nathanael of "An Obscure Man," who achieves unmediated fusion with his natural environment as he is dying; and truly the last representative of liberal subjectivity in mass culture, Eric von Lhomond, the aristocratic rightwing homosexual who is exempt from the dehumanizing demands of (re)productive labor. Every one of these figures tropes a value crucial to some form of fascism: imperialism, the cult of nature and the valorization of the rural peasantry, the elite and misogynist *Männerbund*. Furthermore, as I have suggested before, Yourcenar's idealized rural village substitutes, as does fascism, a conception of class *cooperation* for the Marxist vision of class revolution; in this view, class antagonism is an artificial mediator between individuals who should be bound by their commitment to a shared community, whether defined by blood or by soil.

For Yourcenar, this community is clearly *not* represented by the nation, as it is in fascist thought; she was always unresponsive to nationalist claims and particularly liked to explore the symbolic possibilities offered by regions like Flanders, which confuse national, cultural, and linguistic boundaries. The perimeters of Yourcenar's ideal community are either much smaller than those of the nation (for example, Northeast Harbor) or larger (for example, the "Europe" that figures so powerfully as a trope in and a topos of nearly all of her work). We might ask, indeed, whether "nation" is not simply replaced in her work by "Europe": and also whether this substitution, while erasing the borders of narrowly nationalist fascism, does not reproduce the borders of, for instance, Germany's imperialist imagination.

I have already suggested that Yourcenar's appeal to a rather monolithically defined "Western" or "European" culture, stemming from the classical period, might recapitulate racist and ethnocentric assumptions, as well as miming the fascist effort to define a transhistorical Aryan nation extending from antiquity to the Axis. This is a difficult and complicated point, and it deserves closer examination. In the 1930s it would have been a rare European intellectual who was *not* interested in defining a notion of Europe's cultural heritage, and who would not have traced that heritage to some period of antiquity, whether represented by Periclean Athens, imperial Rome, or Byzantium. In his discussion of Heidegger's ethnocentrism, Richard Wolin claims that it is only in the postcolonial era that we have "become more sensitized to the potentials for exclusion" in this type of discourse about Europe, so prevalent in the 1930s; thus Husserl's notion of a European spiritual community cannot, according to Wolin, be conflated with Heidegger's racist political program (Wolin, xiii–iv).

The same defense might be offered for Yourcenar or Arendt; simply to speak of Europe as some kind of ethnic or spiritual community does not necessarily entail racial discrimination. But at the least, the analyses Yourcenar and Arendt base on assumptions about racial differences lead them to some peculiar conclusions about fascism; at the worst, the exclusion or outright denigration of the non-European is not merely implicit in their focus on Europe, but quite explicit. Furthermore, it is worth remembering that there *were* European intellectuals in the 1930s—among them Woolf, Stephen Spender, and Reich—who were already keenly sensitive to the "potentials for exclusion" in Eurocentric discourse and to the way that racism underpinned both colonialism and fascism. And Arendt's most racist statements, in *Origins of Totalitarianism*, date not from the 1930s but from the 1950s, by which time the risks of racialist thinking were appallingly clear. It is not, then, simply the heightened sensibility of the postfascist, postcolonial age that responds with suspicion to hegemonic notions of "Europe"; it was quite possible to be alert to the danger of that concept before the war, or oblivious to it after.

Now, from Yourcenar's point of view, a loosely defined "Hellenism" was, like Catholicism, an intrinsic part of the European heritage, and also a corrective to fascist idealism. In a letter she wrote in 1937, both appear as bulwarks of the conservative European tradition she contrasts with fascist modernity:

> But along with hellenism, for which it provides all at once the complement and the corrective in my thought, Catholicism represents in my eyes one of the rare values that our epoch has not managed to shatter completely. More and more in the world's current (and perpetual) disorder, I have come to see the Catholic tradition as one of the most precious parts of our complex heritage . . . and the disappearance or the disintegration of these traditions in favor of a crude idealism of force, of race, or of the crowd strikes me as one of the future's worst dangers. (Qtd. in Savigneau, 120)

Yourcenar does not acknowledge that this notion of tradition, of "our complex heritage," could itself reinforce an idealism of race. But the implication, in much of her work, that Greece is the center and source of civilization reminds us of Winckelmann's argument that only the Greek or European type achieves beauty, and that countries distant from Greece, in their climate and soil as well as their culture, produce human and natural deviations from the aesthetic ideal. That idea helped, as we saw in Chapter 2, to support both homosexual aestheticism and Nazism's racist aesthetic ideology.

Yourcenar also seems in many texts to assume a rather Winckelmannian association of soil with cultural or national character, another idea embraced by fascist nationalism. In the second version of *Denier*, for example, Yourcenar contrasts the Italian people and the "powerful" Italian earth with the transitory nature of the fascist regime, a gesture that refutes Italian fascism's claim to represent an authentic Italy at the same time that it affirms the concept of eternal and authentic values invested in the very soil of the *patria* (Yourcenar, *Coin*, 63).

In some manifestations, this notion of the organic and rooted nation simply buttresses distinctions among different European peoples. What is significant for this discussion is that both Yourcenar and Arendt, accepting that soil shapes national character and hence that the Italians are the territorial and racial heirs of Greco-

Roman culture, rely on cultural stereotypes to describe and, in Arendt's case, partially to exonerate Italian fascism. Italy, even during its fascist period, is thus primarily identified with the humane and aesthetic values of the classical tradition. Arendt, like Yourcenar, seems unable to avoid describing Italian fascism according to the same aesthetic criteria it used to describe itself; in *Eichmann*, Arendt indulgently characterizes Mussolini's regime as "farce," while for Yourcenar it evokes the commedia dell'arte, suggesting that both were seduced by Italian fascism's aestheticized and theatrical self-representation. (We recall that decades after the March on Rome, Yourcenar still judged Italian fascism in aesthetic terms, albeit negatively.) Italian fascism is thus made to appear not only comparatively benign, but rather glamorous in contrast to bureaucratic, banal, amoral Nazism.

For her part, furthermore, Arendt clearly admires the Italian fascists; her description of their behavior repeatedly evokes their humor, humanity, and cleverness, as well as their theatricality. Like Yourcenar, Arendt invokes an Italian humanist tradition that protects the "authentic" Italy from its own fascism. The reason for Italian fascism's resistance to Nazi genocidal racial policies was, according to Arendt, the instinctive, "automatic" humanism of the ancient Italian race: "What in Denmark was the result of an authentically political sense, an inbred comprehension of the requirements and responsibilities of citizenship and independence . . . was in Italy the outcome of the almost automatic general humanity of an old and civilized people" (Arendt, *Eichmann*, 179). While few would deny that there are important cultural differences among Europeans, or that Italian fascism was comparatively mild in its treatment of Jews, it nonetheless seems paradoxical to ground an attack on racialist thinking in arguments about the inbred characteristics of different races.

If this line of argument can lead Arendt and Yourcenar into logical impasses in their discussion of fascism, it has more malignant implications when applied not to the differences among Europeans, but to the differences between Europeans, heirs to the classical tradition, and non-Europeans. Like Yourcenar, Arendt implies that there is, if not a "Greek answer" to human problems then "a series of responses which derive from the Greeks and among which one must choose." In *Origins of Totalitarianism*, Arendt repeatedly traces all forms of political philosophy and organization to the Greeks: "forms of government under which men live have been very few; they were discovered early, classified by the Greeks and have proved extraordinarily long-lived" (Arendt, *Origins*, 461). In this analysis, peoples who do not conform to the principles of Aristotelian political philosophy are by definition outside civilization; indeed, they are in some sense nonhuman, lacking, as she says of African "savages," "the specifically human character, the specifically human reality" manifested in self-consciousness, artistic expression, civic responsibility, and "Man's" desire to transform nature through praxis (Arendt, *Origins*, 192). It is here, when Arendt claims that the worst consequence of the colonization of South Africa was to drag the Boers down to the same level of inhumanity as the Africans, that we understand how explicitly racist her sort of "Hellenism" can become (Arendt, *Origins*, 194). Her racism also renders suspect her characterization of fascism as a uniquely evil aberration in Western history, distinct even from imperialism; one might ask whether the horrors of imperialism appeared to be "marked by a certain moderation" to, for instance, Africans in the Belgian Congo, or whether that judgment is not simply based on the extremely different values Arendt places on the lives of Europeans and non-Europeans.

Without ceding to the same overt racism, Yourcenar makes a somewhat similar point when she suggests, in an essay written at about the same time as "European Diagnosis," that great art can only be produced by cultures with a Western concept of the individual, and that tribal, primitive, or folk aesthetic forms reflect the undeveloped humanity of their creators: "There can be no art, without pronounced individuality on the part of the artist; the art of the tribe, of the steppe, of the village, lags thirty centuries behind human individualism" (Yourcenar, "L'improvisation," 52). Indeed, Yourcenar's very emphasis on Enlightenment values of individualism, rationality, and tolerance makes her intolerant of non-Western cultures that she perceives as hostile to these values. More than 50 years after her reference to "barbaric" Afro-American music, for example, she contrasts the "unreason" of Islamic fundamentalism "on moral questions" with a Western humanist discourse, derived from the Greeks, of liberty in sensual choices (Yourcenar, *Open Eyes*, 144). When Yourcenar casts about for an example of sexual intolerance, then, she immediately looks to a non-Western ideology, rather than examining any of the numerous ways that repression has functioned in both European and Greek cultures; cultural and historical variations *within* Islamic and Western ethical traditions are thus elided in favor of a stereotyped contrast *between* the irrational East and the enlightened West.

The *Mémoires d'Hadrien*, perhaps Yourcenar's most beautiful, philosophically rich, and morally compelling work, exemplifies the paradoxes and problems inherent in her liberal humanist project. As we saw above, the novel can be read as an attempt to recuperate the Greco-Roman tradition, represented by Hadrian, in the service of an emancipatory philosophy of nonviolence and cultural tolerance. In this view, the text responds to the ideological explosion of World War II by suggesting that Europe needs to learn to read history another way, to unlearn the ideologies of fascism or imperialism by reinterpreting its own historical narratives. DeJean also argues that in *Hadrien* Yourcenar uses her "eulogy of *pederastia* to subvert the ideology of conquering nationalism and violent militarism that it had previously been made to serve" (DeJean, 297), thus undermining the erotic foundation of fascism's *Männerbund*. Fascism is not, as it presented itself, the heir to Greek civilization, but a total departure from that culture as Yourcenar depicts it.

The novel could also be read, however, as a reactionary attempt to reground "civilization" in a fundamentally oppressive Western tradition that Yourcenar has falsely romanticized. In a sense, both readings are valid; Yourcenar remains entirely committed to the tradition she also critiques, and so her terms of analysis are limited to, and by, the vocabulary of the discourse of humanism. Thus Yourcenar's "monument . . . to the need to preserve civilization" never really questions whether that project does not inevitably preserve some civilizations at the expense of others; even Hadrian is bent on the political subjugation of the cultures he claims to respect. And we might also interrogate Yourcenar's choice of a Greco-Roman, male, homosexual subject to represent that which is both best and most universal in all of human experience.

A final consequence of Yourcenar's commitment to the Hellenic and Enlightenment traditions is that she does indeed privilege male psyches and sexualities in all her works, identifying them with the universal, while she erases the voices and feelings of women, identified with the private and subjective. As an explanation for the dearth of important female characters in her works, Yourcenar frequently offered the excuse that women's lives are too secretive and too particular to be accessible to the writer interested in exploring universal truths. In her autobiography, she says of a female ancestor, "But no life can be judged from the outside, and even less than any other the life of a woman" (Yourcenar, *Archives*, 381). And, explaining why she never wrote a projected response to *Alexis* by his wife Monique, she says, "Nothing is more secret than a woman's existence. The tale of Monique might be more difficult to write than the admissions of Alexis"—particularly, it would appear, for Yourcenar, who seems always to have been unable to project herself into a feminine psyche or, more accurately, to project a feminine psyche into writing (Yourcenar, *Alexis*, xiii).

Yet Yourcenar also became indignant at the accusation that her works or her life were "male-identified."* The subject of gender in her life/texts is certainly complicated, and probably the least one can say is that neither the accusation that Yourcenar is male-identified to the point of misogyny (see, e.g., Stillman) nor Yourcenar's own defensive protest that women are, despite all appearances, central to her texts, entirely suffices as an account of the complex and contradictory deployment of gender models in her work. Let us say, rather, that gender is a point of ideological disruption in the Yourcenarian text, showing the fault lines in her value systems. She uses

* See, for example, *Open Eyes*, 226–27; the same theme can also be found in many of Yourcenar's other interviews and self-commentaries.

gender paradigms in contradictory ways, to attack or defend particular ideologies, and frequently undermines her own ideological positions in the process.

Yourcenar's attitude toward gender difference is, on the one hand, conditioned by her commitment to an abstract liberal notion of equality, a gender "indifference" that inevitably reinscribes the male or masculine as the human norm, in the same way that Yourcenar's political "indifference" in the 1930s aligned her with the supporters of a conservative status quo; the insistence on neutrality in effect leaves the dominant system or term in place. Yourcenar's own gender identification thus frequently appears to be masculine, because she tends to refer to herself in a "neutral" third person represented by masculine nouns requiring masculine articles and pronouns, such as "*auteur*." She also implies at several points in her work, and notably in her autobiography, that gender differences (and gendered oppression) are purely nominal, not to say imaginary, categories: like Mussolini's imperial image, in Massimo's view, oppression is created by those who resist it. She says of herself as a young girl, for instance, speaking in the third person, "She would not be hampered, as so many women still are in our time, by the fact of being a woman, perhaps because it did not occur to her that she ought to be hampered by it" (Yourcenar, *Archives*, 613–14).

On the other hand, Yourcenar gives us in the autobiography a materialist account, as it were, of the formation of her liberal gender (un)consciousness. After her mother's death in childbirth she was raised, in the early 1900s, by her unconventional father, with little interference from educational institutions or the female relatives who would ordinarily have been responsible for socializing a female child into appropriate gender behavior. Thus Yourcenar largely escaped acculturation as an upper-class Catholic woman—and the psychologically stressful rebellion against that acculturation that would probably have erupted at some point in a woman of great intelligence and unconventional sexual preferences. She describes with barely disguised satisfaction the irritation of her relations at the prospect of a girl who preferred Plato and Virgil to dolls, and of a father who encouraged this eccentricity, refusing even to have his daughter confirmed, since she did not wish it (Yourcenar, *Quoi?*, 672–73). In this context, Yourcenar's inability to identify as a woman can be read in somewhat the same sense as Monique Wittig's famous pronouncement that "lesbians are not women." Yourcenar was not raised as a boy, but neither was she raised as a girl of her class and generation; spared the brutal gender socialization that did so much psychological damage to both Barnes and Woolf, Yourcenar was not, indeed, a woman in the sense that they were, forced to struggle against the oppressive rhetoric of religion, female masochism, institutionalized heterosexuality, or maternity. And it is perhaps not surprising, either, that she was so invested in the "culture of the fathers," since it was her own father who protected her, quite literally, from femininity.

Yourcenar's complex and ambivalent feelings about gender are nowhere more obvious than in the highly contradictory attitudes she displays in various texts toward the ideas of maternity, procreation, and childbirth. In the first edition of *Denier du rêve* Yourcenar seems to recapitulate the fascists' opposition between the sterility of liberal emancipatory discourses and the fertility of the essential fascist values of blood and soil. At the same time, she appears in two places to oppose a conception of women's experience, represented especially by childbirth, to the illusory realm of virile, fascist values. The motif of childbirth, though less developed in the first edition than in the second, is nonetheless the only thing in that version that points to a reality outside the hollow politico-cultural world of fascist modernity.

During a discussion between Massimo and Marcella, he suggests that childbirth and murder both appertain to an epistemological space exclusive to women: "Killing, you know all about that, you women, like you know about giving birth. All those bloody operations. You believe too much in life not to take it, or give it" (Yourcenar, *Denier* 1934, 138). This could be interpreted as irony or simple misogyny on Massimo's part, but the idea resurfaces in the last scene, where a worker named "Oreste Marinunzi" gets drunk in a bar while his wife is in labor at home. The name plays out the conflict between maternal/feminine and paternal/virile values: Orestes, the matricide, loyal to Agamemnon; Marinetti and D'Annunzio, loyal to Mussolini, seduced into fascism by the aesthetic bribe and the fascist cult of virility. Marinunzi fantasizes about murdering his mother-in-law, Mother Dida, and frets about his wife's labor. Hostile to the Mother, and excluded from the feminine scene of childbirth, Marinunzi takes refuge in the manly sport of drinking, his intoxication producing increasingly grandiloquent fantasies of glory, war, and death.

> With the second glass of wine, the distance suddenly doubled between him and the room where Attilia was screaming in the hands of women; all that, that was their business. . . . The fifth glass made him powerful. He doubled salaries; he lowered the cost of living by half; he cancelled his debts to the butcher, the milkman, and the landlord; there was a war; he won it; and after that, everybody got a little peace and quiet. (Yourcenar, *Denier* 1934, 231–34)

In the second version of the novel, Marinunzi toasts a photograph of Mussolini hung on the wall before sliding unconscious to the floor. That detail is missing in the first edition, but the description is unchanged of the drunk man, "happy as a king, or perhaps a dictator. . . . happy as a dead man" (Yourcenar, *Denier* 1934, 234–35). The significance of the scene seems clear: the adherents to the virile values of fascism are victims of a kind of drunkenness, unconscious of realities taking place outside the scene of masculinist history, in the hands of women.

The idea that reproduction gives women privileged access to the "real" might seem to echo the fascist mandate to women to fulfill themselves in maternity. Yourcenar's later commentaries on the text also emphasize the connection between all the women characters in *Denier* except Angiola, and the "earth" (de Rosbo, 90). Read in one way, then, Yourcenar's treatment of the themes of reproduction and childbirth in the text could be viewed as a conventional, not to say reactionary, reiteration of the complementary distinction between women/nature on the one hand and men/culture (that is, here, politics and abstract ideologies) on the other. Yet the scene of childbirth appears in the text specifically as the antithesis of, rather than the complement to, the masculine and fascist sphere of values represented by the bar; and in the context of this particular work, culture, politics, and the abstract are hardly valorized categories. Admittedly, the suggestion that childbirth functions in *Denier* as a redemptive locus of authentic meaning appears incongruous, given that Yourcenar's œuvre has so often been characterized as "virile," and that it is so largely concerned with the psychology and sexuality of men. And certainly, we note, the narrative voice does not identify with the laboring woman; she remains outside the plot, as well as outside the bar. But it is difficult to know how to read her intrusion into this final scene, if it is not as a counterpoint to the lethal unreality of fascist idealism.

This ambiguous deployment of the theme of childbirth—the reiteration of a patriarchal or fascist stereotype in the service of an antipatriarchal critique—is typical of Yourcenar's œuvre. Interestingly, although she liked children, in other works and in her own life Yourcenar manifested a pronounced disdain for the processes of procreation. Her biographer claims that "she had a genuine distaste for procreation, one common to many homosexuals—of both sexes—of her generation" (Savigneau, 248). Like the nineteenth-century aesthetes, Yourcenar seems to have viewed the burden of reproduction, especially for women in the conventional world of the landed aristocracy from which she came, as inimical to aesthetic (self) production. She copied into a notebook an aphorism by her friend Natalie Barney that reads in part, "the most beautiful life is one spent creating oneself, not procreating" (qtd. in Savigneau, 485n39). Unlike Barney, Huysmans, Wilde, Barnes, and other aesthetes, Yourcenar never evaded or aestheticized the prospect of human transience, regarding death instead as a sort of exercise in individual self-realization; her response to mortality was not to renounce liberal subjectivity, but, on the contrary, to emphasize the rational contemplation of death as a crucial formative element of that subjectivity. Her horror of procreation was, instead, motivated by her concerns about the ecological problem of overpopulation, the "uglification" of the world, and the devalorization of human life in mass society—concerns that were undoubtedly intertwined with the covert but deeply ingrained hostility of the aristocratic homosexual for the proliferating proletariat.*

We should also, however, read Yourcenar's aversion to procreation in the context of her desire to debunk a sentimental and oppressive ideology of maternity by focusing on the physical details of pregnancy and childbirth. The first chapter of her memoirs is entitled "The Birth" and gives an account of her own mother's agonizing labor and consequent death several days after Yourcenar's birth; she goes on to describe at some length the frequent deaths in childbirth, or following miscarriage or abortion, of women in her family. Yourcenar contrasts the terrible dangers of pregnancy and childbirth, repeatedly identified with "reality," with the sentimental commonplaces that banalize women's physical experiences and assimilate them to abstract patriarchal values like "duty" and "honor."

In this, her deployment of the theme of childbirth rather resembles the opening passage of *Nightwood*, so apparently different from Yourcenar's style and tone; even more pronouncedly, it recalls Augusta's bitter protest in *The Antiphon*: "I've done my duty to the state—in children." For Yourcenar, childbirth represents a scene of essential and authentic values that she opposes, as in *Denier*, to the unreality of fascism. In *Nightwood*, Barnes uses the description of Hedvig's labor to parody the pretensions of militarism, while in *The Antiphon* she more explicitly attacks the exploitation of women's reproductive labor by patriarchal and fascist ideologies. Both women thus employ themes of childbirth and maternity to undermine and ridicule patriarchal or fascist values. Yourcenar, for example, ironically cites her bereaved father, repeating to his brothers-in-law the dictum that "giving birth is the special duty of women: Fernande had died on the field of honor"; and she concludes that "reality had been a hideous chaos: Monsieur de

---

*Yourcenar suggests in an interview that in light of the overpopulation problem "the situation of homosexuality obviously has to be reconsidered," reiterating in the 1970s an argument rooted in the aestheticist tradition of the previous century (qtd. in de Rosbo, 86n1).

C. contained it, after a fashion, within a commonplace of which Théobald and Georges undoubtedly approved" (Yourcenar, *Dear Departed*, 50).

Here and elsewhere in her memoirs, Yourcenar particularly attacks the association of patriotism with the cult of maternity I have termed "matriotism," challenging, as Woolf does in *Three Guineas*, the sex/gender system that compels women to reproduce the *patria*. Yourcenar argues that women's patriotism is not allied to their maternal instinct, but proof instead that they have no such instinct, since they are willing to sacrifice their children to the nation. Women, in fact, have to be conscripted into motherhood, as men are conscripted into military service, and are interpellated into matriotic ideology differently according to, for example, their class status. In this passage she slides neatly from deconstructing patriotism to deconstructing matriotism, as she explains why her parents hesitated to have children:

> Roughly three years in the army had not transformed Monsieur de C. into a patriot ready to give his sons for the sake of recapturing Alsace-Lorraine. . . . The maternal instinct is not as compelling as people like to say it is, for in every age women of the so-called privileged class have blithely entrusted their children, from infancy on, to the care of underlings. . . . Consider, too, the ease with which so many women have offered their children to the Moloch of war and gloried in such sacrifice. (Yourcenar, *Dear Departed*, 15)

In contrast to the hollow abstractions of patriarchal/matriotic rhetoric, however, childbirth itself is usually identified with the "real" or "authentic" and is described throughout Yourcenar's œuvre as ritual and as tradition, both highly valued in her aesthetic ethic. Describing her own birth, she writes, "Once again, the gestures made throughout millennia by generations of women were repeated," recalling the scene taking place in *Denier* "between the hands of women"; in both texts the tone is one of solemnity and respect (Yourcenar, *Dear Departed*, 22). While Yourcenar's hostility toward the idea of procreation might be interpreted, then, as the snobbery of the homosexual aesthete, or as a pathological fear of pregnancy stemming from her mother's death—the theory offered by her biographer—it is perhaps more usefully read as the desire to take apart a falsely romanticized image of the institution of maternity, and especially to attack the patriarchy's manipulations of that image.

It is interesting to note that Yourcenar was eventually to carry this critique of patriarchal ideologies to an attack on De Gaulle's "paternalism" that can be read retrospectively as an attack on fascist hero-worship. In 1968 she said:

> What worries me most in France ... is what the Americans call paternalism. The fact that people say to themselves: here we are, we have someone very good, he's in power, we consider him a kind of father who makes decisions for us. Now, even if this figure were supreme in his genius or honesty, even if he were superhuman, this would still be bad because of what it represents. (Yourcenar, "L'Express va plus loin," 50)

As devoted to the Western culture of "the fathers" as Yourcenar was, it appears that she was wary of the cult of the Father, as well as of its companion cult of matriotism. And, remembering that the disjunction in the final scene between the labor room filled with women and the bar with its tatty photo of Mussolini is made more striking in the second *Denier* than in the first edition, it seems likely too that Yourcenar, like Barnes, arrived retrospectively at an analysis of fascism as the manifestation of a patriarchal phantasm founded on masculinist values as illusory as they are deadly.

The theme of childbirth, then, and the gender difference it represents, is in a sense the materialist impulse that fractures Yourcenar's own ideology of an abstract and neutral liberal humanism. Yourcenar's political ideal is expressed in a neutral language of rights that, as we have seen, masks racial or gendered specificities; her ideal subject is the ζῳον πολιτικον, public, transcendent—and male. Yet she also valorizes women's physical experiences as a way of attacking patriarchal ideologies like fascism to which she is particularly hostile; and while her association of gender difference with reproduction borders on essentialism, her analysis of the politics of reproduction is carefully materialist.

The incongruities in Yourcenar's use of gender models are relevant precisely because they point to larger ideological incongruities, to the tensions between conflicting ideological requirements in her texts. Although she wants to claim a politically centrist, gender-neutral position for the author as indifferent medium, her meticulous construction of herself as historical figure, and her incessant interventions into her own texts, oblige us instead to read her life/works in historical and cultural context. While she rejects fascist idealism, irrationalism, and authoritarianism, her simultaneous refusal of a materialist analysis of class leaves her with a conservative, antimodernist vision of society that realigns itself with reactionary tendencies. When she rejects materialist analyses in favor of the universal(izing) principles of the Enlightenment, the resulting ethnocentrism confounds her own ideals of cultural tolerance; when she adopts a materialist critique of reproduction in order to assault patriarchal ideologies to which she is hostile, she finds herself valorizing a gender-specific experience that she disallows elsewhere.

Obviously, these contradictions do not point to anything so simple as hypocrisy or intellectual fuzziness on Yourcenar's part; they are, rather, intrinsic to the liberal humanist project she elaborated, with great conscientiousness and insight, throughout her life. That project has insisted on identifying fascism (or at least National Socialism), with communism (or at least Stalinism), as twin totalitarian doctrines that assault Western liberal values of individualism and a shared ideal of civilization. The need to define that shared central ground, that ideal of "civilization" where extremisms are balanced and neutralized, has a number of consequences. First, as we have seen, it forestalls investigation of liberalism's own ideological lineages, dismissing the possibility that fascism might have a good deal more to do with "civilization" than civilization can comfortably admit. It fails to acknowledge that a centrist position is not necessarily a neutral one when the two sides between which it stations itself are as morally unequal as were, for example, the Left and the Right in Italy in the early 1930s. And it tends to dismiss out of hand even those leftist analyses that might, on further investigation, turn out to complement and correct liberalism.

Although Yourcenar's critique of fascism also assails leftist "idealism," for example, it could be argued that it is related to the neo-Marxist critique of the Frankfurt School by their shared conceptions of rational subjectivity, their quest for authenticity—in art, the nation, or sexuality—and their rejection of irrationalism and barbarism. In this sense both liberals like Yourcenar and Arendt, and the intellectual Left represented by Frankfurt and Virginia Woolf, are heirs to what one critic calls "the best of the Enlightenment legacy, the admonition to use one's mind" (Berman, "German Primitivism," 66). But Yourcenar and Arendt also embrace the most problematic aspects of the Enlightenment legacy, unable to acknowledge the possibility that the Enlightenment might indeed be dialectical, and fascism no aberration in the development of Western civilization, but rooted in it. And their uncritical commitment to the Enlightenment's aesthetic, ethical, and political values in turn allies them *bon gré mal gré* with the ethnocentric and ultimately racist concept of European culture that also subtends certain fascist ideologies.

In the next chapter we will examine an explicitly materialist critique of fascism, Woolf's *Three Guineas*, and ask whether it, while also in dialogue with fascist themes and rhetorical figures, is not in some ways a more comprehensive response to fascist modernity than Yourcenar's. In the meantime, let us return to *Denier du rêve* and consider it a last time, not as political equivocation or aesthetic failure but as a paradigm for the crisis of liberalism in the 1930s. In *Denier*, Yourcenar addresses the same problems of mass modernity that concerned both Left and Right: alienation, the commercialization of human relations, the commodification of personality. She rejects both right and left "idealisms" without, however, being able to propose any alternative solutions, not even the liberal humanist realism that, while itself problematic, at least gives the second edition of the novel philosophic depth and coherence. The original edition of *Denier* leaves us instead at an ideological dead end: the text is neither antifascist, as Yourcenar would have it, nor complicit with fascism, as André Fraigneau asserted. Nor is it beyond ideology altogether, the goal Yourcenar always claimed for her most ideologically problematic texts, like *Le coup de grâce*. *Denier du rêve* is, rather, ineluctably indeterminate—not indifferent to ideology, but ideologically undifferentiable. And in this it resembles the liberal ideologies and institutions that, confronted with the violently conflicting visions of modernity circulating in the 1930s, could not muster an alternative vision of comparable clarity and force: and so hesitated, appeased, and equivocated, until there no longer seemed any alternative but total war.

CHAPTER 5

*Another Country:
Virginia Woolf's
Disloyalty to Civilization*

The working men have no country.
> Karl Marx and Friedrich Engels,
> *Manifesto of the Communist Party*

Returned from that dishonest country, we
Awake, yet tasting the delicious lie:
And boys and girls, equal to be, are different still.
> W. H. Auden, "Nor was that final,
> for about that time"

Marguerite Yourcenar largely rewrote *Denier du rêve* in 1959 in order to underscore her hostility toward fascism and to emphasize the idea that fascism was a manifestation of masculinist values. Similarly, Djuna Barnes waited until she wrote *The Antiphon* in 1958 to draw an explicit parallel between patriarchy and fascism. For these two writers, the connection between fascism and certain masculinist values or behaviors seems to have been more obvious after the war than before it. We ought perhaps to ask ourselves, then, if our own vision of that connection is not illumined by hindsight as well, and to tread cautiously when invoking potentially anachronistic analytic categories in our discussion of fascism. Yet of the three authors in this study, it is the one who did not live to see the war's worst horrors who wrote the strongest denunciation of fascism, and particularly of fascism as an expression of men's domination of women—which suggests that it is not merely that our current thinking has become sensitized, ex post facto, to the gendered relations of power intrinsic to fascist ideologies, but that the relationship between fascist thought and the politics of gender was already obvious to at least some in the 1930s.

Virginia Woolf's *Three Guineas* endeavors to trace the connections between fascism, patriarchal and capitalist ideologies, and the oppression of the marginalized, particularly women. Woolf's criticism of property relations extends to an analysis of the roots of sexual, racial, and religious oppression as she calls on women of her own class to form what she calls the "Outsiders' Society," arguing that if the "daughters of educated men" reject their affiliations to family and nation, their "disloyalty to civilization" will bring an end to war, which is endemic to patriarchy/patriotism.*

Woolf's analysis of fascism's origins in the material disenfranchisement of women is an ambitious attempt to examine the intersection of the politics of class, gender, and sexuality. This endeavor draws on a long tradition of socialist feminism in England, with which Woolf was associated through her connections with various labor and suffrage groups.† As a theoretical project, it also aligns Woolf with the revisionist tendencies of those left intellectuals who were trying, during the 1920s and especially the 1930s, to break away from the rigid economic determinism of Marxist orthodoxy and to focus instead on the reciprocal interaction of the superstructure and property relations.

This approach is usually identified with figures like Antonio Gramsci, Wilhelm Reich, and the members of the Frankfurt School. I will argue that both Virginia Woolf and the young writers in W. H. Auden's circle, particularly Stephen Spender, also deplored the failure of the orthodox Left to "comprehend ideology as a historical force" (Reich, 14); and so they were also striving, using different tactics and vocabularies of explanation, to account for and counteract fascism's colonization of the territories of culture, psychology, and sexuality, phenomena neglected by both traditional Marxist

*The phrase "disloyal to civilization" is of course borrowed from Adrienne Rich's essay "Disloyal to Civilization: Feminism, Racism, Gynephobia."

†For a discussion of Woolf's involvement with these groups, see Naomi Black, "Virginia Woolf and the Women's Movement."

and liberal analyses. The goal of antifascist criticism, they believed, could not be to disdain or attempt to transcend the emotions fascism exploited so successfully; powerful tropes like nation, race, culture, and sex must instead be recuperated and revised to serve a politics of emancipation.

In Chapter 1, I described this critical enterprise, a project that accepts its own determination by fascism's "recentering of critical focus on the terrain of the politico-cultural." In Heesok Chang's words, fascism has taught critical theory a "formative lesson"; it is, indeed, "the unnamed precondition of critical speculation itself" (Chang, 17–18). This supposition has, of course, been the basis of my own work here. I propose that it was also the basis for Woolf's, and that as fascism extended its control over ever-wider areas of sociocultural life during the 1930s, while Woolf was writing *Three Guineas*, Woolf adapted her own strategies in reaction. *Three Guineas*' historical development was thus determined by developments in fascist ideologies; it is as if Woolf had to keep pace with fascism throughout the decade, to try to respond point by point to the growing arsenal of fascist ideological weaponry.

As we have seen, *Nightwood* reacts to fascism by cycling between fascination and disaffection with fascist themes, where *Denier du rêve* mimes them while explicitly trying to set itself outside and in opposition to them. In contrast, *Three Guineas* assumes a priori that fascism has defined the parameters of political struggle for its day; and so the text embraces, while attempting to reverse or redefine, the terms laid down by fascist ideologies. Woolf neither sympathizes with fascism nor "Others" it; instead, in *Three Guineas* she engages squarely with the problem of the relation between Western "civilization" and fascism. The text signals to us the impossibility of escaping the fascism in modernity and suggests that the most adequate antifascist response, acknowledging this problem from the outset, will set out to analyze and counteract the myriad manifestations of barbarism in civilization.

*Three Guineas* is a polemical work rather than a novel, so its political significations are naturally more explicit than those of *Nightwood* or *Denier du rêve*. It can nonetheless be evaluated, like any of

Woolf's texts, as a formal experiment whose political import is manifested in its form as well as its content. One critic has aptly described "the genre of *Three Guineas* as prophecy, a literary mode peculiar to cultural crisis" (Smith, 225); and in a footnote to the text Woolf slyly comments on the "confusion" in the Bible between "the gift of prophecy and the gift of poetry," between "propagandist poems and novels" and aesthetic artifacts, thus providing her own hybrid work of poetic prophecy with an unimpeachable precedent and anticipating those critics who might accuse her of conflating the two modes of literary production (Woolf, *Three Guineas*, 180n29). We can, then, investigate the literary strategies at play in *Three Guineas* in order to emphasize the way the text's formal innovations may, like *Nightwood*'s, be read themselves as a response to fascist ideologies and aesthetics.

*Three Guineas* could be read partly, for example, as a satire of academic elitism and pomposity, traits Woolf associates with the oppressive hierarchies of patriarchal systems of thought. Thus she refers, tongue in cheek, to "the vast deposit of notes at the bottom of Greek, Latin and even English texts" during a discussion that is itself in one of the footnotes that make up nearly a quarter of her text (Woolf, *Three Guineas*, 181n31). But whereas she equates academic footnotes with other "meaningless but highly ingenious turnings and twistings into which the intellect ties itself," manifestations of a pointless intellectual vanity and frivolity, she uses her own footnotes to discuss some of her most politically controversial material, such as her attacks on organized Christianity.

The book also constitutes a striking reworking of the epistolary novel. It is written as a series of letters, embedded within each other, addressed to the treasurers of several organizations who have previously written to ask the female narrator for money and support. The first letter, which contains the others, is a response to the male treasurer of a pacifist organization; the second and third are addressed to women, treasurers, respectively, of an association to rebuild a women's college and another to help women enter the professions. The narrator sends each a guinea, after discussing the conditions under which it should be used.

Woolf's use of the traditionally female epistolary form, which usually purports to represent an intimate dialogue, could in itself be read as a challenge to the exhortative and monovocal tone of the typical political pamphlet. In keeping with her insistence that private and public spheres are interrelated (a point to which we shall return), she adapts the personal tone of the epistolary form to a polemical, public debate. But Woolf does more than adopt an unconventional form for political writing; she also uses that form to convey a political point that is not simply about gender, but more broadly about the relation of gender to authority, narration, and reading practices.

The intricate layering of voices in *Three Guineas*, the shifting narrative identities, and the convoluted loops of argumentation diffuse and defer narrative authority. The use of embedded narratives and indirect speech makes it difficult to attribute particular political views to particular speakers, let alone to such a fragmented character as the "author." Indeed, any recognizable, singular narrator/author disappears on the fourth page of the work, when the narrator writes, "let us ask . . . Mary Kingsley to speak for us" (Woolf, *Three Guineas*, 4). The use of the plural here is already ambiguous: "we" ought logically to refer to the narrator and the male treasurer whose letter is the pre-text for all of *Three Guineas*, but seems instead to indicate the class of the daughters of educated men, with which the narrator now identifies herself. Through the momentary slippage into another woman's voice, Woolf moves the narrator into the position of spokeswoman for her sex, a position she retains for the rest of the text. Her "I," then, quickly becomes both a royal "we" and a collectivity defined by gender.

Jane Marcus claims that this technique constitutes "a deliberate last attack on authority in narrative, almost postmodern in its insistence that the righteous tone of authority in political pamphlets is a literary form of fascist dictatorship" (Marcus, *Languages*, 146). Woolf may indeed be challenging the unity of voice and the notion of presence embodied in the fascist leader. But it could also be argued that her dispersal of narrative authority ultimately serves to reinstate an omniscient author *behind* the narrator, who generates all the text's putative polyphony herself. Such an argument would lend weight to the objection many have raised to *Three Guineas*, that it tends to take the experiences of a small and relatively privileged class of women as representative, and, despite Woolf's stated intention to the contrary, to universalize the bourgeois woman as the "norm." Woolf's politics of class, in this and other texts, is in fact rather inconsistent, a point we will discuss later. For the moment, however, let us consider whether Woolf's strategy of displacing narrative identity may not actually have a more radical effect on the construction of the *reader* than it does on the role of the author.

Her technique, after all, also implicates the potential readers of the text in a politics whose "postmodernity" is pointedly materialist. The identity of the implicit or explicit readers of the multiple and embedded texts is also unstable; after the first four pages, "you" becomes not just the narrator's male interlocutor but the entire class of educated men. It may also refer, variously, to the narrator, the daughters of educated men, any of the addressees of any of the letters, or the implied readers of the "meta-text," *Three Guineas*. The reader is thus constantly reminded of his or her own class and gender position in relation to the various individuals and classes temporarily nominated as author, or recipient, of any of the letters: he or she may find himself or herself alternately included, excluded, berated, commiserated with, pleaded with, or argued with in the course of reading the text. The "you" and the "we" will mean very different things to women and men readers, or to readers of different classes.

*Three Guineas*, and the way in which we read *Three Guineas*, is, then, structured by the questions the text addresses: who has capital and who needs it, and under what circumstances women can control capital in patriarchal society. Woolf's commitment to a materialist approach underlies her interrogation of the patriarchal institutions that attempt to give women's disenfranchisement the appearance of something "natural"; she is particularly critical of claims grounded in "science" or a concept of Nature, which for her obscure actually existing relations of gender domination based in material inequities. In contrast, Woolf seems at first to intend to argue that the only category of the objective or real is economic. Her repeated appeals to "facts" invariably refer to the economic base that, she claims, conditions superstructural institutions such as science, religion, and the law; referring to existing differences between the sexes, for example, she writes, "to prove this, we need not have recourse to the dangerous and uncertain theories of psychologists and biologists; we can appeal to facts"—that is, to property relations, which are *real* (Woolf, *Three Guineas*, 17). Or again, on the question of the ordination of women, she says, "The argument from nature may seem to us susceptible of amendment; nature, when allied with financial advantage, is seldom of divine origin" (Woolf, *Three Guineas*, 167n38). Thus, although Woolf quickly moves beyond empirical economic analysis, as we will see, she does originally seem to signal her intention to provide a transcendent critique of patriarchy and fascism from that objective standpoint.

In order to discuss gender differences, then, Woolf will need a materialist definition of the genders as classes, formed by the dialectic of praxis, biology, and environment, and with different, gender-specific relations to capital: or, as she puts it, as "a whole made up of body, brain and spirit, influenced by memory and tradition" (Woolf, *Three Guineas*, 18). To define the intersection of class and gender politics, she invents a new gender/class, "the daughters of educated men," to describe those who, owning only an infinitesimal portion of the capital possessed by bourgeois men, cannot, strictly speaking, be considered members of the bourgeoisie (Woolf, *Three Guineas*, 146n2). The relation between fathers and daughters is thus immediately foregrounded, introducing the analogy that the narrator will elaborate throughout the text, between the private world of the patriarchal family and the public world of capitalist property relations.

It can be argued that Woolf's interest in the idea of the patriarchy as a social structure was driven, first and foremost, by her own experience of the oppressiveness and violence of the bourgeois family; certainly, in her published works, her concern with the "private patriarchy" appears chronologically to precede her attack on patriarchal institutions. And she undoubtedly speaks with deep empathy when she writes, explaining why a woman of her class would have thrown herself with enthusiasm into war work during World War I, "so profound was her unconscious loathing for the education of the private house with its cruelty, its poverty, its hypocrisy, its immorality, its inanity that she would undertake any task however menial, exercise any fascination however fatal that enabled her to escape" (Woolf, *Three Guineas*, 39). It is easy enough, furthermore, to find an explanation for the varying attitudes of Woolf, Yourcenar, and Barnes toward the "reign of the fathers" in their biographies. Barnes and Woolf, both sexually and emotionally abused by men in their families, were doubtless more hostile than Yourcenar to patriarchs as such. Yourcenar's father gave her every encouragement to become a writer; Woolf said that if her father had lived, she would never have written a word.

Investigation of these biographical details has provided important new insights into these writers' lives and, more generally, into the sexual struggles inscribed in many women's texts. But to reduce their œuvre, as some criticism has tended to do, to so many instantiations of particular psychological traumas not only belittles the complexity of their work but, particularly in Woolf's case, runs the risk of de-emphasizing a political analysis that draws its force from its very insistence on the connection between private and public spheres. For Woolf, of course, the claim that the "women's" sphere—the home and family relations—is separate from the masculine world of public politics, and vice versa, is itself a tool of the patriarchy and of fascism. The notion of separate spheres is "a principle which is frequently stated and approved by the dictators. Herr Hitler and Signor Mussolini have both often in very similar words expressed the opinion that 'There are two worlds in the life of the nation, the world of men and the world of women'" (Woolf, *Three Guineas*, 180n31).

The behavior of the fathers in private has direct bearing on the behavior of the fathers in public; though the personal and the political cannot be entirely collapsed into each other, they are interdependent. Woolf uses the case of Sophia Jex-Blake, the Victorian daughter of an educated man, to illustrate how authoritarian patriarchy represses women and children sexually, controls them financially, and subjects their sexuality to the economic interests of men. Jex-Blake's father—a benevolent and affectionate man, as Woolf is careful to point out—forbade her to accept payment for tutoring and made his financial support contingent on her selection of a suitable husband. The liberal, bourgeois notion of the family relies on abstract ideals of personal affection that, Woolf reminds us, conceal but do not compensate for the real, material inequality between the parties in this most private of social contracts.

In Woolf's view, the structures of inequity bred within the bourgeois family create the material and psychological conditions for fascism, an extreme manifestation of sexist authoritarianism. The transition in *Three Guineas* from "patriarchal thought" to "fascism" is made gradually; she is already a quarter of the way through *Three Guineas* before she establishes an analogy between foreign dictators—to whom she has not yet given the names Hitler and Mussolini—and an irritable Englishman who announces in a letter to the newspaper that women have too much freedom and should not work outside the home. Woolf is explicitly concerned with refuting H. G. Wells's claim that Englishwomen have done nothing to combat fascism, by arguing that the struggle against male domination amounts to the same thing. From this passage on, battle is joined; foreign fascism and British sexism are both manifestations of authoritarian patriarchy. In the words of the misogynists she has just quoted, Woolf writes,

> is the egg of the very same worm that we know under other names in other countries. There we have in embryo the creature, Dictator as we call him when he is Italian or German, who believes that he has the right, whether given by God, Nature, sex or race is immaterial, to dictate to other human beings how they shall live; what they shall do.... Are they not both the voices of Dictators, whether they speak English or German, and are we not all agreed that the dictator when we meet him abroad is a very dangerous as well as a very ugly animal? And he is here among us, raising his ugly head, spitting his poison, small still, curled up like a caterpillar on a leaf, but in the heart of England.... Is not the woman who has to breathe that poison and to fight that insect, secretly and without arms, in her office, fighting the Fascist or the Nazi

as surely as those who fight him with arms in the limelight of publicity? (Woolf, *Three Guineas*, 53)

This passage marks a crucial trope in Woolf's analogy between the private and the public structures of patriarchy. Woolf's project is, ultimately, to demonstrate that all patriarchal institutions contribute to war; that militarism, sexism, and fascism are all interconnected forms of patriarchal ideology; and that fascism circulates throughout what patriarchy has called "civilization." Even though Woolf has previously dismissed "the dangerous and uncertain theories of psychologists and biologists" in favor of an objective, materialist critique, therefore, she herself soon turns to rhetorical strategies emphasizing psychic and physical interiority and the subjective aspects of structures of domination. She figures capitalism, fascism, and patriarchy as "poison," "infection," and "disease," relying for her strongest images not on the objective class relations that she has posited as her subject, but on a discourse about internal medicine: "the fathers in public, massed together in societies, in professions, were even more subject to the fatal disease than the fathers in private" (Woolf, *Three Guineas*, 138). Poison or infection, we note, are not cancers or what H. R. Kedward called, in the passage cited in Chapter 1, "ulcerous growths"; they are not discrete and alien entities occupying the body of civilization, but influences circulating through its bloodstream. Turning Nordau's organicism back on his most violent heirs, Woolf diagnoses the malaise infecting the social body as fascism.

The groundwork for this approach is laid early on in the text, even as Woolf seems to articulate a different, more empirical strategy. The fact that her argument is couched throughout in terms of the relations between daughters and fathers, for example, will encourage the post-Freudian reader from the outset to anticipate an examination of the *psychic* mechanisms of patriarchal fascism. Thus the "egg" in the passage cited above, the embryo of dictatorship, turns out later in *Three Guineas* to be what Woolf only partly facetiously calls "infantile fixation," a sex taboo that provokes irrational emotion whenever male dominance is threatened (Woolf,

*Three Guineas*, 127). Rooted in the male child's belief in female castration and his own subsequent castration anxiety, this infantile fixation underlies men's sense of shame and outrage when they see women in positions of power.

Sophia Jex-Blake's father was suffering from "infantile fixation" when he attempted to control both her sexual choices and her wage-earning capacity. So were the fathers of Elizabeth Barrett Browning and Charlotte Brontë, who forbade their daughters to marry and yet, as Woolf points out, incurred no public censure for inflicting great personal suffering on them because "society it seems was a father, and afflicted with the infantile fixation too" (Woolf, *Three Guineas*, 135). The "fathers in general," the patriarchy, are subject in Woolf's text to a (psycho)analysis that eventually develops into an interrogation of the psychological motivations for dominance: "what possible satisfaction," the narrator wonders, "can dominance give to the dominator?" (Woolf, *Three Guineas*, 129).

Woolf, then, emphasizes the relationships between male control of female sexuality, fascism, and capitalism and undertakes a psychoanalytic reading of those conjunctions. Her application of both Freudian and Marxist terminologies to a critique of the bourgeois family, and her consequent focus on the psychological bases of oppressive power relations, align her neither with orthodox Marxism nor with psychoanalysis, but rather with the renegade tradition of materialist analyses of gender and sexuality that begins with Engels's "Origin of the Family, Private Property, and the State" and had been applied to the problem of fascist psychology by Reich just a few years before *Three Guineas* was published.* The project of synthesizing the apparently contradictory insights of Marx and Freud, which "was still a butt of ridicule in the 1930's"

---

*It is worth reflecting on the irony of the fact that it was not only the comparative obscurity of the work of Reich and Erich Fromm but also the very lack of education of which Woolf complains in *Three Guineas* that would have prevented her from becoming acquainted with their writing, still untranslated in her time. Had she been able to read German, she might have been heartened to discover that there were at least a few men intellectuals who shared her views on gender.

(Jay, *Dialectical*, 133), was nonetheless being undertaken by a number of people in Woolf's circles, as well as in Germany. In *The Destructive Element* (1935), for example, Stephen Spender writes that the "political artist" is aware that Marxism and Freudianism are the two systems of thought most strongly influencing modern consciousness, and asks, "What happens if, instead of being a propagandist for either point of view, he attempts a synthesis: an understanding of the war, for example, which is in both economic and psychological terms?" Spender claims, furthermore, that Auden is attempting this synthesis (Spender, *Destructive Element*, 257).

A crucial aspect of this endeavor, most forcefully articulated by Reich, was the recognition that, whatever the practical response demanded by the rise of fascist regimes, fascism-as-ideology could be adequately addressed only by recognizing the political valences of realms of experience, such as sexuality, that both bourgeois liberalism and orthodox Marxism defined as "private," peripheral to political institutions and conflicts. In *The Concept of the Political*, published in German in the early 1930s, Carl Schmitt cogently described the goal of the fascist, "total" State as the monopolization of those social forces outside the ken of liberal "politics":

> The equation state = politics becomes erroneous and deceptive at exactly the moment when state and society penetrate each other. What had been up to that point affairs of state become thereby social matters, and, vice versa, what had been purely social matters become affairs of state—as must necessarily occur in a democratically organized unit. Heretofore ostensibly "neutral" domains—religion, culture, education, the economy—then cease to be "neutral," if "neutral" means not pertaining to the state and to politics. As a polemical concept against such neutralizations and depoliticizations of important domains appears the total state, which potentially embraces every domain. (Schmitt, *Concept*, 22)

Reich countered with a call for a revolutionary politics of sexuality and culture, writing that his goal in *The Mass Psychology of Fascism* was

> to investigate the basic elements of political reaction's cultural aims, and to ascertain the emotional factors on which revolutionary work

has to be based. Here, too, we have to adhere to the principle of paying strict attention to everything to which cultural reaction gives prominence; for that to which it gives prominence is not incidental, nor is it a means of "distracting" one's attention. It is the central arena in which the fight between revolutionary and reactionary world philosophy and politics is to take place. (Reich, 125)

In other words, fascism's obvious concern with the aesthetics of spectacle, for example, or the uses and control of the erotic, is not to be dismissed as a mere smokescreen for its maintenance of ruling-class economic interests, or for the degeneration of political institutions into barbarism; fascism's interest in the cultural, the sexual, the psychological is exactly what it appears to be and demands a response that recognizes the centrality of these issues to the political struggles of modernity.

The task of antifascist criticism must be to rectify Marxism's failure to provide an adequate theory of desire, to analyze the libidinal drives that made people find commodities, or nationalism, or Hitler, so compelling. Thus, inverting Woolf's question, theorists like Reich, Adorno, Erich Fromm, Max Horkheimer, and Herbert Marcuse all asked what possible satisfaction dominance can give to the *dominated*, why populations respond willingly to eroticization of and by a Leader, and argued that sexual repression is the basis for the authoritarian personality of the Leader and the feminine masochism of the crowd. In particular, Reich rejected the view derived from Le Bon and espoused by Yourcenar, that the masses are by their nature vulnerable to what he called "befogging." Such theories, which attribute "social catastrophes" like fascism to a kind of mass hypnosis, Reich considered condescending to the masses and ultimately a form of mystification themselves. He asserted instead that the psychological structures of both individuals and classes are created by ideology, and that the dominant classes enforce ruling-class ideology through the sexual repression of the masses (see Reich, 23). By the time Adorno and Horkheimer's *Dialectic of Enlightenment* appeared in 1944, the suppression of eros figures as a constituent element of the "Bad Enlightenment," which they trace back to the roots of Western culture in Homer: Odysseus's rejection of

Circe represents the emergence of the liberal subject and the consequent objectification of the erotic, women, and Nature.*

Broadly construed, these approaches may be seen as an attempt to put the body back into rationalist, materialist critiques in order to undo mind-body dualism, to overcome liberalism's alienating abstractness while counteracting fascism's virtual hegemony over discourses of the body and sexuality. In *Three Guineas*, for example, Woolf uses metaphors of the body to concretize her economic arguments, as when she asks, arguing that the alienated life of the white-collar worker deprives him of sensual and aesthetic pleasure,

> what then remains of a human being who has lost sight, sound, and sense of proportion? Only a cripple in a cave.
>
> That of course is a figure, and fanciful; but that it has some connection with figures that are statistical and not fanciful—with the three hundred millions spent upon arms—seems possible. (Woolf, *Three Guineas*, 72)

Reich insists that fascism's characterization of Marxism as "*lebensfeindlich*" is a valid criticism of Marxist orthodoxy. What caused the collapse of the Worker's International, the crises provoked by World War I, and other apparent failures of Marxism was, in Reich's view, the fact that Marxism had retained liberalism's overemphasis on rationality and ensuing rejection of the body and sexuality. He recognizes fascism as an understandable response to mind-body dualism; his counterstrategy is to recuperate sex from "mysticism," which he defines as the force stemming from repressed sexuality and manipulated by both fascism and the Church. Reich's criticisms of liberalism and "communism," then, explicitly and deliberately resemble those of fascism, even while he argues that fascism itself is fundamentally just another symptom of the same malaise:

> "Away from the animal; away from sexuality!" are the guiding principles of the formation of all human ideology. This is the case whether it

---

*These ideas circulate through numerous texts by members of the Frankfurt School, as well as through Reich's work; some of the more representative are Adorno, "Freudian Theory and the Pattern of Fascist Propaganda"; Adorno and Horkheimer, *Dialectic of Enlightenment*; and Fromm, *Escape from Freedom*.

is disguised in the fascist form of racially pure "supermen," the communist form of proletarian class honor, the Christian form of man's "spiritual and ethical nature," or the liberal form of "higher human values." All these ideas harp on the same monotonous tune: "We are not animals. . . . *And we don't have genitals like the animals!*" All of this adds up to an overemphasis of the intellect, of the "purely" mechanistic; logic and reason as opposed to instinct; culture as opposed to nature; the mind as opposed to the body; work as opposed to sexuality; the state as opposed to the individual; the superior man as opposed to the inferior man. (Reich, 339)

Interestingly, Reich goes on to argue that this kind of binary thinking leads to the projection of animal and sexual characteristics onto the racial Other: "There is a direct connection between the 'dominion' over animals and racial 'dominion' over the 'black man, the Jew, the Frenchman, etc.' " (Reich, 343). In the work of Reich, as well as in many of the other texts discussed here, we frequently find this kind of tacit admission that the category of "class" is too abstract to account for all forms of exploitation and oppression and is therefore inadequate as the basis of either materialist theory or revolutionary praxis. While rarely focusing on race, nearly all these writers acknowledge it as a category intersecting and complicating the notion of class, and thus call into question orthodox Marxism's exclusive concern with the exploitation of the industrial proletariat. After all, a Marxist analysis should recognize not only that workers have bodies, but also that those bodies have different class valences according to their gender and race; leftists were beginning to feel that a comprehensive materialist approach needed to take such specifics into account. For the intellectuals examined here, furthermore, analyses of race and racism frequently encompassed not only Jewishness and anti-Semitism—subjects that were of personal relevance to nearly all of them, and in any case had long been of concern to the Left—but the oppression of colonized peoples and peoples of color as well.

In some cases, particularly Woolf's, this awareness manifests itself simply in passing references to racism or colonialism, as if to acknowledge that these phenomena are relevant to the central problem of class or gender oppression, although the writer is lacking the theoretical vocabulary to explore the problem further. Elsewhere, as in Reich's work, there is a more sustained, if still sketchy, attempt to investigate the correlations among forms of oppression. And the later work of the Frankfurt School ultimately develops this analysis into an investigation of all the manifold forms of domination imbricated with modernity. Their final goal is a thorough transformation of Enlightenment values, a radical fulfillment of the "Good Enlightenment" that would extend the concepts of democracy and rights to the numerous classes of dominated beings that that tradition has historically excluded.

Thus Woolf recognized a danger in an exclusive concern with the oppression of women; though she failed to articulate any thorough analysis of racism, she warned that if white bourgeois women appropriated power for themselves while continuing to replicate patriarchal patterns of discrimination, they would become "just as possessive, just as jealous, just as pugnacious" as bourgeois men (Woolf, *Three Guineas*, 66). The narrator of *Three Guineas* writes that she will lend her support to the association to help women enter the professions only if the professional women pledge to eschew sexism and racism themselves:

> Therefore this guinea, which is to help you to help women to enter the professions, has this condition as a first condition attached to it. You shall swear that you will do all in your power to insist that any woman who enters any profession shall in no way hinder any other human being, whether man or woman, white or black, provided that he or she is qualified to enter that profession, from entering it; but shall do all in her power to help them. (Woolf, *Three Guineas*, 66)

And a few pages later, she admonishes the woman Outsider that her obligation is not merely to help other women, but to "help all properly qualified people, of whatever sex, class or colour, to enter your profession" (Woolf, *Three Guineas*, 80).

For his part, Reich felt the need to develop what he calls in *Mass Psychology* "the social concept of the worker," meaning a proletariat defined not simply by its relation to the mode of production, but as the subaltern more generally. He believed that the ascension to power of a racist, nationalist laboring class could not bring about emancipation: "Organizations of workers that exclude Negroes and practice Hitlerism do not deserve to be regarded as creators of a new and free society" (Reich, xxii). In precisely the same vein, Spender wrote just after the war that proletarian solidarity could not be emancipatory if it was not informed by opposition to other forms of oppression at the same time; he also questioned whether the dictatorship of a racist proletariat could lead society to a freer future: "Yet I am sure it is wrong to assume that proletarian virtues will inevitably remain with the poor when they cease to be oppressed. The selfishness of the trade-unionists who fight for improved standards of living not only against the rich, but also against the poor of other countries, and against the coloured peoples, should demonstrate this" (Spender, *World*, 265–66). We see then, that all these works, whether their primary concern is with gender or class, recognize the interconnections between these issues, and the politics of race that had emerged as the organizing principle of German fascism.

One other point is worth mentioning briefly for what it may indicate about the scope of these emancipatory projects. Without elaborating anything like a theory of "animal rights," these left intellectuals nonetheless evince an interest in the problem of human domination of the natural world, and particularly of animals, as one manifestation of the exploitativeness and alienation of modernity. Interestingly, antidemocratic reactionaries had also been known to suggest, sarcastically, that this was in fact bound to be the next step in an absurd drive toward universal emancipation:

> The lingering medieval veneration of ladies and the modern fanaticism for equality, which pretends that all people, no matter what race or which sex, are "equal" or "of equal worth," have combined with one another to give birth to and rear the greatest, and, in its consequences, the most fateful foolishness of our era. "Equality for everything that bears a human countenance!" Why not rather equality for everything that has a mammalian structure? (B. Friedländer, 210)

To which some responded, why not, indeed? As the passage on dualism quoted above suggests, Reich was especially vocal on this point; he believed that "Man's" preoccupation with distinguishing himself from animals (here Reich refers specifically to the Scopes trial) manifests his inability to accept his own corporeality (Reich, 334). For Reich, such homocentric thinking underwrites the founding mythologies of Western patriarchy: "The biblical legend of the creation of man as an image of God, of his dominion over the animals, clearly reflects the repressive action man carried out against this animal nature" (Reich, 342).

The domination of the natural world also became a recurrent theme in the work of the Frankfurt School. That the objectification and domination of Nature is integral to the "Bad Enlightenment" is, as I mentioned above, a central thesis of *The Dialectic of Enlightenment*. Though only in passing, Woolf also refers several times to blood sports in *Three Guineas*, and decries the quantities of game animals slaughtered by men as a further indictment of the violence and oppression inherent in patriarchal "civilization." Even Auden may have been reflecting the belief that violence against animals is conterminous with other forms of oppression in Western culture in "August for the people," a poem in which he evokes "the distant baying" of sportsmen's hounds that accompanied his idle conversations with Christopher Isherwood during their privileged, protected boyhood. Auden abruptly ends the stanza with the image of the hunted deer "flying through the wood," reminding Isherwood, and the reader, of the fear and pain of their elitist culture's victims (Auden, 156).

Reading *Three Guineas* in the context of this broad theoretical enterprise helps to explain much in the text that has seemed to some illogical or inconsequential, like Woolf's indictment of hunting. Q. D. Leavis, in her famously caustic review of the book in *Scrutiny*, was only the first of many critics to deride Woolf's focus on apparently trivial and benign customs such as the academic dress code. But if Woolf is adhering to, as Reich said, "the principle of paying strict attention to everything to which cultural reaction gives prominence," then we can read her concern with blood sports and dress codes as a direct response to fascism's glorification of violence and spectacle; and, further, as an effort to investigate the full scope of fascist influence in the determination of cultural life. It is significant in this regard that in her review Leavis repeatedly accuses Woolf of behaving like a Nazi, as we might expect this to be precisely the effect of an antifascist critique that attempts to meet fascism on its own grounds. Unlike Yourcenar, for whom fascism is "*le contraire*" of her notion of civilization, Woolf believes with Benjamin that "there is no document of culture which is not at the same time a document of barbarism" (W. Benjamin, "Fuchs," 233) — including, we might surmise, *Three Guineas* itself.*

Woolf is compelled, therefore, to point out the correspondences between the apparently nonfascist and the fascist, between the English and the German, between Us and Them, until she forces the reader, and herself, into an uncomfortable identification with the very figure of the dictator. Describing a photograph of the "Führer or Duce," she says that the picture

> suggests a connection and for us a very important connection. It suggests that the public and the private worlds are inseparably connected; that the tyrannies and servilities of the one are the tyrannies and servilities of the other. . . . It suggests that we cannot dissociate ourselves from that figure but are ourselves that figure. It suggests that we are not passive spectators doomed to unresisting obedience but by our thoughts and actions can ourselves change that figure. (Woolf, *Three Guineas*, 142)

Like Yourcenar, Woolf wants us to recognize the human in the dictator; unlike Yourcenar, Woolf also wants us to recognize the dictator in ourselves, arguing that barbarism is not an aberration in the history of Western civilization but inheres in the culture of the fathers. While she by no means rejects all of "civilization," the Western or Enlightenment tradition, she insists on its dialectical relation to barbarism. Her appeal to the individuality of the dictator does not function, as Yourcenar's does in *Denier du rêve*, to revalorize a notion of the private sphere in opposition to mass society, but rather to mobilize a revolutionary — though certainly rational and free-willed — subject who will understand that the fight

---

*Marie-Luise Gättens draws the same parallel I do here between Woolf and Benjamin and discusses it at greater length; see *Women Writers and Fascism*, 13, 32.

against tyranny demands a radical transformation of the world, *including* the individual and the private sphere.

As Woolf attempts to envision a transformed world, she reproduces themes and images widely found in fascist texts, just as Yourcenar and Barnes do. As they usually do not, however, Woolf explicitly displaces these images in the service of a feminist, antifascist politics, as if to acknowledge their power while turning them to ends very different from those of fascist ideologies. Point by point, Woolf engages with and attempts to redefine many of the categories and concepts that fascism, in the 1930s, had managed to make its own: the nation, the media, art, sexuality, motherhood.

Most obviously, Woolf reformulates the concept of the nation, challenging the assumption that patriotism is equivalent to love of country. In her attack on nationalism, Woolf equates the *patria* and the patriarchy, indicting patriotism in the opening pages of the work as that unanimity of opinion that encourages men to go to war (Woolf, *Three Guineas*, 8). She includes, in this interrogation of patriotism, a passing criticism of colonialism, when she asks what "the testimony of the ruled—the Indians or the Irish" looks like in comparison with the claims of their rulers, thus acknowledging that the narratives of subaltern classes about nationhood may differ from the ruling class perspective (Woolf, *Three Guineas*, 108).

Women, like the colonized, are alienated from national bodies that nominally include them. Excluded from the ownership of capital, from education, and from the other privileges of their fathers and brothers, women are, equally, excluded from the nation and therefore have no cause for patriotism (Woolf, *Three Guineas*, 107–9). Woolf claims that she does not want to belong to the *patria*, at least as it has been defined: the narrator has, she tells her male interlocutor, "no wish to be 'English' on the same terms that you yourself are 'English' " (Woolf, *Three Guineas*, 101).

Woolf finds, in the fact of women's exclusion and disenfranchisement, the potential for a different freedom from that conferred by power: the freedom *from* power, from what she defines as "unreal loyalties." First among these is loyalty to country: "By freedom from unreal loyalties is meant that you must rid yourself of pride of nationality in the first place; also of religious pride, college pride, school pride, family pride, sex pride" (Woolf, *Three Guineas*, 80). While writing *Three Guineas*, Woolf herself had already set about detaching herself from unreal loyalty to the institutions of British patriarchy, refusing degrees and honors and the other "bribes" offered her to persuade her to participate as a token in the structures and rituals of the nation's life. When, in 1935, E. M. Forster told Woolf that the London Library Committee had rejected his suggestion that she be appointed to the committee, on the grounds that "ladies are quite impossible," Woolf responded angrily: "God damn Morgan for thinking I'd have taken that. . . . The veil of the temple—which, whether university or cathedral, was academic or ecclesiastical I forget—was to be raised, & as an exception she was to be allowed to enter in. But what about my civilisation? For 2,000 years we have done things without being paid for doing them. You cant bribe me now" (Woolf, *Diary*, 4: 298). In the same vein, in *Three Guineas* Woolf refers to women like Florence Nightingale, Emily Brontë, and Christina Rossetti as "civilized women," but adds that "whether or not they can rightly be called 'English' women is matter for dispute" (Woolf, *Three Guineas*, 79). Women's civilization, "my civilisation" in Woolf's words, is something entirely different and separate from British civilization; and the daughters of educated men cannot swear allegiance to both.

Woolf's insistence on the need to forswear all affiliations to the *patria*/patriarchy seems to mark one of those moments of mythmaking where she "affirms particular experiences of letting-go, of detaching from male worlds in order to see differently, to think differently" (Smith, 228). Woolf imagines women as a united, international class, fulfilling the hopes dashed by the disintegration of the Second International and uniting in the Outsiders' Society to renounce patriotism and bring an end to war. Her rhetoric reaches a climax in the celebrated passage of *Three Guineas* in which she declares, with what is surely a conscious echo of the *Communist Manifesto*, that "the outsider will say, 'in fact, as a woman, I have no country. As a woman I want no country. As a woman my country is the whole world' " (Woolf, *Three Guineas*, 109). She thus seems to reject definitively any conception of nationalism, whether it be its most extreme manifestation in National Socialism, or the very British patriotism called on in the 1930s to rally against the fascist menace.

Yet Woolf ends the famous passage cited above with a less-quoted appeal to another kind of patriotism, a love of country that moves outward from the motherland to the world. Recognizing the force of fascist nationalism's appeal to the irrational, Woolf attempts to appropriate that power for an ethic of humanitarianism:

> And if, when reason has said its say, still some obstinate emotion remains, some love of England dropped into a child's ears by the cawing of rooks in an elm tree, by the splash of waves on a beach, or by English voices murmuring nursery rhymes, this drop of pure, if irrational, emotion she will make serve her to give to England first what she desires of peace and freedom for the whole world. (Woolf, *Three Guineas*, 109)

Despite her affirmations to the contrary, then, it would seem that not only does Woolf have a country, but that that country is England.\* Instead of dispensing with the nation, Woolf wants to make it her nation, her civilization, to be English on her own terms. Trying to imagine a world without countries, Woolf imagines instead *another* country, another civilization. Furthermore, her love of country, like the fascist's, is rooted in the semiotic seductiveness of archaic orality and the oceanic maternal embrace. But the moment of submission to the symbolic order, to paternal authoritarianism, so crucial to fascism's rigid and conflicted sense of boundaries, never arrives in Woolf's text; for her, any particular motherland is at most the specific source of a nonspecific, undifferentiated love of humanity. Her reappropriated concept of "nation," of what it means to have a national identity, becomes the model for the politics endorsed by her text, a politics that moves constantly from the specific

---

\* For further discussion of Woolf's devotion to England and its relation to her contempt for patriotism, see Karen Schneider, "Of Two Minds"; and Alex Zwerdling, "*Between the Acts*," and the chapter "Pacifism Without Hope" in his *Virginia Woolf and the Real World*.

to the general, working outward from Woolf's own gender/class to a whole world at war.

Woolf also attempts to appropriate for her own political ends the power of visual imagery and *its* appeal to the irrational, which fascism had exploited to such great effect. We recall that in a passage already cited in Chapter 3, Russell Berman described the relation between "paralogic fascism" and "the aestheticist preservation of the image impervious to conceptual scrutiny and outside the venue of any legal rationality," which culminates in "the compulsive fixation on the image and the associated fear of language" (Berman, "Wandering Z," xx). Woolf was only one of many contemporary critics of fascism to respond to fascism's irrational "fixation on the image"; she attacks fascist aestheticism, particularly the use of visual codes, such as distinctions of dress, to enforce social hierarchies and to brainwash the spectator. Like Yourcenar, Adorno, and Isherwood, Woolf associates fascist spectacle, symbolized by the use of visual ornamentation, with the hypnotic effects of commercial advertising: "With the example then, that [the Fascist States] give us of the power of medals, symbols, orders and even, it would seem, of decorated ink-pots to hypnotize the human mind it must be our aim not to submit ourselves to such hypnotism. We must extinguish the coarse glare of advertisement and publicity" (Woolf, *Three Guineas*, 114).

To reinforce an argument that denounces the hypnotizing effects of both mass culture and fascist aestheticism, however, Woolf herself relies on frequent references to photographs, to mechanically reproduced visual images. In the original edition of the book this device was even more obvious, because in addition to the references to photographs, especially of mutilated bodies and houses destroyed in the war in Spain, the volume itself was illustrated with actual photographs of English judges and other figures of patriarchal power. In the text, Woolf adverts to photos of fascist atrocities, but the photos shown in the first edition were those of male figures of power in England, indicating that "we are meant to put the patriarchal horse before the Fascist cart" (Marcus, "No More Horses," 275) and, furthermore, that the war against fascism needs to be fought at home, against the manifestations of patriarchy in England, rather than abroad.

Even in subsequent editions without illustrations, it is striking how often Woolf employs the figure of a visual image to introduce crucial rhetorical turns in her text. In her very first reference to fascism, she mentions the photos she has been sent of the Spanish Civil War (Woolf, *Three Guineas*, 10). Those and other photos continue to reappear, often in order to provide a visual or emotional shortcut through rational argument. The visual image can substitute for logic, memory, and lived experience; for example, it can bridge the ontological gap between women and men: "There is thus no longer any reason to be confined to the minute span of actual experience which is still, for us, so narrow, so circumscribed. We can supplement it by looking at the picture of the lives of others" (Woolf, *Three Guineas*, 7). Photographs also mediate between body and mind, fusing Woolf and her male interlocutor, the eye, the brain, and the nervous system into one emotional response to the "fact" of the image. The image here overcomes class and gender alienation and creates consensus, as fascist iconography strives to; with the clergy and other traditional guarantors of social stability "at loggerheads" over the issue of war, the products of technological innovation can be used to create a new, albeit irrational, social cohesion (Woolf, *Three Guineas*, 11). "Photographs," Woolf concedes,

> are not an argument; they are simply a crude statement of fact addressed to the eye. But the eye is connected with the brain; the brain with the nervous system. That system sends its messages in a flash through every past memory and present feeling. When we look at those photographs some fusion takes place within us; however different the education, the traditions behind us, our sensations are the same; and they are violent. (Woolf, *Three Guineas*, 11)

Yourcenar recognized the similarity between the thrill of fascist ceremony and her own love for aestheticized ritual, while characterizing fascism as a degenerate form of ritual; and she resorted to an argument grounded in aesthetic criteria to denounce fascist spectacle (*"Cela ne m'avait pas paru beau"*). Woolf's use of visual artifacts to provoke the reader's irrational, violent reaction against fascist irrationalism may reveal a similar fault line in her text: after all, it does seem an incongruous strategy in a work that purports to deploy the logocentric tradition of rhetorical argument against an aestheticized and irrational politics.

Yet if Woolf's goal is not to differentiate herself from the fascist Other, but to reappropriate the power of fascism's methodologies for an antifascist politics, then her reliance on the image of the photographs here could be interpreted as a valid maneuver in the battle over the uses of the aesthetic. The particular danger of fascist aestheticism lies not merely in the recourse to image and icon but in the transference of the anti-utilitarian amoralism of *l'art pour l'art* to the sphere of politics. In contrast, Woolf's project, like Reich's, is to make room for the mystical, the emotional, in rationalist discourse; and to that end she attempts to imagine the social uses left criticism might make of irrational appeals to the image.

While Woolf especially emphasizes the connection between fascist aesthetics and advertising, she is also concerned with the corruptibility, and corrupting influence, of other forms of media. Unlike conservatives, however, Woolf recognizes that the mass media *are* cultural forms; she does not disdain them, as Yourcenar does, as mere tools for the obfuscation of the great unwashed, but instead asks why fascist patriarchy has monopolized the mass media and how they may be recuperated by political progressives.

Historically, Woolf writes, journalism and trade writing have been open to women because they are inexpensive professions to enter and have been less susceptible to the pernicious influence of the patriarchy because writing and publishing could to some extent take place outside of institutional structures. But, precisely as fascist cultural critics do, she holds that in the age of mass production and circulation of printed media, the press and publishing houses are manipulated by the financial interests of large-scale capital. Woolf does not, of course, imply that "capital" is equivalent to Jews or freemasons; in Woolf's view, there is indeed a conspiracy to manipulate the media, but the conspirators are patriarchs determined to suppress "discussion of any undesirable subject" (Woolf, *Three Guineas*, 162n16). Woolf envisions in contrast a woman-run newspaper that would be "committed to a conspiracy, not of silence, but of speech" (Woolf, *Three Guineas*, 68).

In order to found such a newspaper, though, women writers would have to have money; and if journalism and other forms of literary production have traditionally been inexpensive professions to practice, they have also been ill paid. Always sensitive to the material conditions of aesthetic production, Woolf develops in *Three Guineas* the analysis of the (gender) politics of culture she had first formulated in *A Room of One's Own* in 1929. At times Woolf is not far, in these works, from the sort of materialist cultural criticism articulated by, for example, Benjamin. In both texts, she questions the validity of the central precepts of autonomy aesthetics, the concepts of the individual genius and the auratic work of art. Like Benjamin, she examines the history of the reception of aesthetic artifacts, asking how reception has been conditioned by, for instance, the gender of the artist. She also criticizes the linear narratives of literary criticism like Eliot's, in which one great writer descends from another. Compare her declaration in *A Room of One's Own* that "masterpieces are not single and solitary births; they are the outcome of many years . . . of thinking by the body of the people," to Benjamin's assertion that "the products of art and science owe their existence not merely to the effort of the great geniuses that created them, but also to the unnamed drudgery of their contemporaries" (Woolf, *Room*, 65; W. Benjamin, "Fuchs," 233).

In *Three Guineas*, furthermore, Woolf examines the material conditions of production, not only of art works, but of artists as members of classes, arguing that in England's class-based educational institutions, artists and intellectuals are also produced as commodities. Her economic metaphors for cultural processes underline her materialist critique of the politics of "culture," as when she asks, of a university education, "What is this mysterious process that takes about three years to accomplish, costs a round sum in hard cash, and turns the crude and raw human being into the finished product—an educated man or woman?" (Woolf, *Three Guineas*, 24).

Yet despite a thoroughgoing commitment to a materialist analysis of culture, Woolf's interest in questions of aesthetics, the media, and culture inspire in her the same concern with authenticity we find in liberal, conservative, and fascist cultural criticism, the same desire to recuperate a "disinterested," "pure," or "authentic" art that would not be mediated by social or material considerations. This impulse seems at times to overwhelm the explicit political import of the text: Woolf asserts at one moment that the work of art must always reflect the social conditions of its own creation, and in the next expresses her preference for art works that are not "mutilated" by either financial considerations (that is, the constraints of liberal capitalism) or polemical criteria (the requirements of socialist realism). In her vehement rejection of both forms of mediation she invokes images of usury and sterility not unlike those we find in, for instance, Pound's work. She writes in one footnote that "the reduction of English literature to an examination subject must be viewed . . . with profound regret by all who wish to keep one art at least out of the hands of middlemen and free, as long as may be, from all association with competition and money making," and then asserts a few lines later, "if we use art to propagate political opinions. . . . literature will suffer the same mutilation that the mule has suffered; and there will be no more horses" (Woolf, *Three Guineas*, 155n30, 170n39).

Woolf's ideal, unmediated culture would, furthermore, be high rather than low, virile rather than effeminate, in the tradition of the "classics" of English literature. If writers were freed from both material and political constraints, she writes,

> "culture," that amorphous bundle, swaddled up as she now is in insincerity, emitting half truths from her timid lips, sweetening and diluting her message with whatever sugar or water serves to swell the writer's fame or his master's purse, would regain her shape and become, as Milton, Keats and other great writers assure us that she is in reality, muscular, adventurous, free. (Woolf, *Three Guineas*, 99)

One critic has argued that Woolf's "desire for historical revision warred against the unchallengeable supremacy of 'Art' and its accompanying (and unavoidable) dependence upon hierarchy" (Mudge, "Burning," 233). According to this theory, Woolf's materialism is inevitably in conflict with her tendency to exile minor art works, particularly those written by women, and to reinscribe the self-evident, universally valid truth values of the canonical, auratic work of art. Ultimately, it does seem that Woolf accepts the objective existence of "great works" and of "genius," interrogating the conditions of possibility for their production or fruition rather than, like Benjamin, going on to ask how and why certain names are fetishized and reproduced by other writers or artists.

It might also be possible, however, to read Woolf's apparently liberal ideal of unmediated art as a gesture toward a socialist aesthetics in the tradition of Morris and Wilde. At one point she reinscribes the distinction between private and public in the aesthetic realm, by contrasting "pageantry"—that is, masculinist, patriarchal, institutional spectacle—to the "private" aesthetic praxis of the women of the Outsiders' Society. This aesthetics, however, does not recapitulate a bourgeois vision of auratic art works to be consumed in private by an educated elite; it is, instead, an ideal of a totally aestheticized life that Woolf espouses:

> The outsiders will dispense with pageantry not from any puritanical dislike of beauty. On the contrary, it will be one of their aims to increase private beauty; the beauty of spring, summer, autumn; the beauty of flowers, silks, clothes; the beauty which brims not only every field and wood but every barrow in Oxford Street; the scattered beauty which needs only to be combined by artists in order to become visible to all. (Woolf, *Three Guineas*, 113–14)

Here Woolf anticipates fascism's claim that materialism is essentially anti-aesthetic and anhedonic, counteracting the fascist aestheticization of technology and violence with her own picture of a feminist, socialist utopia in which the aesthetic potential of both metropolis and countryside, art(ifice) and nature, is made available to the masses through the art work. If this vision still relies, like bourgeois aesthetics, on the privileged ideals of Art and Artist, it is nonetheless a move toward an aesthetics that captures the spirit of fascism's aesthetic power and appeal, without allying it to an amoral or authoritarian politics.

Woolf is also self-consciously critical of her own idealism, retreating ironically from her own utopic visions time and time again as she admits that, whatever art and life might look like after the revolution, her immediate concern must be instead with establishing the conditions for that revolution. Her fantasies of burning down the universities, or, more modestly, of encouraging "the disinterested pursuit of reading and writing the English language," are repeatedly interrupted "because of facts again"—that is, because of her awareness of the material constraints on women who, without access to education or capital, are frequently in no position even to join the revolution, much less to finance it, and who have, therefore, to write for money—to prostitute their intellectual labor.

> So to ask the daughters of educated men who have to earn their livings by reading and writing to sign your manifesto would be of no value to the cause of disinterested culture and intellectual liberty, because directly they had signed it they must be at the desk writing those books, lectures and articles by which culture is prostituted and intellectual liberty is sold into slavery. (Woolf, *Three Guineas*, 92)

Woolf thus reiterates the association, by now familiar, between the corruption of culture and the commodification of sexuality. Prostitution circulates in *Three Guineas* as both example of and metaphor for the processes of mediation and commodification in alienated society, just as it does in *Denier du rêve*—or *Mein Kampf*. Far from being a reflexive invocation of a standard and ultimately misogynist trope, however, Woolf's use of such metaphors is highly self-conscious, culminating in an explicit investigation into the politico-cultural meanings of illicit female sexuality. At first, prostitution is introduced as a figure for women's alienation from the political institutions of liberal democracy. The political power that women are supposed to have through their influence over their husbands is inauthentic, because their relation to the State is mediated by men who control them economically. Marriage itself is, as Engels noted, no more than a form of privatized prostitution under the conditions of capitalist patriarchy; the bourgeois ideal of a contract between equals is rendered purely formal by the material inequality between the two parties. Only the influence of a woman who is financially independent and has the right to vote can be "disinterested," authentic; without these rights, says Woolf, she would do better openly to declare herself a prostitute than to rely on the "influence" of personal charm.

> If such is the real nature of our influence, and we all recognize the description and have noted the effects, it is either beyond our reach, for many of us are plain, poor and old; or beneath our contempt, for many of us would prefer to call ourselves prostitutes simply and to take our stand openly under the lamps of Piccadilly Circus rather than use it. (Woolf, *Three Guineas*, 15)

Having thus turned the metaphor of prostitution into an explicit equation between the legitimate and illegitimate uses of female sexuality under patriarchy, Woolf passes to the metaphor of adultery, which metamorphoses into adulteration; she thus compares illicit sexuality (which involves a third element, outside the authentic couple) to commodified culture, where the financial element enters in illegitimately. "Advertisement and publicity are also adulterers. Thus, culture mixed with personal charm, or culture mixed with advertisement and publicity, are also adulterated forms of culture" (Woolf, *Three Guineas*, 93). This argument culminates in an indictment of commodified culture that resembles conservative cultural critiques in its association of illicit sexuality, degeneration, and the lack of love in contemporary art and sexual relations:

> Just as for many centuries . . . it was thought vile for a woman to sell her body without love, but right to give it to the husband whom she loved, so it is wrong, you will agree, to sell your mind without love, but right to give it to the art which you love . . . to sell a brain is worse than to sell a body, for when the body seller has sold her momentary pleasure she takes good care that the matter shall end there. But when a brain seller has sold her brain, its anaemic, vicious and diseased progeny are let loose upon the world to infect and corrupt and sow the seeds of disease in others. (Woolf, *Three Guineas*, 93)

Unlike conservatives, though, Woolf, like other left theorists of sexuality, analyzes commodified sexuality/culture as a consequence of inequitable power relations. As we have seen, Reich also produces a diagnosis of the inauthentic sexual relations at the heart of commodified culture that focuses not on the erosion of "traditional" cultural values, as fascist and conservative critiques do, but on sexual repression as a symptom of oppression. Reich, however, tends to rely on what Marcuse and others have found an overly simplified notion of "repression," to be counteracted by an equally simplistic vision of a sexual "liberation" effected through sexual education and widespread distribution of contraceptives.

Woolf's analysis of the function of repression, and its antidotes, is more subtle. She compares "prostitution" and "chastity," the roles of whore and virgin, as the two modes of sexual being that patriarchy allows to women. In several long footnotes, Woolf investigates the myriad religious, social, and financial pressures on women to be physically "chaste" (see, e.g., Woolf, *Three Guineas*, 166–69n38); and throughout the text she decries the hypocrisy that defines the "unchaste" woman as a prostitute, as if all women were not at all times subject to men's sexual and economic power. For Woolf, as for Reich, male control of female sexuality is one of the foundations of fascist patriarchy. Instead of attempting to escape the patriarchal paradigm of chastity and prostitution, however, Woolf displaces it by defining chastity and unchastity in psychological rather than physical terms.* She concludes at the end of one footnote that "the real nature of chastity" is still "highly conjectural" (Woolf, *Three Guineas*, 158n34); in the text which this footnote accompanies, of course, she has described in detail her own conception of real chastity, which she defines as the refusal "to sell your brain for the sake of money" (Woolf, *Three Guineas*, 80).

Woolf's strategy works on several levels here. She combines a Marxist notion of unalienated labor with the insight that women under patriarchy are alienated from their sexuality, and with a feminist vision of unalienated sexuality in the form of psychological chastity. She thus tacitly recognizes that the putative sexual "liberation" espoused by Reich or—to use an example with which Woolf would have been familiar—the free-love advocates of her day, was not necessarily a solution to the problem of women's repression, tending instead to have the effect of pressuring women to be more

* Jane Marcus discusses this and other examples of Woolf's use of the concept of chastity at greater length in *Virginia Woolf and the Languages of Patriarchy*, 115–19.

sexually available to more men for less money than they could have earned honestly under the lamps at Piccadilly. Her advocacy of psychological chastity reflects her recognition that chastity might be transformed from a mode of male domination, into a space women could create for their own psychic and physical independence.

We might go on enumerating the concepts that Woolf thus seeks to reclaim from fascist patriarchy and to transform in her effort to describe the future of *her* civilization, the outsiders' country; in addition to the nation, the media, the arts, and sexuality, they include education and religion, as Woolf envisages the creation of the Outsiders' University and "a new religion based, it might well be, upon the New Testament, but, it might well be, very different from the religion now erected upon that basis" (Woolf, *Three Guineas*, 113). I will conclude the list, however, with one of Woolf's most important projects, and the point where she converges with Barnes and Yourcenar. Like them, Woolf wants to recuperate childbirth and maternity from the cultural discourses of patriarchal fascism. She adapts images of childbirth, maternity, and the analogy between childbirth and military service to an argument that is both angry and parodic, as it is in Barnes and Yourcenar. For Barnes, labor and childbirth can represent a sardonic inversion of militarist values, or, more straightforwardly, fascist patriarchy's appropriation of women's reproductive labor; for Yourcenar, childbirth is the materialist subplot that offers an alternative to fascist idealism. Woolf, too, more consciously preoccupied with the issue of maternity than either of the others, invokes the themes of pregnancy, labor, and childrearing to ridicule patriarchal and fascist aesthetics, ethics, and concepts of nature; she then goes on to develop an argument about the place of reproductive labor in socialist feminism.

This is a crucial aspect of the strategy of reintroducing the body (and, along with it, both sexuality and sexual difference) into materialist discourse. Fascist ideologies were often able to appeal to women by acknowledging their bodily difference, their specific contribution to the nation in the form of maternal labor. In its abstract neutrality, fascists argued, liberalism overlooked the particular, physical species being of women; fascism, in contrast, promised to recognize and reward it. A materialist discourse of female sexuality, then, would also have to recognize gendered difference, but without limiting the scope of women's gender-specific experience exclusively to their maternal labor within the patriarchal family.

Woolf initially advances this point humorously, in an implicit analogy between motherhood and patriarchal professions. Poking fun at the elaborate semiotics of clothing in academia, the military, and the legal profession, Woolf says, "A woman who advertised her motherhood by a tuft of horsehair on the left shoulder would scarcely, you will agree, be a venerable object" (Woolf, *Three Guineas*, 20–21). She thus calls into question the priority given to masculine achievement in patriarchal culture, while laying the groundwork for a more serious analogy between reproductive and other forms of labor. She first argues that reproductive labor is, or ought to be treated as, a profession when she compares the "intensive childbirth of the unpaid wife" to "the intensive money-making of the paid husband in the Victorian age" (Woolf, *Three Guineas*, 78–79). From this point, she works her way up to the demand that the State remunerate women's unpaid labor in the home, particularly their labor as mothers. Wages for maternal labor would guarantee women independent minds and wills; furthermore, if mothers were salaried, fathers would have to work fewer hours outside the home to support families, and so men too could begin to overcome reified consciousness: "the half-man might become whole" (Woolf, *Three Guineas*, 112).

Woolf also invokes the kind of eugenicist argument so common to the discourses about sexuality, both reactionary and radical, that stemmed from nineteenth-century organicism: wages for mothers would, she asserts, increase the birthrate in the educated classes, "the very class where births are desirable" (Woolf, *Three Guineas*, 111). In the same slightly facetious tone, she then resorts to an analogy, half-ironic and half-serious, with military service; if childbirth is to women what fighting is to men, she seems to say, then let it be at least as well compensated by the State, whom both are supposed to serve: "Just as the increase in the pay of soldiers has resulted, the papers say, in additional recruits to the force of arms-bearers, so the same inducement would serve to recruit the child-bearing force, which we can hardly deny to be as necessary and as honourable, but which, because of its poverty, and its hardships, is now failing to attract recruits" (Woolf, *Three Guineas*, 111).

Like Yourcenar's association of women's role in reproduction with the "natural" and the "real," this appeal to the State to recognize women's contribution to the Improvement of the Race may appear dubious, easily adapted to a rhetoric of *"Kinder, Kirche, Küche."* As one critic notes, "This solution is problematic because it replaces women's economic dependency on an individual patriarch with that of the patriarchal state, whose legitimacy Woolf proceeds to dismantle" (Gättens, 17). The fascist states did, after all, experiment with recompensing maternal labor in the form of bonuses and prizes for prolific childbearing; the consequences can hardly be considered to have been emancipatory. For Woolf, however, as for Yourcenar, childbearing is not to be viewed as the complement to the masculine realm of the military, within an ideology of rigidly separate spheres; it can be, instead, a powerful antidote to patriarchal and fascist values. Early in the text, Woolf inserts a footnote in which she argues that the principal, indeed the only, form of political power wielded by women of her class is the ability to withhold their reproductive labor as an antimilitaristic strategy: "one method by which [women] can help to prevent war is to refuse to bear children" (Woolf, *Three Guineas*, 147n10).

It is also important to note that, in opposition to fascist ideologies of maternity, Woolf specifies that she does not consider that maternity is either women's duty or the only labor suited to them. As we have seen, she mistrusts the concept of "nature" and is quick to point out that bodies and natures are not outside of historical processes. In Woolf's model, women's "nature" is produced by the dialectic of praxis, biology, and environment; women's biological functions are influenced both by their agency as subjects, and by their position as subjects of history. The material conditions of childbirth, for example, can change: to cite only one obvious transformation in the technologies of reproduction, the introduction of chloroform and other medical advances in the late nineteenth and early twentieth centuries meant that childbirth in the 1930s was no longer as dangerous and exhausting as it had been.

> And when at last the daughters interposed, But are not brain and body affected by training? Does not the wild rabbit differ from the rabbit in the hutch? And must we not, and do we not change this unalterable nature? . . . Then the priests and professors in solemn unison intoned: But childbirth itself, that burden you cannot deny, is laid upon woman alone. Nor could they deny it, nor wish to renounce it. Still they declared, consulting the statistics in books, the time occupied by woman in childbirth is under modern conditions—remember we are in the twentieth century now—only a fraction. (Woolf, *Three Guineas*, 140)

Woolf thus launches a direct assault on one of fascist patriarchy's most carefully shored-up positions, its idealization of maternity as the counterpart to militarism, in order, like Yourcenar, to take apart both matriotism and patriotism: and, furthermore, to come to a new conception of maternity as praxis—as conscious, creative, unalienated labor in the most literal sense.

The emphasis on gender difference marked by women's role in reproduction, together with Woolf's insistence on women's agency in transforming that role, illumine her specifically materialist and feminist treatment of gender. Undoing mind-body dualism, for Woolf, means refusing to cede either to fascism's biological determinism, or to liberalism's abstract rationalism. Instead, Woolf wants to undermine patriarchal narratives of difference that use allegedly natural distinctions between the sexes to demonstrate women's intellectual or moral inferiority to men, while at the same time reinscribing a feminist conception of difference that would valorize and utilize those distinctions where they might be of benefit to women or society as a whole. As Auden writes in the poem quoted at the beginning of this chapter, "boys and girls," while perhaps "equal to be" under a more egalitarian political dispensation, are nonetheless "different still"; where Auden celebrates the erotic dimension of this difference, Woolf emphasizes its value to a politics of transformation.

It is not finally of significance to that politics whether gender difference is "innate or accidental" (Woolf, *Three Guineas*, 6). History and biology operate reciprocally on one another, for the difference of women's bodies is material, and yet "history is not without its effect upon mind and body" (Woolf, *Three Guineas*, 9). Difference, then, emerges at the intersection of biology, culture, and history. What is important for Woolf is, first, the recognition that gender differences need not motivate a hostile discrimination. On the contrary, Woolf claims, a fuller appreciation of the differences between the sexes might encourage respect and communication between them: "If it were possible not only for each sex to ascertain what laws hold good in its own case, and to respect each other's laws; but also to share the results of those discoveries, it might be possible for each sex to develop fully and improve in quality without surrendering its special characteristics" (Woolf, *Three Guineas*, 184–85n42).

Where difference is pernicious, of course—as in the case of men's greater tendency toward violence—it is worthwhile for men to try to overcome the "laws" of their sex: "a very strong movement is on foot towards emancipating man from the old 'natural and eternal law' that man is essentially a fighter; witness the growth of pacifism among the male sex today." In short, Woolf concludes dryly, when the future of life on earth is at stake, "some alteration in the hereditary constitution may be worth attempting" (Woolf, *Three Guineas*, 186–87n48). Women, on the other hand, are advised to maintain their marginality and their detachment from masculinist institutions. Woolf realizes that hegemonic institutions require the manufactured consent of and even token participation by members of classes marginal to those institutions. While she wavers on the question of the degree to which biological sex determines behavior, she understands that any individual may participate in social formations largely dominated by the other gender and worries therefore that women who join patriarchal institutions will be assimilated into them rather than changing them. What women must do instead is to work first within their own gender/class, to form their own Outsiders' Society in order "to defend culture and intellectual liberty by defending our own culture and our own intellectual liberty" (Woolf, *Three Guineas*, 88). Woolf's model of nationalism, which takes a specific love of place as the starting point for a love of humankind, informs this model of gender politics, which takes solidarity with a specific gender/class as the starting point for a broader politics of emancipation.

The goal of such a politics, Woolf makes clear, is not separatism in any rigorous sense. But though she can envision coalitions between the sexes, "men and women working together for the same cause" (Woolf, *Three Guineas*, 102), she does not want women subordinating their own interests to masculinist politics. Instead, she finally outmaneuvers H. G. Wells by arguing that it is not women who should join men's antifascist struggle, but men who should join women's. The antifascist cause represents, for Woolf, the fight against all forms of discrimination; she names fascism as that which, while stemming from the material oppression of women, has developed into a system of oppressive hierarchical relations that demands the concerted response of all subaltern classes.

> The daughters of educated men who were called, to their resentment, "feminists" were in fact the advance guard of your own movement. They were fighting the same enemy that you are fighting and for the same reasons. They were fighting the tyranny of the patriarchal state as you are fighting the tyranny of the Fascist state. . . . Abroad the monster has come more openly to the surface. There is no mistaking him there. He has widened his scope. He is interfering now with your liberty; he is dictating how you shall live; he is making distinctions not merely between the sexes, but between the races. You are feeling in your own person what your mothers felt when they were shut out, when they were shut up, because they were women. Now you are being shut out, you are being shut up, because you are Jews, because you are democrats, because of race, because of religion. (Woolf, *Three Guineas*, 102–3)

This strategy allows both for intersections between women as a gender/class and other subaltern classes, and for certain differences within the class of women. The first time Woolf uses the word "outsider," for instance, it is to refer to a woman who has not been to college, as distinguished not from a man, but from a woman who has had that privilege (Woolf, *Three Guineas*, 31). By the end of the text she describes a progressive nineteenth-century school as an "outsiders' school" because it admitted both sexes, members of different socioeconomic classes, and Jews.

Woolf displays, however, a certain inconsistency about the definition of the outsider that reflects an ambivalence in her attitudes toward class and toward the role of class politics in her own antifascist feminism. The Outsiders' Society is defined both as a sort of "coalition of the marginal" and as a group of "educated men's daughters working in their own class—how indeed can they work in any other?—and by their own methods for liberty, equality and peace" (Woolf, *Three Guineas*, 106). This movement from the specific to the general is not always philosophically coherent, unlike her movement from love of country to love of humanity. Instead, Woolf seems to waver between insisting, on the one hand, that the text is only addressed to other women of her own class, and, on the other hand, championing the notion of women as an international class, whose oppression *qua* women gives them common ground with workers.

Queenie Leavis was perhaps not entirely unjustified in criticizing Woolf for building a universal theory on the very particular, and relatively privileged, case of bourgeois women; it has been one of the most common complaints lodged against *Three Guineas* ever since, not just by anti-Bloomsbury Leavisites but also by socialist feminists. The history of the text's composition, which helps to explain its innovative strategies for challenging fascism, may also account for its lacunae as a work of materialist feminist theory. Woolf's diaries indicate that *Three Guineas*, which was originally called "On Being Despised," was conceived in the early 1930s as a feminist pamphlet on women in the professions, not as an antifascist work. As the decade wore on, the connection between sexism and fascism became more apparent to her, and the broader concern with attacking fascism's hydra-headed manifestations in the spheres of culture and sexuality became more central to her text. Hence *Three Guineas*' somewhat uneven development, from a manifesto for the daughters of educated men to a work of antifascist theory. Woolf's interest was indeed, initially, in the concerns of quite a narrow class of women; a more radical analysis expanded from the original problem of the material inequality of middle-class women, but retained it as its *causa prima*.

This arguably skewed perspective on the relation between gender and class privileges and oppressions leads Woolf to claim, for example, that the daughters of educated men constitute the least influential and most oppressed of all classes, since the State does not even rely on their labor, as it does on that of working women (Woolf, *Three Guineas*, 13). Not surprisingly, Woolf's analysis seemed flawed to at least some working women, like Agnes Smith, who wrote to her that she "felt Woolf had ignored the fact that the daughter of the workingman not only faced the same problems of family dominance and subservience at work as the daughter of the educated man but, being forced to work no matter what the job, faced them in greater degree" (Silver, 268).* Woolf's response has been lost, but her biographer Quentin Bell writes that "Virginia replied that *Three Guineas* had been explicitly addressed to women in a more fortunate social position" (Bell, 205), an answer that begs the question of the degree to which Woolf universalizes the experience and oppression of middle-class women.

Woolf was not entirely unaware of this problem. In a long footnote, she notes her aversion to "slumming," to the liberal or left-wing bourgeois who wears "pro-proletarian spectacles" and claims to understand or identify with the oppression of the working classes. The note is worth quoting at length for what it reveals, both of one of Woolf's passionately held convictions and of her inconsistency and blind spots when discussing class issues. The daughters of educated men, she says,

> can work much more effectively by remaining in their own class and using the methods of that class to improve a class which stands much in need of improvement. If on the other hand the educated (as so often happens) renounce the very qualities which education should have bought—reason, tolerance, knowledge—and play at belonging to the working class and adopting its cause, they merely expose that cause to the ridicule of the educated class, and do nothing to improve their own. But the number of books written by the educated about the

---

*For Smith's depiction of working women's lives, perhaps inspired by *Three Guineas*, see Agnes Smith, *A Worker's View of the Wool Textile Industry*.

> working class would seem to show that the glamour of the working class and the emotional relief afforded by adopting its cause, are today as irresistible to the middle class as the glamour of the aristocracy was twenty years ago.... Meanwhile it would be interesting to know what the true-born working man or woman thinks of the playboys and playgirls of the educated class who adopt the working-class cause without sacrificing middle-class capital, or sharing working-class experience. (Woolf, *Three Guineas*, 177n13)

Woolf apparently does not recognize herself in this description, perhaps because she did not consider herself a member of the "educated class": her focus on a university education and the right to earn a wage as the only measures of emancipation precludes her recognition of her own advantages over working men and women and prevents her from developing her economic analysis fully. She dismisses, for example, the larger question of the exploitation involved in wage labor per se, saying simply that "if... you object that to depend upon a profession is only another form of slavery, you will admit from your own experience that to depend upon a profession is a less odious form of slavery than to depend upon a father" (Woolf, *Three Guineas*, 16).

The theorists of the Frankfurt School claimed that the forms of exploitation particular to capitalism constitute a specific historical instantiation of domination, a mode of human relations intrinsic to Western civilization. In contrast, Woolf fails to consider any forms of gender discrimination other than those specific to bourgeois women under capitalism, and yet traces all other forms of oppression—racism, colonialism, anti-Semitism—to this single and historically recent manifestation of domination. She does not explain why, if economic discrimination against women is at the root of all other oppression, and the right of women to earn a living has been won, oppression has not simply come to an end.

Woolf's dilemma was, as she herself admitted, that in trying to move from "the private house" into "the public world" she was trapped "between the devil and the deep sea." Women can only be freed from private patriarchal institutions through some participation in public patriarchal institutions, like higher education and the professions. Of these, however, there seems no doubt that Woolf felt that the institutions of capital were the more dangerous. We note that the question of racism enters only into her discussion of the professions, not of education; and while the second guinea, for the women's college, has no strings attached to it, the conditions under which she agrees to donate the third guinea, to help women in the professions, are very stringent. The choice between the patriarchal system of which she is a victim and the capitalist system of which she may, Woolf fears, eventually become the champion is, she fully acknowledges, "a choice of evils" (Woolf, *Three Guineas*, 67, 74). She chose, with great reluctance and many precautions, to pursue some of the privileges of class as the only way for her and other women to free themselves from the constraints of gender.

This ambivalence about class may also have contributed to the vicissitudes of Woolf's relations with the Auden group, whose antifascist political and aesthetic project closely corresponded to hers in the 1930s. In addition to Stephen Spender, several of the other members of Auden's circle—Cecil Day Lewis, Isherwood, John Lehmann, and Louis MacNeice—became Woolf's friends, antagonists, coworkers, rivals, protégés, and comrades-in-arms during the last decade of her life. Recent accounts of that relationship have frequently relied on Woolf's essay "The Leaning Tower," a lecture delivered to the Workers' Educational Association in 1940, in which Woolf took issue with the younger writers' approach to literature and politics. Contemporary critics have, for the most part, unquestioningly accepted and even exaggerated Woolf's criticisms of the Auden Generation in that piece, accepting at face value the harshness of her attack, a bitterness which is neither justified by more careful readings of their work nor expressed in her personal relations with the group.

Shari Benstock and Quentin Bell, for example, both make the unfounded claim that Woolf attacked the group for "refusing to acknowledge their own privileged place in the social scheme," for being blind "to the effects of class and education," whereas Woolf's point in "The Leaning Tower" was exactly the opposite one—that they were *too* conscious of their privilege (see Benstock, *Women*, 408; Bell, 219). It is likely, indeed, that what particularly antagonized Woolf was the group's insistence on their own class privilege and their efforts to reconcile their bourgeois upbringing and their radical politics. She seems unable, in her essay, to interpret their politics as anything other than hypocrisy; and this I think is not in spite of, but precisely because of the fact that as left-wing bourgeois artists they were engaged in a political project very similar to hers, but approached it with an honesty about their own class status that she did not share and could not bear to be confronted with.

We should treat with some caution as well Benstock's assertion that, despite their efforts to differentiate themselves from "the presumed elitism of early Modernism," the Auden Generation produced heavily encoded coterie literature that reproduced that elitism, as well as the misogyny of the older men modernists. Marcus has also argued, with reference to the older men in Woolf's sphere, that, unlike "homosexuals of more vulnerable classes," the men of Bloomsbury were not "the natural allies of women, fellow outsiders" (Marcus, *Languages*, 76). The younger men, those in Auden's group, were certainly not the "natural allies" of women either, any more than Woolf was the "natural ally," by virtue of her own lesbian inclinations, of male homosexuals of any class. But then there is no such thing as a "natural" alliance: all communities are imagined. And I would argue that both the Auden Generation and Woolf were beginning in the 1930s to imagine the horizons of a political community in which they might find themselves united by a common commitment to the struggle against fascism in all its forms.

The evidence of biography is that, despite some of their clashes in print, Woolf and the members of the Auden group did in fact understand themselves to be allies in that struggle. Bell says that Woolf's "relationship with the anti-Fascist poets was, on the whole, easy, friendly and cordially appreciative. They, knowing her, must also have known that . . . her attitude to politics was of a kind that they found sympathetic" (Bell, 186). They also defended one another both publicly and privately. In his later years Isherwood recorded retrospectively his awestruck admiration for Woolf (while also admitting that as an insecure budding writer he had "sometimes used Virginia as an enemy image of the ivory-tower intellectual," just as she used him) (Isherwood, *Christopher*, 114). Spender published a strong defense of Woolf in the *Spectator*, in response to *Men Without Art*, Wyndham Lewis's scathing attack on Bloomsbury (see Spender, "One Way Song"). For her part, Woolf approved of Spender's *Destructive Element*, one of his treatises on socialist aesthetics. After reading it in 1935, Woolf indicated in a diary entry her sense that she and Spender were engaged in the same political and aesthetic project, though they approached it with the different perspectives created by sex and age:

> It has considerable swing & fluency; & some general ideas; but peters out in the usual litter of an undergraduates table. Wants to get everything in & report and answer all the chatter. But I want to investigate certain questions: why do I always fight shy of my contemporaries? What is really the woman's angle? . . . But I admire Stephen for trying to grapple with these problems. . . . And—there are incessant conversations—Mussolini, Hitler, Macdonald. All these people incessantly arriving at Croydon, arriving at Berlin, Moscow, Rome; & flying off again—while Stephen & I think how to improve the world. (Woolf, *Diary*, 4: 303)

"Improving the world," in the face of the rise of fascism and the constant threat of world war: such was their common end, and to a certain extent they agreed on the means to achieve it.

The Auden group were, like Woolf, part of that revisionist tendency I have associated particularly with Reich and the Frankfurt School. Some have characterized the left poets as essentially liberal, rather than "communist," a view that has been encouraged by the tendency of the members of the group themselves to disavow Marxism after World War II, as did some members of the Frankfurt School (see Hynes, 300–301). Yet the Auden group and Frankfurt School stood, like Woolf, in a long tradition of socialists who have attempted to combine "the best of the Enlightenment legacy," a commitment to rationality, tolerance, and egalitarianism, with the Marxist insight that the material oppression of subaltern classes has excluded most human beings from that legacy. They were committed to the achievement of both negative, or liberal, and positive freedoms, recognizing that the "formal" freedoms are necessary though insufficient to guarantee an emancipated society, and that to suppress them in the name of socialism, as was then being done in the Soviet Union, could only reproduce the Enlightenment's structures of domination without providing any means of critiquing them. While such "liberal" values were discounted by the "communist" (i.e., Stalinist or orthodox) Left of the period, they are perfectly compatible with a genuine commitment to a materialist analysis of property relations.

In *Forward from Liberalism*, for example, Spender argued that liberal democracies had a choice between genuine democracy and liberal economics. They could ally themselves with fascism in order to preserve bourgeois privilege, or they could admit that communism was the "logical conclusion" of a fulfilled liberalism, that "whatever is said, liberal democracy contains the idea of economic democracy, and there is still time in which to make this idea real" (Spender, *Forward*, 121, 280). Woolf, too, insisted that in order to be radically fulfilled liberal democracy must be examined for its lacunae, its specific historical failings. In one passage of *Three Guineas* she describes the goals of her male interlocutor's peace society, with which she also agrees, and which are in essence the traditional goals of liberal democracy: "What then are the aims of your society? To prevent war, of course. And by what means? Broadly speaking, by protecting the rights of the individual; by opposing dictatorship; by ensuring the democratic ideals of equal opportunity for all" (Woolf, *Three Guineas*, 100). But Woolf also distinguishes herself from her male correspondent, and by implication from the whole tradition of male-dominated liberalism, by reminding him incessantly that, in the words of one critic, "since the days of Aristotle the notion of democracy had been able to coexist very comfortably with complete subordination of women" (Black, 191–92).

If Woolf's personal insights into the failings of liberalism were motivated by her sensitivity to gender politics, the Auden Generation's were, in several cases, motivated by their consciousness of the politics of sexuality. Like Woolf, all of the members of the Auden group were attracted to radical politics in the 1930s by their desire for social justice, a loathing for the hypocrisy and oppressiveness of their own class, and the fear, rapidly becoming a certainty, that the institutional structures of liberal capitalist democracy had been and would be powerless to prevent the rise of international fascism. But some of them had, in addition, a more personal reason for their deep alienation from bourgeois patriarchy, in the knowledge that patriarchal institutions threatened their sexual and love relationships with other men with legal interdiction and social scandal, and that their privilege as bourgeois men was entirely contingent on their willingness to conceal this aspect of their lives.

Benstock and others have described the political rhetoric of the Auden Generation's work as a "code" for homosexuality: "W. H. Auden, Christopher Isherwood, and Stephen Spender developed poetic styles that simultaneously mapped and masked homosexuality. . . . Their writing was indeed subversive, as commentators were quick to perceive, but it was subversive in ways that eluded readers who accepted the coded political rhetoric at face value" (Benstock, *Women*, 398). But a richer interpretation is that, rather than being a simple mask or code for the private experiences of the body, the Auden Generation's radical political rhetoric was deeply informed by and imbricated with their knowledge that those experiences constituted an expression of disloyalty, indeed of treason, to the civilization they had been raised to rule. Alienated by the hypocrisy of the ruling-class values that permitted almost any degree of exploitation, deception, or brutality within the confines of institutionalized heterosexuality, but punished love between men with forced labor camps, they perceived themselves either as exiles or as spies, either banished from the *patria*/patriarchy entirely or admitted to it only under false pretenses, on condition that they never expose "the delicious lie."

The homosexual or bisexual members of the Auden group, then, shared Woolf's understanding that the "private" realm of sexuality is inherently political, and that the regulation of sexual expression is one of the critical functions of patriarchal structures of domination. Like both Woolf and the Frankfurt School, they were interested in the synthesis of Freud and Marx necessary to a radical politics of gender and sexuality. They realized, as she did, that to be disloyal to patriarchy—by flouting the paradigms of compulsory heterosexuality or refusing to participate in other patriarchal institutions—is ultimately to be disloyal to the *patria*, to call into question the terms of one's membership in the national community.

They also understood the ways that fascist nationalism, in particular, both used and disciplined (homo)eroticism. Years later Isherwood remembered the reaction of homosexual men in Berlin when Hitler came to power—the reaction both of those who, like the members of the *Gemeinschaft der Eigenen*, hoped for a renaissance of Hellenic *pæderastia*, and of the others, like the young "Christopher" himself, who realized that open expressions of tenderness and desire between men would constitute an intolerable violation of the authoritarian structures of the National Socialist *Vaterland*:

> No doubt the prudent ones were scared and lying low, while the silly ones fluttered around town exclaiming how sexy the Storm Troopers looked in their uniforms. [Christopher] knew only one pair of homosexual lovers who declared proudly that they were Nazis. Misled by their own erotic vision of a New Sparta, they fondly supposed that Germany was entering an era of military man-love, with all women excluded. They were aware, of course, that Christopher thought them crazy, but they dismissed him with a shrug. How could *he* understand? This wasn't his homeland... No, indeed it wasn't. Christopher had realized that for some time already. But this tragic pair of self-deceivers didn't realize—and wouldn't, until it was too late—that this wasn't their homeland, either. (Isherwood, *Christopher* 124–25; his ellipses)

Women, as Woolf points out, are excluded officially or unofficially from many of the institutions of national life; in England, they had no right to formal participation in its political structures until after World War I, and if they marry a foreigner their affiliation within institutionalized heterosexuality takes precedence over their affiliation with the nation, and they change citizenship. Inversely, the obsession in the poetry and prose of the Auden group with "frontiers," and the concomitant images of visas and passports, reminds us that the "private" world of their relationships with men is constantly intersected and disrupted by the boundaries of the nation, that their national affiliation always takes precedence over love relations that cannot be institutionalized.

Thus, while Auden could contract a *mariage blanc* with Erika Mann, whom he barely knew, in order to provide her with a passport, Isherwood's repeated attempts to obtain a visa or change of citizenship for his German lover failed, exposing the couple to humiliation and eventually to prosecution. Condemned by the institutions of the *patria*/patriarchy to ignominy and duplicity, their sense that the nation had betrayed them, and that their existence constituted a betrayal of the nation, was perhaps even more profound than Woolf's. Auden probably did not exaggerate when he compared Guy Burgess's defection to the Soviet Union to his own adoption of American citizenship, both desperate efforts "to break away from it all" (Maugham, 203); he understood that both of them were spies, agents of another country, owing no more allegiance to the British *patria* than Woolf felt.

The principal ideological divergence between Woolf and the Auden group lay, in fact, neither in their class politics nor in their relation to the patriarchal nation-state, but in their different attitudes toward the use of violence. It has often been assumed, perhaps because Woolf herself believed it, that this disagreement was based in gender difference, in the propensity of men for warfare. But Woolf also admitted that it had at least as much to do with a generational difference: many men in her circles had been radical pacifists for years and were involved in, even founders of, organizations like the Peace Pledge Union and the League of Nations Society.* Woolf was certainly not the only intellectual of the 1930s, of either gender, who believed that writing letters and signing petitions could be an effective political tool in the struggle against fascism and militarism: "Most of those who joined the Peace Pledge

---

* See her memoir of Julian Bell, killed in Spain in 1937, in which she asks, "What made him do it? I suppose its a fever in the blood of the younger generation which we can't possibly understand. I have never known anyone of my generation have that feeling about a war" (qtd. in Bell, 258).

Union . . . did so in the belief that if they gathered enough members war would become impossible" (J. Symons, 41).

The younger generation, in contrast, felt that this attitude was outdated and naive, indeed dangerous given the magnitude of the fascist threat and the consequences if it were not averted. In a well-known exchange, Day Lewis responded to Aldous Huxley's pacifist pamphlet *What Are You Going to Do About It?* with a work titled *We Are Not Going to Do Nothing*, a justification of the use of violence under certain circumstances. He believed that at times the conscientious intellectual had to accept what Auden, in his famous poem "Spain 1937," called "guilt in the necessary murder"—a line Auden later amended to read "guilt in the fact of murder," without really managing to change the tone of emotional ambivalence that the poem conveys (see Auden, 210–12).

For although the Auden group came to advocate taking up arms as the only possible hope of stopping Franco, they arrived at that conclusion reluctantly. The Spanish Civil War, after all, was not fought to achieve a proletarian revolution but to stop a fascist one, and so they recognized that that war, and the larger crisis impending in Europe, were likely to create enormous suffering without bringing about anything like a genuinely socialist or democratic society. Furthermore, like Woolf, they yearned for the return of peace, for the private satisfactions of artistic creation or love. They all knew, and regretted, that the times would not allow them to retreat into such private utopian visions; they all felt compelled to answer the conflicts of their day with what they interpreted as *realpolitik*. Woolf writes to her male correspondent at the end of *Three Guineas*:

> Even here, even now your letter tempts us to shut our ears to these little facts, these trivial details, to listen not to the bark of the guns and the bray of the gramophones but to the voices of the poets, answering each other, assuring us of a unity that rubs out divisions as if they were chalk marks only; to discuss with you the capacity of the human spirit to overflow boundaries and make unity out of multiplicity. But that would be to dream—to dream the recurring dream that has haunted the human mind since the beginning of time; the dream of peace, the dream of freedom. But, with the sound of the guns in your ears you

have not asked us to dream. You have not asked us what peace is; you have not asked us how to prevent war. (Woolf, *Three Guineas*, 143)

She continues, "Let us then leave it to the poets to tell us what the dream is"; but the poets too had the sound of guns in their ears, and were forced to respond, to try to imagine how war could be prevented or at least contained. They did not generally favor violence as a means to achieve socialism, any more than Woolf would have; but unlike hers, their version of *realpolitik* suggested that only the use of force could stop fascism, not in the wide ideological sense but in the very concrete form of the fascist armies massing on the Continent. It is still difficult, in good conscience, to say who was right, if any of them were: since, in the event, history proved only that they were all helpless. As Hitler marched across Europe and the Wehrmacht strafed London, it must have seemed that signing petitions, writing pamphlets, and driving ambulances for the International Brigade had been equally futile. Woolf killed herself; and Isherwood and Auden—refusing to fight for a nation that was not their own, against men who had been their lovers—abandoned England for another country.

If I have suggested that the ideological tendency represented by Virginia Woolf, the Auden Generation, and the Frankfurt School was a more adequate or comprehensive response to fascism than Barnes's pessimistic Catholicism or Yourcenar's liberal humanism, it is not, then, because I believe that widespread dissemination and adoption of their ideas could in any literal sense have halted the advance of Europe's fascist regimes. No intellectual group or movement alone could have achieved that in 1938, or at any point in the 1930s. The real struggle for ideological control of Europe had taken place in the previous decade, and indeed in the previous half-century. By 1933 it was already, at least in Italy and Germany, largely a question of consolidating the political power of the fascist parties and leaders; intellectuals, whether antifascist or fascist, were becoming increasingly superfluous.

But in a broader sense the task of the Left in the 1930s was to continue to combat the cultural influence of fascism in countries like England, where the fascist leader Oswald Mosley was still only a provocateur and not a dictator; to offer an analysis of fascism that adequately explained the depth and force of its appeal to wide sectors of the population; and to envision the forms and directions the struggle to improve the world would need to take even if the immediate threat of fascist aggression could be vanquished. This wider project required a critique that would acknowledge that fascism addresses deep inadequacies in liberalism's account of human experience, and that could account for fascism's ability to extend into vast areas of life that had not previously been thought of as political territory. It had to provide not simply an alternative political programme, but an ideological vision that accepted the terms of debate that fascism had laid down and transcended them.

The left intellectuals discussed here embraced many of the same values as liberals like Yourcenar. They generally posited a rational subject, for them necessary as the agent of meaningful political action. They valued ideals of tolerance and democratic egalitarianism, and of personal as well as collective freedom. At the same time they recognized that the reifying tendencies of instrumental reason had produced enormous classes of objectified and dominated beings—workers, colonized peoples, women, animals—and alienated humans from the products of their labor, their own bodies, each other, and the natural world. The history of Western civilization that culminates in capitalism and liberal parliamentary democracy has created the conditions of possibility, both economic and psychological, for fascist domination.

In works like *Three Guineas*, *The Mass Psychology of Fascism*, and *Forward from Liberalism*, the Enlightenment begins to take itself apart. These texts endeavor to replace, within a discourse of rationality, the elements that rationalism in the West has tended to suppress: the mystical, the aesthetic, the sexual. By focusing on the experiences of specific kinds of bodies, for example, Reich, the members of the Auden group, and Woolf put the body back into materialist discourse: thus Reich defends the sexual needs of the workers, while Auden, Spender, and Isherwood inscribe the relationship of male homosexuals to political institutions, and Woolf articulates a materialist theory of maternity, of women's actually existing experiences of pregnancy, childbirth, and motherhood.

These texts represent critical points of engagement in the immanent critique of fascism, a critique that investigates the roots of barbarism in its own civilization. Woolf felt that few of her contemporaries understood the relevance of her analysis to the political struggles of their age. Yet "if it were taken seriously enough," a reviewer for the *Times Literary Supplement* wrote in 1938, "this brilliant and searching pamphlet might mark an epoch in the world's history" ("Women in a World of War," 379). And indeed it does: it marks the dawning of the realization that we cannot understand fascism without understanding its broad manifestations in the realms of culture, psychology, and sexuality—a perception that had to wait three decades to be rediscovered by a new generation of cultural critics. If less than a definitive response to the rise of fascist regimes and the threat of imminent war, *Three Guineas* nonetheless adds a vital dimension, in its exploration of fascist gender politics, to our current analyses of fascist ideologies. The question today, as in 1938, is whether we are prepared to take that insight, in its full scope and with all its implications, seriously.

CODA

## Back to the Future

My goal in this book was to examine the relationships between women intellectuals of the interwar period, fascism, and modernity. In so doing, I have raised a number of questions that I hope have been usefully elaborated, if not answered, in the preceding pages: questions about the function of gender, gender roles, and sexuality in the works of Barnes, Yourcenar, and Woolf; about their engagement with themes and images also commonly found in texts by writers identified with fascism; and, thus, more broadly, about the relation between fascist and nonfascist modernity. Here I would like to summarize some of the results of my speculations about these questions.

I have found that the manner of approaching issues of gender and sexuality forms at best a tenuous link between these three women writers. The only significant point of convergence in their treatment of gender, and the thing that differentiates them most sharply from many of their male contemporaries, is not any kind of thematics or politics of Sapphism, as we might expect, but rather their view of the relation between matriotism and patriotism. As we have seen, the responses of Barnes, Yourcenar, and Woolf to fascism coincide at the moment when all three undertake a critique of the sexual politics of fascism, describing fascism as a patriarchal politics, a loyalty to the fathers, and a corresponding contempt for, rejection, or misuse of the mother and maternity.

This can hardly be attributed to any shared beliefs among the three writers about women's or maternal nature: in fact, all of them—Barnes as a skeptic, Yourcenar as a humanist, and Woolf as a materialist—would probably have rejected the idea that women were "by nature" opposed to fascism or even that there was such a thing as "women's nature." Furthermore, when we consider the fact that Woolf was the only one of the three who took the oppression of women as a principal theme of her work, that none of them had children, and that Barnes and Yourcenar manifested a pronounced distaste for childbearing and -rearing, this convergence in their approaches seems rather surprising. For Barnes and Yourcenar at least, the emphasis on childbirth certainly had nothing to do with any sentimentality about the experiences of pregnancy or motherhood, or regret about their own childlessness. Indeed, it may have been the very fact of their childlessness that gave them such a sharply unsentimental, objective awareness of the dangers and difficulties of maternity, and inspired such a vehement rejection of fascist patriarchy's ideological manipulations of that experience.

For each of these three women did choose, in her own manner, to oppose to fascist ideology an image of childbirth, of maternity, or of values associated with the maternal. It is possible that this was because fascism itself took maternity and matriotism as categories essential to its thought and its functioning; it would seem that perhaps the fight against fascism necessitated an engagement with these issues. It is worth reiterating, however, that with a few important exceptions it was rare for men writers, even antifascist men, to choose a similar approach to these problems, or for them to use themes of feminine values or of maternity to defy masculinist values without, at the same time, re-inscribing a regressive conception of women's nature or the maternal instinct. It can be proposed, then, that at least these three women intellectuals responded to the concept of maternity, and fascism's uses of motherhood, in a markedly different way from the majority of their male contemporaries; and that the significance of themes of pregnancy, childbirth, and maternity in modernist writing by women, particularly lesbian and childless women, is a subject that bears further investigation.

In approaching the second question, about the engagement of these writers with cultural discourses they shared with fascist thinkers, I have tried to stress that each employed typically fascist themes and tropes while also departing sharply from fascist rhetoric in some manner. Barnes shares fascism's romantic and decadent influences, particularly its love of ritual, its obsession with death, and its desire to overcome individuality; but she retains a pessimism that negates fascism's specific prescriptions for the "universal malady." Yourcenar displays the elitism, the nostalgia for the past, and the hostility to modernity that inform fascism's most reactionary tendencies. But she also guards a deep commitment to certain Enlightenment values antipathetic to fascism: individualism, rationality, and sexual liberalism. Woolf, like fascism, is concerned with the prostitution of culture, the mediation and commodification of art and sexuality. And she employs typically fascist methodologies as well as a typically fascist vocabulary of purity, irrationality, conspiracy, and "muscularity" in her analysis of commodified culture—but uses them in the service of a rhetoric of emancipation, stressing egalitarianism and the liberation of subaltern classes like women, concepts that are anathema to most fascist thought.

This brings me to my third point, the question of the relation between fascist and nonfascist modernity. It is not a matter of banalizing fascism, or of excusing it, to say that fascist writers and intellectuals—and even fascist ideologues—shared the preoccupations of other writers and movements of the interwar period. It is, rather, a question of admitting that fascism represented not only a brutal response to economic crisis or an appeal to humanity's worst instincts—although it was both—but also a system of ideas, even, one might say, a metaphysics, that addressed widespread desires and fears. Commenting on fascist irrationalism, Berman claims that "irrationality as a refusal of knowledge or an intentional restriction of cognitive capacity is necessarily regressive and a retreat from the best of the Enlightenment legacy, the admonition to use one's mind: *aude sapere*." But, he goes on to say, "the critique of reason that is driven by a genuine discontent with characteristics of modern society—alienated labor, the loss of community, the domination of nature—can hardly be denounced as fascist" (Berman, "German Primitivism," 66). The question Berman elides, however, is whether fascism itself can be "denounced as fascist" for providing such a critique of reason. The discovery that Barnes, Yourcenar, and Woolf all share certain concerns about modernity with fascist writers may not lead us to label them fascists; it ought instead to provoke us to acknowledge that fascism, too, was an answer to the "genuine discontents" of the post-Enlightenment era. We cannot hope to understand the phenomenon, or rather the phenomena, of fascism without taking account of the crucial role played in European culture by the problems to which fascism responded.

Acknowledging this, one theorist has written that "whereas the errors of political fascism were singular, horrific, and unquestionable, it has yet to be determined what constituted the errors of intellectual fascism" (Chang, 32). While I believe that there is still a pressing need to answer this implicit challenge with increasingly detailed investigations of fascist culture and intellectual life, my own analysis suggests that, finally, no single ideological point in the repertoire of "thinking fascism" will be found to be specifically fascist, or singularly erroneous. Even anti-Semitism—which is not, in any case, characteristic of all fascisms—is, as we saw in Chapter 2, organically related to discourses of Semitism that Jews and others used to emancipatory ends. Instead, it is the conjunction, the accumulation, of the ideologemes discussed herein that is more characteristic of the hybridity of intellectual fascism; it is the combination of Barnes's aestheticism, Yourcenar's conservatism, Woolf's rejection of commodified culture, all at once and without the balance provided, in their work, by anti-authoritarian, humanist, or emancipatory impulses. But more important, I would stress that, however we characterize fascist thought, it may still be that the "errors of intellectual fascism" will turn out to lie *not* in any particular philosophical fallacy or theoretical flaw, but very precisely in the alliance fascist intellectuals forged between their various ideological and philosophical tendencies, and an amoral and authoritarian politics: it may be, in other words, that there are no errors of intellectual fascism that are not also, and primarily, political errors.

But such a conclusion is speculative, and probably premature. For the time being, I will end this discussion by considering some implications of the arguments I have made for our own putatively "postfascist" age. It has been suggested with increasing frequency that perhaps, in some very real sense, the Axis lost the battle—World War II—but not the ideological war (see, e.g., Valesio, 183). Most obviously, liberal capitalism and Stalinism both took crucial lessons from fascism in techniques of media manipulation and deployed them with increasing sophistication and effectiveness after World War II. Certainly the members of the Frankfurt School became increasingly pessimistic about the possibility of mobilizing any resistance to the ravages of capital and the State, believing fascist techniques of thought control had so permeated mass culture as to create almost irresistible consensus for domination. Furthermore, the virtual collapse of class-based political movements and organizations in the United States after the war, or the shift in Western Marxism away from a class-centered analysis, could be and have been analyzed as a regressive retreat, an acknowledgment of defeat in the face of the fascist/capitalist onslaught.

But more optimistically, we might point out, for example, that the politics of spectacle developed by fascist regimes has since been used to great effect by media-savvy antiwar demonstrators as well as by the U.S. and Soviet military machines, by AIDS activists as well as Latin American dictators, by the African National Congress as well as the Pepsi-Cola Corporation. Similarly, we might ask whether the liberation movements of the 1960s were not enabled by fascism's "recentering of critical focus on the terrain of the politico-cultural," as well as by the priority fascist thought gave to race, gender, and sexuality—the ontological and epistemological categories that have emerged as the privileged sites of political discourses, both reactionary *and* progressive, in the West in the second half of this century. Paradoxically, it might be argued that it was the need to respond to fascism that allowed antifascist and progressive critiques to move beyond an overly reductive focus on class oppression, and, after the war, to articulate increasingly comprehensive analyses of other forms of domination. If the Axis "won," in this case, it could only be in the sense that it provided the tools for a more effective rebuttal of the ideology it represented.

Today, as in the 1930s, political affiliations and accountability cannot be a question simply of the technologies employed, the vocabulary of explanation exercised, or the categories of thought invoked, but of the uses to which they are put. As one writer has put it, the true heirs of the legacy of fascist erotics are not aficionados of sadomasochism with a taste for Nazi regalia, but the U.S. military officials who scrawled obscene valentines to Saddam Hussein on bombs before dropping them on Iraq (Klotz, 79). The style, methods, and vocabulary—indeed, the very conditions of possibility—of our own antifascist critique are, I have argued, a legacy from fascism; it is not necessarily those influences that ought to concern us. We need instead to be alert to the fascist influence manifested in the institutions, movements, and ideologies that legitimate and eroticize violence; that inscribe any form of domination by certain classes of human beings over others; or that are allied with authoritarian, dictatorial, and patriarchal politics. Whether or not we label such ideologies and institutions "fascist," it is these fundamental questions about the uses and abuses of power, violence, and authority that should concern us as we continue, as we must, thinking fascism.

*Reference Matter*

# Bibliography

This bibliography is by no means an exhaustive listing of the available work on any of the subjects treated; I list here only the works that I have cited or consulted in writing this book. I hope, however, that it will serve to guide interested readers in compiling a more thorough listing.

When listing works originally written in languages other than English, I have generally supplied bibliographical information for the English translation; in cases where I have relied on both the original and a translation, I provide the information for both. In a few cases I have given information only for the text in the original language, either because no translation exists or because I referred only to the original. All translations in the body of the text for which no bibliographical information is supplied are my own.

Abraham, Julie L. " 'Woman, Remember You': Djuna Barnes and History." In *Silence and Power: Djuna Barnes, a Reevaluation*, ed. Mary Lynn Broe, 252–68. Carbondale: Southern Illinois University Press, 1991.

Adamson, Walter L. "Modernism and Fascism: The Politics of Culture in Italy, 1903–1922." *American Historical Review* 95, no. 2 (April 1990): 359–90.

Adorno, Theodor W. *Aesthetic Theory*. London: Routledge and Kegan Paul, 1984.

——. "Freudian Theory and the Pattern of Fascist Propaganda." In *The Essential Frankfurt School Reader*, 118–37. Ed. Andrew Arato and Eike Gebhardt. New York: Continuum, 1982.

Adorno, Theodor, and Max Horkheimer. *Dialectic of Enlightenment*. Trans. John Cumming. New York: Continuum, 1989.

Arendt, Hannah. *Eichmann in Jerusalem*. New York: Penguin Books, 1977.

——. *The Origins of Totalitarianism: Antisemitism, Imperialism, Totalitarianism*. New York: Harcourt Brace Jovanovich, 1979.

Aschheim, Steven E. " 'The Jew Within': The Myth of 'Judaization' in Germany." In *The Jewish Response to German Culture: From the Enlightenment to the Second World War*, ed. Jehuda Reinharz and Walter Schatzberg, 212–41. Hanover, N.H.: University Press of New England, 1985.

Auden, W. H. *The English Auden: Poems, Essays and Dramatic Writings, 1927–1939*. Ed. Edward Mendelson. London: Faber and Faber, 1977.

Barbey d'Aurevilly, Jules. *Le roman contemporain*. Paris: Alphonse Lemerre, 1902.
Barnes, Djuna. *The Antiphon*. London: Faber and Faber, 1958.
———. *I Could Never Be Lonely Without a Husband*. Ed. Alyce Barry. London: Virago Press, 1987.
———. *Ladies Almanack*. 1928. New York: Harper and Row, 1972.
———. *Nightwood*. 1936. New York: New Directions, 1961.
———. *Nightwood*. Typescript. Djuna Barnes Papers. McKeldin Library, University of Maryland, College Park.
Barney, Natalie [Tryphô, pseud.]. *Cinq petits dialogues grecs*. Paris: Éditions de la plume, 1902.
———. *Éparpillements*. Sansot, 1910.
Barrès, Maurice. *Les déracinés*. 1897. Paris: Plon, 1920.
Barron, Stephanie. "Modern Art and Politics in Prewar Germany." In *"Degenerate Art": The Fate of the Avant-Garde in Nazi Germany*, by Stephanie Barron et al., 9–23. Los Angeles: Los Angeles County Museum of Art, 1991.
Baudelaire, Charles. "L'École Païenne." 1851. In *Oeuvres*, vol. 2, ed. Y.-G. Dantec, 419–25. Paris: Pléiade, 1951.
———. "The Painter of Modern Life." 1863. In *The Painter of Modern Life and other Essays*, trans. and ed. Jonathan Mayne. London: Phaidon, 1965.
Beckson, Karl, ed. *Aesthetes and Decadents of the 1890s: An Anthology of British Poetry and Prose*. New York: Vintage Books, 1966.
Bell, Quentin. *Virginia Woolf: A Biography*. San Diego: Harvest–Harcourt Brace Jovanovich, 1972.
Ben-Ghiat, Ruth. "Italian Fascism and the Aesthetics of the 'Third Way.'" *Journal of Contemporary History* 31, no. 2 (April 1996): 293–316.
Benjamin, Jessica, and Anson Rabinbach. Foreword to *Male Bodies: Psychoanalyzing the White Terror*, ix–xxv. Vol. 2 of *Male Fantasies*, by Klaus Theweleit. Trans. Erica Carter and Chris Turner. Minneapolis: University of Minnesota Press, 1989.
Benjamin, Walter. "Eduard Fuchs: Collector and Historian." 1937. In *The Essential Frankfurt School Reader*, ed. Andrew Arato and Eike Gebhardt, 225–53. New York: Continuum, 1982.
———. "The Work of Art in the Age of Mechanical Reproduction." 1936. In *Illuminations*, 217–51. New York: Schocken Books, 1968.
Benstock, Shari. "Expatriate Sapphic Modernism: Entering Literary History." In *Lesbian Texts and Contexts: Radical Revisions*, 183–203. New York: New York University Press, 1990.
———. "Paris Lesbianism and the Politics of Reaction, 1900–1940." In *Hidden from History: Reclaiming the Gay and Lesbian Past*, ed. Martin Duberman, Martha Vicinus, and George Chauncey, Jr., 332–46. New York: NAL-Penguin, 1989.
———. *Women of the Left Bank*. Austin: University of Texas Press, 1986.
Bergonzi, Bernard. *Reading the Thirties: Texts and Contexts*. London: Macmillan, 1978.
Berlin, Isaiah. "Joseph de Maistre and the Origins of Fascism." In *The Crooked Timber of Humanity*, 91–174. London: John Murray, 1990.

Berman, Russell. "German Primitivism / Primitive Germany: The Case of Emil Nolde." In *Fascism, Aesthetics, and Culture*, ed. Richard J. Golsan, 56–66. Hanover, N.H.: University Press of New England, 1992.
———. *The Rise of the Modern German Novel*. Cambridge, Mass.: Harvard University Press, 1986.
———. "The Wandering Z: Reflections on Kaplan's *Reproductions of Banality*." In *Reproductions of Banality*, by Alice Kaplan, xi–xxiii. Minneapolis: University of Minnesota Press, 1986.
Black, Naomi. "Virginia Woolf and the Women's Movement." In *Virginia Woolf: A Feminist Slant*, ed. Jane Marcus, 180–97. Lincoln: University of Nebraska Press, 1983.
Brand, Adolf. "Political Criminals: A Word About the Röhm Case." 1931. In *Male Bonding in Pre-Nazi Germany*, ed. Harry Oosterhuis and Hubert Kennedy, 235–39. New York: Harrington Park Press, 1991.
———. "What We Want." 1925. In *Male Bonding in Pre-Nazi Germany*, ed. Harry Oosterhuis and Hubert Kennedy, 155–66. New York: Harrington Park Press, 1991.
Broe, Mary Lynn, ed. *Silence and Power: Djuna Barnes, a Reevaluation*. Carbondale: Southern Illinois University Press, 1991.
Broe, Mary Lynn, and Angela Ingram, eds. *Women's Writing in Exile*. Chapel Hill: University of North Carolina Press, 1989.
Burke, Carolyn. " 'Accidental Aloofness': Barnes, Loy, and Modernism." In *Silence and Power: Djuna Barnes, a Reevaluation*, ed. Mary Lynn Broe, 67–79. Carbondale: Southern Illinois University Press, 1991.
Burke, Kenneth. "Version, Con-, Per, and In- (Thoughts on Djuna Barnes' Novel *Nightwood*)." In *Language as Symbolic Action*, 240–53. Berkeley: University of California Press, 1966.
Bush, Ronald. Introduction. "Ezra Pound." In *The Gender of Modernism*, ed. Bonnie Kime Scott, 353–59. Bloomington: Indiana University Press, 1990.
Caesaréon [pseud.]. "A Word in Advance to the Better Ones." 1903. In *Homosexuality and Male Bonding in Pre-Nazi Germany*, ed. Harry Oosterhuis and Hubert Kennedy, 93–94. New York: Harrington Park Press, 1991.
Carroll, Berenice. " 'To Crush Him in Our Own Country': The Political Thought of Virginia Woolf." *Feminist Studies* 4 (1978): 99–131.
Carroll, David. "Literary Fascism or the Aestheticizing of Politics: The Case of Robert Brasillach." *New Literary History* 23, no. 3 (Summer 1992): 691–726.
Caserta, Ernesto G. "Croce and Marxism: The Fascist Period." *Italian Quarterly* 28, no. 107 (Winter 1987): 33–45.
Casillo, Robert. "Fascists of the Final Hour: Pound's Italian *Cantos*." In *Fascism, Aesthetics, and Culture*, ed. Richard J. Golsan, 98–127. Hanover, N.H.: University Press of New England, 1992.
———. "Nature, History and Anti-Nature in Ezra Pound's Fascism." *Papers on Language and Literature* 22, no. 3 (Summer 1986): 284–311.
Céline, Louis-Ferdinand. *Bagatelles pour un massacre*. Paris: Éditions Denoël, 1937.
Chang, Heesok. "Fascism and Critical Theory." *Stanford Italian Review* 8, no. 1–2 (1990): 13–33.

Craig, Cairns. *Yeats, Eliot, Pound and the Politics of Poetry*. London: Croom Helm, 1982.
Curry, Lynda. " 'Tom, Take Mercy': Djuna Barnes' Drafts of *The Antiphon*." In *Silence and Power: Djuna Barnes, a Reevaluation*, ed. Mary Lynn Broe, 286–98. Carbondale: Southern Illinois University Press, 1991.
D'Annunzio, Gabriele. *The Child of Pleasure*. 1889. Trans. Georgina Harding; verses trans. Arthur Symons. New York: Howard Fertig, 1990.
———. *The Triumph of Death*. 1894. Trans. Arthur Hornblow. New York: Boni and Liveright, 1923.
Dasenbrock, Reed Way. "Wyndham Lewis's Fascist Imagination and the Fiction of Paranoia." In *Fascism, Aesthetics, and Culture*, ed. Richard J. Golsan, 81–97. Hanover, N.H.: University Press of New England, 1992.
Day Lewis, Cecil. "We're Not Going to Do Nothing." London: Left Review, 1936.
De Grand, Alexander. *Italian Fascism: Its Origins and Development*. Lincoln: University of Nebraska Press, 1982.
De Grazia, Victoria. *How Fascism Ruled Women: Italy, 1922–1945*. Berkeley: University of California Press, 1992.
DeJean, Joan. *Fictions of Sappho 1546–1937*. Chicago: University of Chicago Press, 1989.
DeKoven, Marianne. " 'Excellent Not a Hull House': Gertrude Stein, Jane Addams, and Feminist-Modernist Political Culture." In *Rereading Modernism: New Directions in Feminist Criticism*, ed. Lisa Rado, 321–50. New York: Garland, 1994.
DeSalvo, Louise A. " 'To Make Her Mutton at Sixteen': Rape, Incest and Child Abuse in *The Antiphon*." In *Silence and Power: Djuna Barnes, a Reevaluation*, ed. Mary Lynn Broe, 300–315. Carbondale: Southern Illinois University Press, 1991.
Drieu La Rochelle, Pierre. *Chronique Politique 1934–1942*. Paris: Gallimard, 1943.
Eliot, T. S. "A Commentary." *Criterion* 3, no. 2 (April 1925): 341–44.
———. Introduction to *Nightwood*, by Djuna Barnes, xi–xvii. New York: New Directions, 1961.
———. "Tradition and the Individual Talent." 1919. In *Selected Prose of T. S. Eliot*, ed. Frank Kermode, 37–44. San Diego: Harcourt Brace Jovanovich, 1975.
Engels, Friedrich. "The Origin of the Family, Private Property, and the State." 1884. In *The Marx-Engels Reader*, 2d ed., ed. Robert C. Tucker, 734–59. New York: W. W. Norton, 1978.
Faderman, Lillian. *Surpassing the Love of Men*. New York: William Morrow, 1981.
Farrell, C. Frederick, Jr., and Edith R. Farrell. *Marguerite Yourcenar in Counterpoint*. Lanham, Md.: University Press of America, 1983.
Felski, Rita. "Modernism and Modernity: Engendering Literary History." In *Rereading Modernism: New Directions in Feminist Criticism*, ed. Lisa Rado, 191–208. New York: Garland, 1994.
Field, Andrew. *Djuna*. Austin: University of Texas Press, 1985.
Fletcher, Ian. "Some Aspects of Aestheticism." In *Twilight of Dawn: Studies in*

*English Literature in Transition*, ed. O. M. Brack, Jr., 1–33. Tucson: University of Arizona Press, 1987.
Foucault, Michel. *The History of Sexuality: An Introduction*, trans. Robert Hurley. New York: Vintage Books, 1980.
Frank, Joseph. "Spatial Form in Modern Literature." In *The Widening Gyre: Crisis and Mastery in Modern Literature*, 3–49. New Brunswick, N.J.: Rutgers University Press, 1963.
Freud, Sigmund. "Group Psychology and the Analysis of the Ego." 1921. In *A General Selection from the Works of Sigmund Freud*, ed. John Rickman, 169–209. Garden City, N.Y.: Doubleday, 1957.
Friedländer, Benedict. "Male and Female Culture: A Causal-Historical View." 1906. In *Homosexuality and Male Bonding in Pre-Nazi Germany*, 207–17. Ed. Harry Oosterhuis and Hubert Kennedy. New York: Harrington Park Press, 1991.
Friedländer, Saul. *Reflets du nazisme*. Paris: Éditions du Seuil, 1982.
Friedman, Susan Stanford. "Exile in the American Grain: H.D.'s Diaspora." *Women's Writing in Exile*, ed. Mary Lynn Broe and Angela Ingram, 87–112. Chapel Hill: University of North Carolina Press, 1989.
———. "Modernism of the 'Scattered Remnant': Race and Politics in the Development of H.D.'s Modernist Vision." In *H.D.: Woman and Poet*, ed. Michael King, 91–116. University of Maine at Orono: National Poetry Foundation, 1986.
Fromm, Erich. *Escape from Freedom*. New York: Holt, Rinehart and Winston, 1941.
Gagnier, Regenia. Introduction to *Critical Essays on Oscar Wilde*, ed. Gagnier. New York: G. K. Hall–Maxwell Macmillan International, 1991.
Garmann, Gerburg. "Tragische Heiterkeit und zynische Tragik: Ideologische Gemeinsamkeiten in Ernst Jüngers 'Auf den Marmorklippen' und Marguerite Yourcenars 'Le Coup de Grâce.'" *Germanisch Romanische Monatsschrift* 40, no. 1 (1990): 85–100.
Gättens, Marie-Luise. *Women Writers and Fascism: Reconstructing History*. Gainesville: University Press of Florida, 1995.
Gaudin, Colette. "Marguerite Yourcenar's Prefaces: Genesis as Self-Effacement." *Studies in Twentieth Century Literature* 10, no. 1 (Fall 1985): 31–55.
Gautier, Théophile. Introduction to *Mademoiselle de Maupin*. 1835. Paris: Bibliothèque Charpentier, Eugène Fasquelle, 1922.
Geller, Jay. "Blood Sin: Syphilis and the Construction of Jewish Identity." *faultline* 1 (1992): 21–48.
Gelpi, Albert. *A Coherent Splendor: The American Poetic Renaissance, 1910–1950*. Cambridge, Eng.: Cambridge University Press, 1987.
Gentile, Giovanni. *Che cosa è il fascismo: Discorsi e polemiche*. Florence: Vallecchi, 1925.
Gerstenberger, Donna. "The Radical Narrative of Djuna Barnes's *Nightwood*." In *Breaking the Sequence*, ed. Ellen G. Friedman and Miriam Fuchs, 129–39. Princeton, N.J.: Princeton University Press, 1989.
Gide, André. *Corydon*. 1924. Trans. Richard Howard. New York: Farrar, Straus and Giroux, 1983.

Gilbert, Sandra M., and Susan Gubar. *No Man's Land I: The War of the Words.* 3 vols. New Haven, Conn.: Yale University Press, 1987.

Gilman, Sander L. *Jewish Self-Hatred: Anti-Semitism and the Hidden Language of the Jews.* Baltimore, Md.: Johns Hopkins University Press, 1986.

Gindin, James. "Politics in Contemporary Woolf Criticism." *Modern Language Quarterly* 47, no. 4 (Dec. 1986): 422–32.

Golsan, Richard J., ed. *Fascism, Aesthetics, and Culture.* Hanover, N.H.: University Press of New England, 1992.

Goodstein, E. S. " 'The Most Mendacious Prototypes Have Been Stolen from Life: Femininity and Spectacle in Siegfried Kracauer's Reading of Weimar Mass Culture." *faultline* 1 (1992): 49–67.

Gorman, Kay. "Marguerite Yourcenar's Encounter with a Feminist Critic." *A.U.M.L.A.* 73 (1990): 59–73.

Green, Martin. *Children of the Sun: A Narrative of "Decadence" in England After 1918.* New York: Basic Books, 1976.

Green, Mary Jean. "Toward an Analysis of Fascist Fiction: The Contemptuous Narrator in the Works of Brasillach, Céline and Drieu La Rochelle." *Studies in Twentieth Century Literature* 10, no. 1 (Fall 1985): 81–92.

Gubar, Susan. "Blessings in Disguise: Cross-Dressing as Re-dressing for Female Modernists." *Massachusetts Review* 22, no. 3 (Autumn 1981): 477–508.

———. "Sapphistries." *Signs* 10, no. 1 (Autumn 1984): 43–62.

Guenther, Peter. "Three Days in Munich, July 1937." In *"Degenerate Art": The Fate of the Avant-Garde in Nazi Germany*, by Stephanie Barron et al., 33–43. Los Angeles: Los Angeles County Museum of Art, 1991.

Hamilton, Alastair. *The Appeal of Fascism: A Study of Intellectuals and Fascism 1919–1945.* Dublin: Anthony Blond, 1971.

Hansen, Miriam. "Benjamin, Cinema and Experience." *New German Critique* 40 (Winter 87): 179–224.

Harrison, John R. *The Reactionaries: A Study of the Anti-Democratic Intelligentsia.* New York: Schocken Books, 1966.

Henke, Suzette A. "(En)Gendering Modernism: Virginia Woolf and Djuna Barnes." In *Rereading the New: A Backward Glance at Modernism*, ed. Kevin J. H. Dettmar, 325–41. Ann Arbor: University of Michigan Press, 1992.

Herf, Jeffrey. *Reactionary Modernism: Technology, Culture, and Politics in Weimar and the Third Reich.* Cambridge: Cambridge University Press, 1984.

Hewitt, Andrew. *Fascist Modernism: Aesthetics, Politics, and the Avant-Garde.* Stanford, Calif.: Stanford University Press, 1993.

———. "Fascist Modernism, Futurism, and 'Post-modernity.' " In *Fascism, Aesthetics, and Culture*, ed. Richard J. Golsan, 38–55. Hanover, N.H.: University Press of New England, 1992.

———. "Wyndham Lewis: Fascism, Modernism, and the Politics of Homosexuality." *English Literary History* 60 (1993): 527–44.

Hitler, Adolf. *Mein Kampf.* Trans. Ralph Manheim. London: Hutchinson, 1969. [Orig. pub. as *Mein Kampf.* Munich: Zentralverlag der NSDAP Franz Eher Nachf., 1925–1927.]

Horn, Pierre L. *Marguerite Yourcenar.* Boston: Twayne–G. K. Hall, 1985.

Hussey, Mark, ed. *Virginia Woolf and War.* Syracuse, N.Y.: Syracuse University Press, 1991.

Huysmans, Joris-Karl. *Against Nature*. Trans. Robert Baldick. London: Penguin Books, 1959.
———. *A Rebours*. 1884. Paris: Éditions Fasquelle, 1965.
Hynes, Samuel. *The Auden Generation: Literature and Politics in England in the 1930s*. London: Bodley Head, 1976.
Isherwood, Christopher. *The Berlin Stories*. New York: New Directions, 1935.
———. *Christopher and His Kind*. New York: Farrar, Straus and Giroux, 1976.
———. *Down There on a Visit*. New York: Farrar, Straus and Giroux, 1959.
Jacobs, Deborah F. "Feminist Criticism / Cultural Studies / Modernist Texts: A Manifesto for the '90s." In *Rereading Modernism: New Directions in Feminist Criticism*, ed. Lisa Rado, 273–95. New York: Garland, 1994.
Jay, Martin. *The Dialectical Imagination*. Boston: Little, Brown, 1973.
———. "Postmodern Fascism? Reflections on the Return of the Oppressed." *Tikkun* 8, no. 6 (Nov.–Dec. 1993): 37–41.
Johnston, Judith L. "Marguerite Yourcenar's Sexual Politics in Fiction, 1939." In *Faith of a (Woman) Writer*, ed. Alice Kessler-Harris and William McBrien, 221–28. New York: Greenwood Press, 1988.
Jünger, Ernst. *Der Kampf als inneres Erlebnis*. 1922. Berlin: Mittler, 1928.
Kannenstine, Louis F. *The Art of Djuna Barnes: Duality and Damnation*. New York: New York University Press, 1977.
Kaplan, Alice Yaeger. *Reproductions of Banality*. Minneapolis: University of Minnesota Press, 1986.
Katz, Jonathan. *Gay American History*. New York: Crowell, 1976.
———. *Gay/Lesbian Almanac: A New Documentary*. New York: Harper and Row, 1983.
Kedward, H. R. *Fascism in Western Europe, 1900–45*. Glasgow: Blackie, 1969.
Kent, Kathryn R. " 'Lullaby for a Lady's Lady': Lesbian Identity in *Ladies Almanack*." *Review of Contemporary Fiction* 13, no. 3 (Fall 1993): 89–96.
Klotz, Marcia. "The Question of Fascist Erotics." *faultline* 1 (1992): 69–81.
Lacoue-Labarthe, Philippe, and Jean-Luc Nancy. "The Nazi Myth." Trans. Brian Holmes. *Critical Inquiry* 16 (Winter 1990): 291–312.
Laity, Cassandra. "H.D. and A. C. Swinburne: Decadence and Modernist Women's Writing." *Feminist Studies* 15, no. 3 (Fall 1989): 461–84.
Laqueur, Walter, ed. *Fascism: A Reader's Guide*. Berkeley: University of California Press, 1976.
Leavis, Q. D. "Caterpillars of the Commonwealth Unite!" *Scrutiny* 7, no. 2 (September 1938): 203–14.
Lee, Judith. *"Nightwood*: 'The Sweetest Lie.' " In *Silence and Power: Djuna Barnes, a Reevaluation*, ed. Mary Lynn Broe, 207–18. Carbondale: Southern Illinois University Press, 1991.
Lewis, Wyndham. *Men Without Art*. 1934. Ed. Seamus Cooney. Santa Rosa, Calif.: Black Sparrow Press, 1987.
Louÿs, Pierre. *Les chansons de Bilitis*. 1895. Paris: Gallimard, 1990.
Loy, Mina. "Gertrude Stein." 1924. In *The Last Lunar Baedeker*, ed. Roger L. Conover, 289–99. Highlands, N.C.: Jargon Society, 1982.
Lydon, Mary. "Calling Yourself a Woman: Marguerite Yourcenar and Colette." *Differences* 3, no. 3 (Fall 1991): 26–44.

Lyon, Janet. "Women Demonstrating Modernism." *Discourse* 17, no. 2 (Winter 1994–95): 6–25.
Macciocchi, Maria-Antonietta. "Female Sexuality in Fascist Ideology." *Feminist Review* 1 (1979): 67–82.
Maccoby, Hyam. "The Jew as Anti-Artist: The Anti-Semitism of Ezra Pound." *Midstream* 22, no. 3 (March 1976): 59–71.
Madou, Jean-Pol. "L'art du secret et le discours de l'aveu." In *Marguerite Yourcenar: une écriture de la mémoire*, ed. Daniel Leuwers and Jean-Pierre Castellani. Marseille: Sud, 1990.
Marcus, Jane. "Laughing at Leviticus: *Nightwood* as Woman's Circus Epic." In *Silence and Power: Djuna Barnes, a Reevaluation*, ed. Mary Lynn Broe, 221–50. Carbondale: Southern Illinois University Press, 1991.
——. " 'No More Horses': Virginia Woolf on Art and Propaganda." *Women's Studies* 4 (1977): 265–89.
——. *Virginia Woolf and the Languages of Patriarchy*. Bloomington: Indiana University Press, 1987.
——, ed. *Virginia Woolf: A Feminist Slant*. Lincoln: University of Nebraska Press, 1983.
——, ed. *Virginia Woolf and Bloomsbury: A Centenary Celebration*. London: Macmillan, 1987.
Marcuse, Herbert. *Eros and Civilization*. Boston: Beacon, 1955.
Marks, Elaine. " 'Getting away with Murd(h)er': Author's Preface and Narrator's Text. Reading Marguerite Yourcenar's *Coup de Grâce* 'After Auschwitz.' " *Journal of Narrative Technique* 20, no. 2 (Spring 1990): 210–20.
Martin, Elaine, ed. *Gender, Patriarchy and Fascism in the Third Reich: The Response of Women Writers*. Detroit, Mich.: Wayne State University Press, 1993.
Maugham, Robin. *Escape from the Shadows*. London: Hodder and Stoughton, 1972.
Maurras, Charles. *Enquête sur la monarchie*. 2d ed. Paris: Nouvelle Librairie Nationale, 1909.
——. *Les pièces d'un procès*. Paris: Flammarion, 1927.
——. *Pour un jeune français: mémorial en réponse à un questionnaire*. Paris: Amiot-Dumont, 1949.
Meyer, Michael. "A Musical Facade for the Third Reich." In *"Degenerate Art": The Fate of the Avant-Garde in Nazi Germany*, by Stephanie Barron et al., 171–83. Los Angeles: Los Angeles County Museum of Art, 1991.
Mohler, Armin. "Der Faschistische Stil." In *Von rechts gesehen*, 179–221. Stuttgart: Seewald Verlag, 1974.
Mosse, George. "Beauty Without Sensuality." In *"Degenerate Art": The Fate of the Avant-Garde in Nazi Germany*, by Stephanie Barron et al., 25–31. Los Angeles: Los Angeles County Museum of Art, 1991.
——. *Nationalism and Sexuality: Respectability and Abnormal Sexuality in Modern Europe*. New York: Howard Fertig, 1985.
Mudge, Bradford K. "Burning Down the House: Sara Coleridge, Virginia Woolf, and the Politics of Literary Revision." *Tulsa Studies in Women's Literature* 5, no. 2 (Fall 1986): 229–50. [Rev. and rpt. as "Exiled as Exiler: Sara Coleridge, Virginia Woolf, and the Politics of Literary Revision." In *Women's*

*Writing in Exile*, ed. Mary Lynn Broe and Angela Ingram, 200–223. Chapel Hill: University of North Carolina Press, 1989.]

Mussolini, Benito. "The Political and Social Doctrine of Fascism." *International Conciliation* 306 (January 1935): 5–17.

Nadeau, Robert L. "*Nightwood* and the Freudian Unconscious." *International Fiction Review* 2 (1975): 159–63.

Nolte, Ernst. *Three Faces of Fascism: Action Française, Italian Fascism, National Socialism.* Trans. Leila Vennewitz. New York: Holt, Rinehart and Winston, 1965.

Nordau, Max. *Degeneration.* Translation of 2d German ed. New York: D. Appleton, 1895.

Oosterhuis, Harry, ed. *Homosexuality and Male Bonding in Pre-Nazi Germany.* Trans. Hubert Kennedy. New York: Harrington Park Press, 1991.

Pearlman, Daniel. "The Anti-Semitism of Ezra Pound." *Wisconsin Studies in Contemporary Literature* 22, no. 1 (Winter 1981): 104–15.

Pellizzi, Camillo. *Problemi e realtà del fascismo.* Florence: Vallecchi, 1924.

Pickering-Iazzi, Robin, ed. *Mothers of Invention: Women, Italian Fascism, and Culture.* Minneapolis: University of Minnesota Press, 1995.

Pochoda, Elizabeth. "Style's Hoax: A Reading of Djuna Barnes's *Nightwood.*" *Twentieth Century Literature* 22, no. 2 (May 1976): 179–91.

Praz, Mario. *The Romantic Agony.* 1933. Trans. Angus Davidson. London: Collins-Fontana, 1962.

Proust, Marcel. *Sodome et Gomorrhe.* 1921–22. Paris: Gallimard, 1985.

Prouteau, Marie-Hélène. "*Denier du rêve* de Marguerite Yourcenar: Comparaison des versions de 1934 et de 1959." *Bulletin de la société internationale d'études yourcenariennes* 13 (June 1994): 47–62.

Rado, Lisa. "Lost and Found: Remembering Modernism, Rethinking Feminism." In *Rereading Modernism: New Directions in Feminist Criticism*, ed. Lisa Rado, 3–19. New York: Garland, 1994.

Rahv, Philip. "The Taste of Nothing." *New Masses* 23, no. 7 (May 4, 1937): 32–3.

Rathenau, Walter [W. Hartenau, pseud.] "Höre Israel!" *Die Zukunft* 18 (1897): 454–62.

Reich, Wilhelm. *The Mass Psychology of Fascism.* 1933. Trans. Vincent R. Carfagno. New York: Farrar, Straus and Giroux, 1970.

Rentschler, Eric. "The Ministry of Emotion: How Nazi Cinema Recast Hollywood." Fascism(s) conference. University of Oregon, Eugene, April 3, 1992.

Restori, Eurica. "Statues et fantômes dans *Denier du rêve.*" In *Marguerite Yourcenar et l'art; l'art de Marguerite Yourcenar.* Tours: Société internationale d'études yourcenariennes, 1990. 121–27.

Retallack, Joan. "One Acts: Early Plays of Djuna Barnes." In *Silence and Power: Djuna Barnes, a Reevaluation*, ed. Mary Lynn Broe, 46–52. Carbondale: Southern Illinois University Press, 1991.

Rich, Adrienne. "Disloyal to Civilization: Feminism, Racism, Gynephobia." In *On Lies, Secrets and Silence: Selected Prose 1966–1978*, 275–310. New York: W. W. Norton, 1979.

Rich, B. Ruby. "From Repressive Tolerance to Erotic Liberation." *Jump Cut* 24/25 (March 1981): 44–50.

Rosbo, Patrick de. *Entretiens radiophoniques avec Marguerite Yourcenar.* Mercure de France, 1972.
Rosenberg, Alfred. *Alfred Rosenberg: Selected Writings.* Ed. Robert Pois. London: Jonathan Cape, 1970.
——. *Blut und Ehre: Ein Kampf für deutsche Wiedergeburt: Reden und Aufsätze von 1919–1933.* Munich: Zentralverlag der NSDAP, Franz Eher Nachf., 1939.
——. "Der Jude." 1918. In *Schriften aus den Jahren, 1917–1921.* Munich, 1943.
Ruthven, K. K. "Ezra's Appropriations." *Times Literary Supplement,* November 20–26, 1987: 1278.
Saalmann, Dieter. "Fascism and Aesthetics: Joseph Goebbel's Novel *Michael: A German Fate Through the Pages of a Diary.*" *Orbis Litterarum* 41, no. 1 (1986): 213–28.
Savigneau, Josyane. *Marguerite Yourcenar: Inventing a Life.* Trans. Joan E. Howard. Chicago: University of Chicago Press, 1993. [Orig. pub. as *Marguerite Yourcenar: L'invention d'une vie.* Paris: Gallimard, 1990.]
Schmitt, Carl. *The Concept of the Political.* Trans. George Schwab. New Brunswick, N.J.: Rutgers University Press, 1976. [Orig. pub. as *Der Begriff des Politischen.* Berlin: Duncker and Humblot, 1932.]
Schnapp, Jeffrey T. "18 BL: Fascist Mass Spectacle." *Representations* 43 (Summer 1993): 89–125.
——. "Epic Demonstrations: Fascist Modernity and the 1932 Exhibition of the Fascist Revolution." In *Fascism, Aesthetics, and Culture,* ed. Richard J. Golsan, 1–37. Hanover, N.H.: University Press of New England, 1992.
——. "Fascinating Fascism." *Journal of Contemporary History* 31, no. 2 (April 1996): 235–44.
Schneider, Karen. "Of Two Minds: Woolf, the War and *Between the Acts.*" *Journal of Modern Literature* 16, no. 1 (Summer 1989): 93–112.
Schnurer, Herman. "The Intellectual Sources of French Fascism." *Antioch Review* 1 (1941): 35–49.
Scott, Bonnie Kime. *Refiguring Modernism.* 2 vols. Bloomington: Indiana University Press, 1995.
——, ed. *The Gender of Modernism.* Bloomington: Indiana University Press, 1990.
Scullion, Rosemarie. "Style, Subversion, Modernity: Louis-Ferdinand Céline's Anti-Semitic Pamphlets." In *Fascism, Aesthetics, and Culture,* ed. Richard J. Golsan, 179–97. Hanover, N.H.: University Press of New England, 1992.
Shaw, George Bernard. "The Sanity of Art." 1895/1907. In *Major Critical Essays,* 281–332. London: Constable; rep. St. Clair Shores, Mich: Scholarly Press, 1978.
Silver, Brenda R. "*Three Guineas* Before and After: Further Answers to Correspondents." In *Virginia Woolf: A Feminist Slant,* ed. Jane Marcus, 254–76. Lincoln and London: University of Nebraska Press, 1983.
Sinclair, May. "The Poems of 'H.D.' " 1927. In *The Gender of Modernism,* ed. Bonnie Kime Scott. Bloomington: Indiana University Press, 1990. 453–67.
Sitwell, Osbert. "Fiume and d'Annunzio." 1925. In *Discursions on Travel, Art and Life.* New York: George Duran Company, [1925]. 217–41.

Smith, Catherine F. "*Three Guineas*: Virginia Woolf's Prophecy." In *Virginia Woolf and Bloomsbury: A Centenary Celebration*, ed. Jane Marcus, 225–41. London: Macmillan, 1987.
Sontag, Susan. "Fascinating Fascism." In *Under the Sign of Saturn*, 71–105. New York: Farrar, Straus and Giroux, 1980.
———. "Notes on 'Camp.'" In *Against Interpretation*, 275–92. New York: Delta-Dell, 1966.
Soucy, Robert. *Fascism in France: The Case of Maurice Barrès*. Berkeley: University of California Press, 1972.
———. *French Fascism: The First Wave, 1924–1933*. New Haven, Conn.: Yale University Press, 1986.
Spackman, Barbara. *Decadent Genealogies: The Rhetoric of Sickness from Baudelaire to D'Annunzio*. Ithaca, N.Y.: Cornell University Press, 1989.
———. "The Fascist Rhetoric of Virility." *Stanford Italian Review* 8, no. 1–2 (1990): 81–101.
Spender, Stephen. *The Destructive Element*. London: Jonathan Cape, 1935.
———. *Forward from Liberalism*. New York: Random House, 1937.
———. "One Way Song." *Spectator* (October 19, 1934): 574–76.
———. *World Within World*. London: Reader's Union, 1953.
Spengler, Oswald. *The Decline of the West*. 2 vols. Trans. Charles Francis Atkinson. New York: Alfred A. Knopf, 1926. [Orig. pub. as *Der Untergang des Abendlandes*. 1918. Munich: Beck, 1920–1923.]
Steakley, James D. *The Homosexual Emancipation Movement in Germany*. New York: Arno Press, 1975.
Sternhell, Zeev. "Fascist Ideology." In *Fascism: A Reader's Guide*, ed. Walter Laqueur, 315–76. Berkeley: University of California Press, 1976.
———. *Maurice Barrès et le nationalisme français*. Paris: Presses de la fondation nationale des sciences politiques, 1972.
———. *Neither Right Nor Left: Fascist Ideology in France*. Trans. David Maisel. Princeton, N.J.: Princeton University Press, 1986.
Stillman, Linda K. "Marguerite Yourcenar and the Phallacy of Indifference." *Studies in Twentieth Century Literature* 9, no. 2 (Spring 1985): 261–77.
Stimpson, Catharine. Afterword. *Silence and Power: Djuna Barnes, a Reevaluation*, ed. Mary Lynn Broe, 370–73. Carbondale: Southern Illinois University Press, 1991.
Surette, Leon. "Pound, Postmodernism, and Fascism." *University of Toronto Quarterly* 59, no. 2 (Winter 1989–90): 334–55.
Symonds, John Addington. *A Problem in Greek Ethics: Being an Inquiry into the Phenomenon of Sexual Inversion Addressed Especially to Medical Psychologists and Jurists*. 1873. London: Areopagitica Society, 1908.
Symons, Arthur. "A Note on George Meredith." 1897. *Studies in Prose and Verse*, 143–51. London: J. M. Dent, 1904.
Symons, Julian. *The Thirties: A Dream Revolved*. London: Cresset Press, 1960.
Theweleit, Klaus. *Male Fantasies*. 2 vols. Trans. Erica Carter and Chris Turner. Minneapolis: University of Minnesota Press, 1989.
Transue, Pamela J. *Virginia Woolf and the Politics of Style*. Albany, N.Y.: State University of New York Press, 1986.

Tucker, William R. "Politics and Aesthetics: The Fascism of Robert Brasillach." *Western Political Quarterly* 15, no. 4 (December 1962): 605–17.

Valesio, Paolo. "The Beautiful Lie: Heroic Individuality and Fascism." In *Reconstructing Individualism: Autonomy, Individuality, and the Self in Western Thought*, ed. Thomas C. Heller, Morton Sosna, and David E. Wellbery. Stanford, Calif.: Stanford University Press, 1986. 163–84.

Van der Starre, Evert. "*Denier du rêve* et *Rendre à César.*" *Recherches sur l'œuvre de Marguerite Yourcenar: Cahiers de recherches des instituts neerlandais de langue et littérature françaises* 8 (1983): 50–79. Ed. Henk Hillenaar. Département de littérature française, Université de Leyde.

Waldecke, St. Ch. [pseud.]. "Eros in the German Youth Movement." 1925. In *Homosexuality and Male Bonding in Pre-Nazi Germany*, ed. Harry Oosterhuis and Hubert Kennedy, 199–206. New York: Harrington Park Press, 1991.

Wasserfallen, François. "D'un art protoromanesque à un art romanesque: l'étape *Denier du rêve*." In *Marguerite Yourcenar et l'art; l'art de Marguerite Yourcenar*, 309–18. Tours: Société internationale d'études yourcenariennes, 1990.

Weber, Eugen. *Varieties of Fascism*. New York: D. Van Nostrand, 1964.

Weininger, Otto. *Sex and Character*. Trans. of 6th German ed. London: William Heinemann, 1908. [Orig. pub. as *Geschlecht und Charakter: eine prinzipielle Untersuchung*. Vienna: Wilhelm Braumüller, 1903.]

Wilde, Oscar. *The Picture of Dorian Gray*. 1891. Ed. Peter Ackroyd. London: Penguin Books, 1985.

Winckelmann, Johan Joachim. *Histoire de l'art chez les anciens*. Trans. Huber. Paris: Barrois, Savoye, 1789.

———. *History of Ancient Art*. 1764. 4 vols. Trans. G. Henry Lodge. New York: Frederick Ungar, 1968.

Wolin, Richard, ed. *The Heidegger Controversy: A Critical Reader*. 1991. Cambridge, Mass.: MIT Press, 1993.

"Women in a World of War: A 'Society of Outsiders.'" *Times Literary Supplement* 1896 (June 4, 1938): 379.

Woolf, Leonard. *Quack, Quack!* London: Hogarth Press, 1937.

Woolf, S. J., ed. *European Fascism*. New York: Random House, 1968.

Woolf, Virginia. *The Common Reader*. 1925. Ed. Andrew McNeillie. San Diego, Calif.: Harcourt Brace Jovanovich, 1984.

———. *The Diary of Virginia Woolf*. 1915–1941. 5 vols. Ed. Anne Olivier Bell. San Diego, Calif.: Harcourt Brace Jovanovich, 1977–1984.

———. "The Leaning Tower." 1940. In *The Moment and Other Essays*, 128–54. San Diego: Harcourt Brace Jovanovich, 1948.

———. *A Room of One's Own*. 1929. San Diego, Calif.: Harvest–Harcourt Brace Jovanovich, 1981.

———. *Three Guineas*. 1938. San Diego, Calif.: Harcourt Brace Jovanovich, 1966.

———. *The Years*. 1937. San Diego, Calif.: Harcourt Brace Jovanovich, 1965.

Yourcenar, Marguerite. *Alexis / Le coup de grâce*. 1929/1939. Paris: Gallimard-Folio, 1988.

———. "A quelqu'un qui me demandait si la pensée grecque vaut encore pour nous." 1936. In *En pèlerin et en étranger*, 14–16. Paris: Gallimard, 1989.

———. *Archives du Nord*. 1977. In *Le Labyrinthe du monde*, 309–616. Paris: Gallimard, 1990.

———. *A Coin in Nine Hands*. Trans. Dori Katz. New York: Farrar, Straus and Giroux, 1982.

———. *Dear Departed*. Trans. Maria Louise Ascher. New York: Farrar, Straus and Giroux, 1991. [Orig. pub. as *Souvenirs Pieux*. 1974. In *Le Labyrinthe du monde*. Paris: Gallimard, 1990.]

———. *Denier du rêve*. Paris: Éditions Bernard Grasset, 1934. Rev. 1959; Paris: Gallimard, 1971.

———. "European Diagnosis." In *Marguerite Yourcenar: Inventing a Life*, by Josyane Savigneau, 444–50. Trans. Joan E. Howard. Chicago: University of Chicago Press, 1993. [Orig. pub. as "Diagnostic de l'Europe." 1929. In *Marguerite Yourcenar: L'invention d'une vie* by Josyane Savigneau, 492–98. Paris: Gallimard, 1990.]

———. "L'Express va plus loin avec Marguerite Yourcenar." *L'Express* (February 10–16, 1969): 47–52.

———. *Feux*. 1936. Paris: Gallimard, 1974.

———. "Forces du passé et forces de l'avenir." 1940. In *En pèlerin et en étranger*, 57–62. Paris: Gallimard, 1989.

———. "L'improvisation sur Innsbruck." 1929. In *En pèlerin et en étranger*, 43–54. Paris: Gallimard, 1989.

———. *Mémoires d'Hadrien*. 1951. Paris: Gallimard-Folio, 1974.

———. "An Obscure Man." Ca. 1935. *Two Lives and a Dream*. Trans. Walter Kaiser. New York: Farrar, Straus and Giroux, 1987.

———. *L'Œuvre au Noir*. Paris: Gallimard, 1968.

———. *Quoi? L'Éternité*. 1988. In *Le labyrinthe du monde*, 617–918. Paris: Gallimard, 1990.

———. *With Open Eyes: Conversations with Matthieu Galey*. Trans. Arthur Goldhammer. Boston: Beacon, 1984. [Orig. pub. as *Les yeux ouverts: Entretiens avec Matthieu Galey*. Paris: Le Centurion, 1980.]

Zwerdling, Alex. "*Between the Acts* and the Coming of War." *Novel* 10 (Spring 1977): 220–36.

———. *Virginia Woolf and the Real World*. Berkeley: University of California Press, 1986.

# Index

In this index an "f" after a number indicates a separate reference on the next page, and an "ff" indicates separate references on the next two pages. A continuous discussion over two or more pages is indicated by a span of page numbers, e.g., "57–59." *Passim* is used for a cluster of references in close but not consecutive sequence.

Abraham, Julie, 82
Adorno, Theodor W., 8, 50, 73, 99–102 *passim*, 149n, 158; *Dialectic of Enlightenment*, 148, 149n
Advertising, 102, 158ff, 165
Aestheticism, 32–33, 93, 100, 111, 121, 158ff, 190; and Barnes, Djuna, 43–51, 55f, 76–79 *passim. See also* Art; Decadence; *L'art pour l'art*
Aestheticization of politics, 24, 57, 85, 111, 158ff. *See also* Benjamin, Walter
Anarchism, 21, 34, 108
Anti-Semitism, 23–29 *passim*, 34, 76, 114, 150, 175, 190. *See also* Jews; Judaization; Race; Racism
Arendt, Hannah, 27, 87, 98, 116–23 *passim*, 134; *Eichmann in Jerusalem*, 15, 98, 117–18, 120–22; *Origins of Totalitarianism*, 98, 120, 123

Art, 5, 8–9, 30ff, 58, 85, 102, 111, 134, 189; and aestheticism, 44–50 *passim*, 60f; in *Nightwood*, 67–70 *passim*, 79; and Yourcenar, Marguerite, 116, 123; and Woolf, Virginia, 155, 161–65 *passim. See also* Aestheticism; Decadence; *L'art pour l'art*
Aryan, 28, 37f, 43, 68, 76, 80ff, 120
Auden, W. H., 26, 136, 147, 153, 170, 176–85 *passim*
Auden Generation, 176–85
Authenticity, 38–41 *passim*, 65ff, 78–81 *passim*, 99, 122, 134, 162; and culture, 23ff, 38–39, 86, 98–101 *passim*; and sexuality, 39–40, 164–65; in Yourcenar's work, 104–7 *passim*, 121, 129–34 *passim*
Avant-garde, *see* Modernism
Axis, the, 120, 191f

209

Barbarism, 12, 61, 98, 112–16 *passim*, 134, 138, 154, 186
Barbey d'Aurevilly, Jules, 59–60
Barnes, Djuna, 1f, 7, 26f, 42–85, 143, 155, 184; and fascism, 5–6, 10, 42f, 55, 59, 77, 83–84, 189; and homosexuality, 6, 33, 51–56, 72, 76, 84; and maternity, 7, 130, 167, 187–88; *Ladies Almanack*, 33, 51–55 *passim*, 82; and liberalism, 40, 64, 68ff; and aestheticism, 44, 50–51, 55–56, 80, 190; *The Antiphon*, 82ff, 130, 136; and Yourcenar, Marguerite, 93, 107, 111, 115, 127ff
—*Nightwood*, 1, 6–7, 42ff, 51–57 *passim*, 63–83 *passim*, 87, 105–6, 130, 138f
Barney, Natalie, 47–52 *passim*, 88, 129
Barrès, Maurice, 22, 87, 93f, 99, 114f
Baudelaire, Charles, 44–49 *passim*, 58–62 *passim*
Beardsley, Aubrey, 32, 44n, 50
Belgium, 25, 89, 114
Bell, Julian, 182n
Bell, Quentin, 174–77 *passim*
Benjamin, Jessica, 73
Benjamin, Walter, 13n, 24, 57, 102, 111, 154, 161ff. *See also* Aestheticization of politics
Benn, Gottfried, 15
Benstock, Shari, 2, 6, 176–80 *passim*
Berlin, 22–25 *passim*, 181
Berman, Russell, 11–12, 76–77, 158, 189–90
Biology, 18–21, 142–45 *passim*, 169ff. *See also* Organicism
Blood (and soil), 22–25 *passim*, 42, 65, 69–70, 75–80 *passim*, 106f, 119, 127
Bloomsbury, 27, 173, 177f
Bloy, Léon, 59
Blum, Léon, 30
Bolshevism, 25, 91–96 *passim*
Brand, Adolf, 34–37 *passim*. *See also* Gemeinschaft der Eigenen
Breton, André, 89, 95

British Union of Fascists, *see* Mosley, Oswald
Brooks, Romaine, 49
Burgess, Guy, 182
Burke, Kenneth, 42, 75

Capitalism, 20–28 *passim*, 33, 38ff, 58, 78, 180, 185, 191; and Woolf, Virginia, 41, 137–46 *passim*, 160–64 *passim*, 175–76; and Yourcenar, Marguerite, 86, 98, 103
Catholicism, 7, 43, 59–68, 76–79 *passim*, 112, 121, 184
Céline, Louis-Ferdinand, 11ff, 23ff, 74–75, 80, 84, 89
Chang, Heesok, 16, 138
Childbirth, 7, 52ff, 81, 126–32, 167–70, 186ff. *See also* Maternity
Christianity, 23, 36, 48, 59–64 *passim*, 78, 139, 150, 167
Cities, 21–25 *passim*, 38f, 77, 98–99, 110, 118f, 163. *See also* Urbanization
Class, 3, 18ff, 55, 148–52 *passim*, 176–77, 182, 191–92; and Yourcenar, Marguerite, 87, 96–99 *passim*, 119, 131ff; and Woolf, Virginia, 137, 140–45 *passim*, 150–51, 156–61 *passim*, 171–77 *passim*, 182. *See also* Proletariat
Claudel, Paul, 94
Colonialism, 29, 120ff, 150, 155, 175, 185. *See also* Imperialism
Commodification, 5, 25, 38–39, 87, 98–103 *passim*, 134, 164f, 189f
Communism, 1, 87, 99, 112, 133, 149–50, 178f. *See also* Bolshevism; Marxism; Stalinism
Conservatism, 19–25 *passim*, 36, 45, 55–58 *passim*, 68; and modernism, 5, 9; and Yourcenar, Marguerite, 5, 87, 94–99 *passim*, 112–19 *passim*, 133, 190; and Woolf, Virginia, 160–65 *passim*
Croce, Benedetto, 9, 55, 87
Culture, *see* Commodification; Fas-

cism and culture; Mass culture; Media; *and under* Authenticity

Dandies, 45, 49, 59–62 *passim*
D'Annunzio, Gabriele, 13, 24, 57, 61, 80, 93, 128
Dasenbrock, Reed Way, 4–5
Day Lewis, Cecil, 176, 183
Decadence, 7, 43–53 *passim*, 55–61 *passim*, 65–66, 74, 80, 111, 189. *See also* Aestheticism; Art; *L'art pour l'art*
Degeneration, 18ff, 29, 39, 45f, 52, 74, 95, 105, 165. *See also* Disease; Nordau, Max
DeJean, Joan, 33, 48–49, 124
DeKoven, Marianne, 4
De Man, Paul, 16
Democracy, 20, 32–36 *passim*, 56, 60, 77f, 87, 115, 164, 185; and modernism, 8f, 56, 78; and the Left, 151f, 179–85 *passim*
Derrida, Jacques, 16
DeSalvo, Louise, 83
Disease, 18f, 45f, 56, 74, 100, 145, 165. *See also* Degeneration; Health; Neurasthenia; Syphilis
Doolittle, Hilda (pseud. H.D.), 2f, 49
Doriot, Jacques, 10
Drieu La Rochelle, Pierre, 38
Dualism, mind-body, 33, 38ff, 149–52 *passim*, 170
Duce, *see* Mussolini, Benito

Eliot, T. S., 2, 8, 32, 39, 50, 62–66 *passim*, 80, 87, 161
Elitism, 9, 35, 58, 87, 94f, 114–19 *passim*, 153, 163, 189; of modernism, 8f, 56, 177
Engels, Friedrich, 39, 136, 146, 164
England, 26, 35, 44, 137, 144, 157–61 *passim*, 181–85 *passim*
Enlightenment, 23, 30, 35, 92, 133f, 178f, 185, 189f; and Barnes, Djuna, 64; and Yourcenar, Marguerite, 113–16 *passim*, 123ff, 133f, 189; and

Woolf, Virginia, 134, 154, 185; and Frankfurt School, 148–53 *passim*
Erotic, the, 34–40 *passim*, 69, 91–92, 124, 148. *See also* Sexuality
Ethnocentrism, 14, 87–90 *passim*, 120, 133f
Europe, 17–20 *passim*, 26–33 *passim*, 47, 58, 87–96 *passim*, 112f, 119–24 *passim*, 134; and fascism, 10–17 *passim*, 24–27 *passim*, 134, 183f, 190
Exile, 26f, 41, 180. *See also* Expatriation; Nation
Expatriation, 26, 89; expatriate writers, 2, 26, 49. *See also* Exile; Nation

Fascism, *see* Fascism and culture; Fascism and sexuality; French fascism; German fascism; Italian fascism
Fascism and culture, 1, 7–11 *passim*, 16, 24–25, 40f, 100f, 184ff, 190; in *Denier du rêve*, 93–94, 103, 107–109 *passim*, 117, 127; leftist analyses of, 102, 138, 147–48, 153, 173. *See also* Mass culture
Fascism and sexuality, 34–39 *passim*, 102, 137f, 146–50 *passim*, 165f, 181, 191f; and Barnes, Djuna, 59, 65f, 84; and Yourcenar, Marguerite, 91, 105, 119, 124; and Woolf, Virginia, 137f, 146, 155, 165f, 173
Feminism, 1–4 *passim*, 8, 34f, 43, 48f, 84; and Woolf, Virginia, 1, 7, 137, 155, 163–73 *passim*
Field, Andrew, 42–43
Film, 25, 94, 100–106. *See also* Media
Flanders, 89, 119
Flanner, Janet, 49, 93
Forster, E. M., 156
Foucault, Michel, 18–21 *passim*, 61, 92
Fraigneau, André, 97, 134
France, 22–25 *passim*, 29f, 35, 59, 75, 88, 132
Franco, Francisco, 183
Frank, Joseph, 65–66

Frankfurt School, 107, 134–37 *passim*, 149n, 151ff, 175–80 *passim*, 184, 191; Erich Fromm, 146n, 148f; Max Horkheimer, 148; Herbert Marcuse, 148, 166. *See also* Adorno, Theodor W.
Freemasons, 29, 160
French fascism, 10, 22–27 *passim*, 38, 43, 75, 87, 96, 100
Freud, Sigmund, 82, 86, 99, 145ff, 181. *See also* Psychoanalysis; Psychology
Frick, Grace, 88
Friedländer, Benedict, 34. *See also Gemeinschaft der Eigenen*
Führer, *see* Hitler, Adolf
Futurism, 9, 24, 57, 70, 101, 115

Galey, Matthieu, 112–13
Gättens, Marie-Luise, 5n, 154n
Gautier, Théophile, 44–48 *passim*, 61
*Gemeinschaft der Eigenen*, 34–36, 181. *See also* Brand, Adolf; Friedländer, Benedict
Gender, 2–7 *passim*, 18ff, 34, 48ff, 137, 187, 191; leftist analyses of, 39, 146, 150ff, 168, 181; in Yourcenar's work, 125–33; in Woolf's work, 140ff, 158–61 *passim*, 168–82 *passim*, 186. *See also* Women
Gentile, Giovanni, 12, 62n
German fascism, 9ff, 15f, 22, 27, 36, 117f, 133, 142–57 *passim*; and homosexuality, 37–38, 181; and Barnes, Djuna, 42f, 59, 68ff, 84; and Yourcenar, Marguerite, 87, 96, 107, 113ff, 121f
Germany, 19, 23–29 *passim*, 33–40 *passim*, 59, 68–69, 92, 114, 147, 181–84 *passim*
Gerstenberger, Donna, 78, 84
Gide, André, 30ff, 91–94 *passim*
Gilbert, Sandra, 2
Gilman, Sander, 19
Gobineau, Joseph-Arthur de, 19
Goebbels, Joseph, 25, 100n

Gramsci, Antonio, 137
Greece, classical, 30–38 *passim*, 69, 82, 89–92 *passim*, 110, 116, 121–25 *passim*. *See also* Hellenism
Green, Martin, 49, 60f
Gubar, Susan, 2
Gypsies, 19ff

Harrison, John R., 87, 115
H.D., *see* Doolittle, Hilda
Health, 22, 28, 35–39 *passim*, 46, 55f, 74, 80. *See also* Disease
Heidegger, Martin, 13, 16, 120
Hellenism, 28–34 *passim*, 61, 90ff, 120–25 *passim*, 181. *See also* Greece, classical
Hemingway, Ernest, 80
Herf, Jeffrey, 40, 58, 67f, 119
Himmler, Heinrich, 22, 52
Hirschfeld, Magnus, 34f. *See also* Homosexual emancipation movements
Hitler, Adolf, 14, 37ff, 73f, 83, 97, 143f, 148, 154, 181–84 *passim*; *Mein Kampf*, 39, 74, 164
Holocaust, 9–14 *passim*
Homosexual emancipation movements, 34–36, 63. *See also Gemeinschaft der Eigenen*
Homosexuality, 4, 18–22 *passim*, 27–41 *passim*, 46–52 *passim*, 56, 61ff, 66, 121, 177–85 *passim*; medical models of, 34, 49, 91; and Barnes, Djuna, 51–59 *passim*, 65–66, 72, 76; and Yourcenar, Marguerite, 88–92 *passim*, 99, 119, 125, 129ff; and Woolf, Virginia, 177. *See also* Lesbianism; Pæderastia; Sapphism
Hulme, T. E., 50
Husserl, Edmund, 120
Huxley, Aldous, 183
Huysmans, Joris-Karl, 45–46, 52, 59ff, 129

Idealism, 36, 99, 108f, 121, 129, 133–34, 167

Imperialism, 27, 110, 116–19 *passim*, 123f. *See also* Colonialism
Incest, 74, 105
Industrialization, 19ff, 33, 87, 106, 113ff, 120
Irrationalism, 36, 47, 58, 74f, 99–102 *passim*, 117, 134; and fascism, 36, 58, 68ff, 74f, 83–84, 96, 114–17 *passim*, 133, 157–60 *passim*, 189; in *Nightwood*, 70f, 83–84; and Yourcenar, Marguerite, 92–99 *passim*, 114–17 *passim*, 124, 133; and Woolf, Virginia, 157–60 *passim*, 189. *See also* Rationalism
Isherwood, Christopher, 26, 40, 102, 153, 158, 176–85 *passim*
Italian fascism, 9–15 *passim*, 24–27 *passim*, 42, 62, 77, 101, 122; and Yourcenar, Marguerite, 86–87, 97f, 103–6 *passim*, 110, 121f
Italy, 11, 15, 24–27 *passim*, 62, 122, 184; and Yourcenar, Marguerite, 86, 97, 110, 121f, 133

Jewification, *see* Judaization
Jews, 18–30, 35, 39ff, 122, 150, 160, 172f, 190; in *Nightwood*, 76–80 *passim*; in *Denier du rêve*, 101–6 *passim*. *See also* Anti-Semitism; Judaization
Joyce, James, 2, 26
Judaization, 23f, 39, 101, 105
Jünger, Ernst, 11–15 *passim*, 25, 58, 67–68, 73f, 91ff, 100, 108n, 115

Kannenstine, Louis, 75
Kaplan, Alice, 10n, 27, 70n, 73f, 100
Katz, Dori, 86n
Kedward, H. R., 1, 145
Kenner, Hugh, 2

La Fontaine, Jean de, 88
*L'art pour l'art*, 32, 44–47 *passim*, 57, 160. *See also* Aestheticism; Decadence
League of Nations Society, 182
Leavis, Q. D., 153–54, 173

Le Bon, Gustave, 99, 148
Lehmann, John, 176
Lesbianism, 3–6 *passim*, 47–55 *passim*, 61, 72, 84, 88, 105, 126f, 189. *See also* Homosexuality; Sapphism
Lewis, Wyndham, 87, 178
Liberalism, 5, 9, 23, 28, 32ff, 40–43 *passim*, 59, 70, 134–38 *passim*, 191; and fascism, 38ff, 58–63 *passim*, 68f, 87, 133f, 167, 180, 185, 191; and Barnes, Djuna, 40, 55, 68ff; and Yourcenar, Marguerite, 40–41, 87, 107, 113–19 *passim*, 124–35 *passim*, 184f; and Arendt, Hannah, 87, 116; and the Left, 133f, 147–50, 178ff; and Woolf, Virginia, 144, 162ff, 170, 174, 179f
Lombroso, Cesare, 29, 46
Louÿs, Pierre, 53
Loy, Mina, 2, 8–9
Lukács, Georg, 8, 55

MacNeice, Louis, 176
Madonna, the, 52–53, 71, 98
Malaparte, Curzio, 13
Malraux, André, 112
Mann, Erika, 182
Mann, Thomas, 93
*Männerbund*, 63, 91, 115n, 119, 124
March on Rome, 97, 111, 122
Marcus, Jane, 2n, 4n, 42, 55n, 80, 140, 166n, 177
Marinetti, F. T., 9, 13ff, 24, 70n, 78, 128
Marx, Karl, 136, 146, 181. *See also* Marxism
Marxism, 24, 38, 58–62 *passim*, 67f, 107, 134–38 *passim*, 146–50 *passim*, 178–81 *passim*, 191; and Barnes, Djuna, 43, 55–56, 70, 77, 84; and Yourcenar, Marguerite, 107, 119, 134; and Woolf, Virginia, 146, 166, 181. *See also* Materialism
Masculinism, 3f, 128, 132, 136, 163, 171f, 188
Mass culture, 8f, 23ff, 158, 191; Mar-

guerite Yourcenar and, 41, 87, 94–103 *passim*, 107ff, 113, 119
Materialism, 35f, 150, 179, 185; and Barnes, Djuna, 56; and Yourcenar, Marguerite, 96, 107, 126, 132f, 167; and Woolf, Virginia, 134, 141–49 *passim*, 161ff, 167–73 *passim*, 185–88 *passim*. *See also* Marxism
Maternal, the, 71–77 *passim*, 82, 128–31 *passim*, 157, 188. *See also* Maternity; Mothers and motherhood
Maternity, 7, 48, 53, 70, 127–32 *passim*, 167–70 *passim*, 186–89 *passim*. *See also* Childbirth; Madonna, the; Mothers and motherhood; Reproduction, sexual
Matriotism, 7, 131f, 170, 187f. *See also* Maternity; Mothers and motherhood
Maurras, Charles, 22, 75, 87, 99, 114f
Media, 24–25, 94, 102, 155, 160ff, 167, 191. *See also* Film
Metropolis, *see* Cities
Militarism, 24, 34f, 90, 115, 124, 191f; and Woolf, Virginia, 1, 41, 145, 182; and maternity, 7, 130, 167–70 *passim*
Miscegenation, 25, 74, 105
Mishima, Yukio, 115n
Misogyny, 2f, 49, 69, 91, 120, 125ff, 144, 164, 177
Modernism, 1–9 *passim*, 16f, 26, 32, 41, 56, 177, 189; and sexuality, 2ff, 32–33, 49–50, 56; Sapphic, 2–6 *passim*, 70, 88–93 *passim*; conservative/fascist, 4–9 *passim*, 41, 67ff, 75, 113; and Yourcenar, Marguerite, 88–96 *passim*, 113f, 133
Montherlant, Henri de, 93
Morel, B.-A., 19
Morris, William, 55, 163
Mosley, Oswald, 10, 185
Mosse, George, 19–22 *passim*
Mothers and motherhood, 7, 52–53, 71–75 *passim*, 78, 82ff, 128–31 *passim*, 155, 168, 186–89 *passim*. *See also* Madonna, the; Maternal, the; Maternity

Mussolini, Alessandra, 15
Mussolini, Benito, 26f, 81, 101, 113, 122, 143f, 154, 178; and *Denier du rêve*, 11, 86, 97, 108ff, 126ff, 132

Nation, 8, 19–27 *passim*, 35, 41, 68, 101, 134, 181–84 *passim*; and Yourcenar, Marguerite, 89, 119–21 *passim*, 131; and Woolf, Virginia, 137f, 155ff, 167. *See also* Nationalism
National Socialism, *see* German fascism
Nationalism, 19–27 *passim*, 34ff, 57, 121, 148–51 *passim*, 181; and Yourcenar, Marguerite, 89–92 *passim*, 96, 115, 119–24 *passim*; and Woolf, Virginia, 155–58, 171. *See also* Nation; Patriotism
Nature, 21f, 36, 44–47 *passim*, 55, 67f, 74–77 *passim*, 119, 123, 128; Woolf and concepts of, 141–44 *passim*, 163, 167ff; human domination of, 149–53 *passim*, 185, 190
Neurasthenia, 19, 57, 64, 94f
Nietzsche, Friedrich, 13n, 36, 93
Nolde, Emil, 13
Nordau, Max, 19ff, 29, 46, 52–55 *passim*, 94f, 145. *See also* Degeneration

Organicism, 20–23 *passim*, 28–31 *passim*, 46f, 51–52, 75f, 94, 121, 145, 168. *See also* Biology
Outsiders' Society, 41, 137, 151, 156, 163, 167, 171ff

Pæderastia, 35, 48, 92, 124, 181
Paris, 6, 88
Patriarchy, 7, 19, 76–77, 153, 164, 180ff, 187f, 192; and Woolf, Virginia, 41, 137–76, 180ff; and Barnes, Djuna, 76–77, 83f, 136; and Yourcenar, Marguerite, 129–33 *passim*

Patriotism, 7, 27, 34, 131, 137, 155ff, 170, 187. *See also* Nationalism
Peace Pledge Union, 182–83
Pellizzi, Camillo, 62n
Pius XI, 101
Pochoda, Elizabeth, 69
Positivism, 43–46 *passim*, 55–59 *passim*, 63
Pound, Ezra, 2f, 8–15 *passim*, 26, 39, 50, 61, 73–78 *passim*, 162
Praz, Mario, 44, 52n, 61
Proletariat, 35, 41, 94, 99, 130, 150ff, 174, 183. *See also* Class
Prostitution, 28, 39, 98ff, 103n, 105, 164–66, 189
Protestantism, 60–65 *passim*
*Protocols of the Elders of Zion*, 29
Proust, Marcel, 18, 29–30, 91, 95
Psychoanalysis, 32, 54, 64, 146. *See also* Freud, Sigmund; Psychology
Psychology, 70–76 *passim*, 82, 129, 137, 142–48 *passim*, 185f. *See also* Freud, Sigmund; Psychoanalysis
Puritanism, *see* Protestantism

Rabinbach, Anson, 73
Race, 3, 8, 18–21 *passim*, 27, 69–70, 74f, 101, 109, 191; and Barnes, Djuna, 69, 75–76, 84; and Yourcenar, Marguerite, 94, 116, 121, 132; and the Left, 138, 150; and Woolf, Virginia, 172. *See also* Anti-Semitism; Jews; Judaization; Racism
Racine, Jean, 88
Racism, 14f, 19–23 *passim*, 27ff, 75, 120–23, 150–52; and Yourcenar, Marguerite, 94–95, 112ff, 120, 134; and Woolf, Virginia, 137, 150–51, 175–76. *See also* Anti-Semitism; Jews; Judaization; Race
Rahv, Philip, 56–57
Rathenau, Walter, 21
Rationalism, 33–36 *passim*, 43–47 *passim*, 58, 62–71 *passim*, 76f, 149f, 178, 185; and subjectivity, 40, 70, 98, 116f, 134, 154, 185; and Yourcenar, Marguerite, 98, 113–17 *passim*, 123, 134, 189; and Woolf, Virginia, 154, 160, 170, 178. *See also* Irrationalism
Reich, Wilhelm, 39f, 74, 92, 120, 137, 146–53 *passim*, 160, 165–66, 178, 185
Reification, 40, 67–70 *passim*, 86, 102f, 119, 168, 185
Reproduction, sexual, 7, 32, 47–48, 53, 70, 106, 128–33 *passim*, 167–70 *passim*. *See also* Maternity
Retallack, Joan, 51
Rexist movement, *see* Belgium
Riefenstahl, Leni, 36, 68, 101
Röhm, Ernst, 36–37
Romanticism, 33–38 *passim*, 43f, 58–61 *passim*, 65–68 *passim*, 94, 114, 189
Rome, 20, 87ff, 97ff, 110f, 120ff
Rosenberg, Alfred, 24, 96, 101
Rousseau, Jean-Jacques, 94
Ruskin, John, 55

SA, *see* Storm Troopers
Saalmann, Dieter, 13n
Sapphic Modernism, *see under* Modernism
Sapphism, 6, 33, 47ff, 189. *See also* Lesbianism
Sappho, 6, 33, 47ff, 90
Savigneau, Josyane, 27n
Schlumberger, Jean, 93
Schmitt, Carl, 68, 147
Scott, Bonnie Kime, 2–5 *passim*
Second International, 149, 156
Sexuality, 4f, 18ff, 29, 38ff, 46–47, 53, 134, 146–50 *passim*, 165ff, 179–87 *passim*. *See also* Erotic, the; Fascism and sexuality; Homosexuality; Lesbianism; Prostitution; Reproduction, sexual; Sapphism; Technology of sex; *and under* Authenticity; Modernism; Woolf, Virginia; Yourcenar, Marguerite
Sinclair, May, 65ff

Sitwell, Osbert, 57
Socialism, 21, 33–36 *passim*, 55, 108, 163, 178f, 183f; socialist feminism, 7, 137, 167, 173; socialist realism, 8, 107, 111, 162
Sorel, Georges, 73
Spanish Civil War, 97, 158f, 183
Spender, Stephen, 8, 120, 137, 147, 152, 176–80 *passim*, 185
Spengler, Oswald, 22f, 68, 74, 78, 87, 94, 99, 114
Staël, Madame de, 59, 65
Stalinism, 116f, 133, 179, 191. *See also* Communism
State, the, 7, 48, 73, 77, 83, 147–50 *passim*, 164, 168–74 *passim*, 191
Stein, Gertrude, 8, 49
Sterility, 28, 47–54 *passim*, 76, 105–6, 127, 162
Sternhell, Zeev, 10n, 58
Stimpson, Catharine, 78
Storm Troopers, 36f, 181
Suarès, André, 93
Surette, Leon, 14n
Surrealism, 88, 95
Swinburne, Algernon Charles, 44n, 49
Symonds, John Addington, 31ff, 47
Symons, Arthur, 42ff, 50
Syphilis, 18, 39, 105

Technology of sex, 18–21 *passim*, 39
Theweleit, Klaus, 73, 78
Third Reich, 22, 82
Totalitarianism, 87, 100, 111, 117, 133, 147
Trebitsch, Arthur, 29

Urbanization, 19ff, 33, 39, 87, 115. *See also* Cities

*Verjudung*, *see* Judaization
Verlaine, Paul, 44n, 59
Virgin Mary, *see* Madonna
Vivien, Renée, 32, 47–49
*Volk*, 21, 25, 39, 65, 75, 102

Weimar Republic, 24f, 34ff, 58
Weininger, Otto, 23, 27
Wells, H. G., 144, 172
West, Dorothy, 5
Wilde, Oscar, 32–35 *passim*, 44–47 *passim*, 55–58 *passim*, 61, 129, 163
Wilson, Edmund, 2
Winckelmann, Johan Joachim, 30ff, 37, 46, 121
Winsloe, Christa, 40
*Wissenschaftlich-humanitäres Komitee*, *see* Hirschfeld, Magnus; Homosexual emancipation movements
Wolin, Richard, 120
Women: writers, 1–8 *passim*, 41, 47–50, 143, 160–63 *passim*, 187; and fascism, 4–5, 41, 73, 83ff, 91, 136–37, 143ff, 181, 187ff; in Barnes's work, 52–55 *passim*, 73, 81ff; in Yourcenar's work, 91, 125–32; in Woolf's work, 27, 136–51 *passim*, 155–81 *passim*, 186; and homosexuals, 28, 34f, 177, 181; as dominated class, 142–44, 149ff, 166, 179, 185, 189. *See also* Gender; Misogyny; Patriarchy
Wood, Thelma, 60, 84
Woolf, Virginia, 1, 5–10 *passim*, 26–27, 39ff, 62, 70, 93, 120, 127, 131–34 *passim*, 136–86; *Mrs. Dalloway*, 3; and fascism, 5, 10, 41, 120, 137f, 143f, 153–73 *passim*, 177f, 186–90 *passim*; and maternity, 7, 131, 167–70, 185–88 *passim*; and nationalism, 26–27, 155–58, 171, 181; *A Room of One's Own*, 27, 161; *The Years*, 27; *Between the Acts*, 27; and Yourcenar, Marguerite, 93, 120, 127f, 131; and sexuality, 137f, 143–46 *passim*, 164–68 *passim*, 180–81, 189; "The Leaning Tower," 176. *See also* Auden Generation; Frankfurt School; Outsiders' Society
—*Three Guineas*, 1, 5ff, 27, 41, 131–41 *passim*, 146–49 *passim*, 153f, 173f, 185f

World War I, 23–26 *passim*, 71–72, 115, 143, 149, 181
World War II, 2, 10f, 14, 83, 89f, 97, 107ff, 124, 178, 191

Yeats, W. B., 8, 50, 80, 87
Yourcenar, Marguerite, 1, 70, 86–136 *passim*, 143, 148, 154–60 *passim*, 158f, 167–70 *passim*, 184–90 *passim*; and sexuality, 6, 88–92 *passim*, 99–100, 103–6 *passim*, 114ff, 124f, 129–34 *passim*, 189; and fascism, 7–11 *passim*, 86–99 *passim*, 113–24 *passim*, 130–34 *passim*, 158f, 187–89 *passim*; and maternity, 7, 127–33 *passim*, 167–70 *passim*, 188; and nationalism, 26–27, 89–90, 119, 124, 134; *Coup de grâce*, 34, 91ff, 112–15 *passim*, 134; and liberalism, 40–41, 87, 107f, 113–19 *passim*, 124ff, 132–35 *passim*, 184f; and Arendt, Hannah, 87, 98, 116–23 *passim*, 134; *Mémoires d'Hadrien*, 89–92 *passim*, 119, 124–25; *L'Œuvre au noir*, 89–92 *passim*; *La nouvelle Eurydice*, 90; *Pindare*, 90; *Feux*, 90–93 *passim*; *Alexis ou le traité du vain combat*, 91ff, 125; "Diagnostic de l'Europe," 94–96, 114ff, 123
—*Denier du rêve*, 1, 6, 11, 86–87, 93–94, 96–112 *passim*, 116–21 *passim*, 127–38 *passim*, 154, 164

Library of Congress Cataloging-in-Publication Data
Carlston, Erin G.
  Thinking fascism : sapphic modernism and fascist modernity / Erin G. Carlston.
     p.    cm.
  Includes bibliographical references and index.
  ISBN 0-8047-3088-1 (cl.)   :   ISBN 0-8047-4167-0 (pbk.)
  1. Barnes, Djuna. Nightwood.  2. Yourcenar, Marguerite. Denier du rêve.  3. Woolf, Virginia, 1882–1941. Three guineas.  4. Fiction—Women authors—History and criticism.  5. Fiction—20th century—History and criticism.  6. Fascism and literature.  7. Feminism and literature.  8. Modernism (Literature)   I. Title.
PN 3401.C37   1998
809.3'9358—dc21                                                    97-28947
                                                                      CIP

∞ This book is printed on acid-free, recycled paper.

Original printing 1998
Last figure below indicates year of this printing:
07  06  05  04  03  02  01  00

The authorized representative in the EU for product safety and compliance is:
Mare Nostrum Group
B.V Doelen 72
4831 GR Breda
The Netherlands

www.ingramcontent.com/pod-product-compliance
Lightning Source LLC
Chambersburg PA
CBHW022058160426
43198CB00008B/271